Blogging FOR DUMMIES®

2ND EDITION

by Susannah Gardner

Author of *Buzz Marketing with Blogs For Dummies*

and Shane Birley

BICENTENNIAL
1807
WILEY
2007
BICENTENNIAL

Wiley Publishing, Inc.

Blogging For Dummies,® 2nd Edition

Published by
Wiley Publishing, Inc.
111 River Street
Hoboken, NJ 07030-5774

www.wiley.com

For general information on our other products and services, please contact our Customer Care Department within the U.S. at 877-762-2974, outside the U.S. at 317-572-3993, or fax 317-572-4002.

For technical support, please visit www.wiley.com/techsupport.

Wiley also publishes its books in a variety of electronic formats. Some content that appears in print may not be available in electronic books.

Library of Congress Control Number: 2007942521

ISBN: 978-0-470-23017-6

Manufactured in the United States of America

10 9 8 7 6 5

WILEY

About the Authors

Susannah Gardner is the co-founder and creative director of Hop Studios Internet Consultants (www.hopstudios.com), a Web design company specializing in custom Web solutions for content publishers.

Susannah is also a freelance writer and author; she is the author of *Buzz Marketing with Blogs For Dummies*, co-author of *BitTorrent For Dummies*, *Dreamweaver MX 2004 For Dummies*, and *Teach Yourself Visually: Dreamweaver MX 2004*, all from Wiley Publishing.

From 1997 to 2003, Susannah was an adjunct professor at the University of Southern California School for Communication, where she taught in the School of Journalism. Her classes in online publishing took students from zero to Web site in a semester.

Prior to running Hop Studios, Susannah worked in the Online Journalism and Communication Program at the University of Southern California, writing curriculum, teaching, and conducting research at the intersection of technology and journalism. She was a senior editor of the Online Journalism Review (www.ojr.org), the media industry's only Internet-focused journalism publication. Susannah also spent four years at *The Los Angeles Times*, one of six editors responsible for launching that newspaper's Web site. During her time at LATimes.com she established the site's multimedia lab, which produced ground-breaking Web audio, video and animation. She also launched and edited MetaHollywood, an online-only publication that covered new Hollywood technology and was LATimes.com's single largest revenue source in 1998.

Susannah earned bachelor's degrees in Print Journalism and American literature at USC. Today she is pursuing a master's degree in Public Art Studies, examining issues that cross the traditional of boundaries of Internet publishing, journalism and art. To learn more about her Web design company, visit www.hopstudios.com. Susannah keeps a poorly updated personal blog at www.unfavorablepink.com.

Shane Birley is a Vancouver-based Web developer, creative writer and blog consultant with more than 14 years of experience in developing Web sites. In January 2006, he co-founded Left Right Minds Initiatives with his partner Allyson McGrane.

Left Right Minds is a creative solutions company for nonprofit societies, charities, and businesses. The business evolved from Shane's work with developing Web sites (through his previous company, Vicious Bunny Creative) and Allyson's ongoing work with nonprofit arts groups. Both partners have experience giving workshops about their areas of expertise and in training others to use new technology and business skills. In addition to Web development, the company manages and represents performing artists with the support of the Canada Council for The Arts.

As a partner in Left Right Minds, Shane is now working to develop Web sites using content management systems that let his clients edit and update their own Web content. He regularly gives workshops on blogging and did extensive research for *BitTorrent For Dummies*. Shane has a background in improvisational theatre and a B.A. in English – these qualifications enable him to translate difficult computing concepts into easy plain language. To learn more about his Web company, visit `www.leftrightminds.com`. He also writes a personal blog at `www.shanesworld.ca`.

Authors' Acknowledgments

Susannah: As with every book I have worked on, I find it unfair that my name is on the cover when so many people played such an important role in getting this book finished.

My husband and business partner, Travis Smith, deserves a huge portion of my thanks. Without his help in keeping our home and company running smoothly, I would have lost much more sleep than I did writing this book. His help late at night when I couldn't decide how to explain a technology or just to give me a little extra encouragement is noted, appreciated, and loved.

Thanks are also due to Shane Birley, a good friend, who is my co-author on this book. He met deadlines, turned in screenshots, and was generally so on top of the process that he put me to shame at times! I look forward to working on more writing projects with him in the future. Thanks are due also to Shane's life and business partner Allyson McGrane, who kept him fed and functioning during deadlines.

As always, special thanks go to Janine Warner, *For Dummies* author extraordinaire, who invited me to co-author *Dreamweaver MX 2004 For Dummies* with her and started me down this road. Her recent books – *Dreamweaver CS3 For Dummies* and *Creating Family Web Sites For Dummies* are great resources.

This book would never have been possible without the patience and good humor of Rebecca Senninger, my editor, and acquisitions editors Melody Layne and Tiffany Ma at Wiley. There are many at Wiley Publishing whose names I don't know but who nonetheless played an important role in making this book possible: Thank you to all of you.

Paul Chaney, Internet marketing director at Bizzuka, Inc., took time from his busy schedule to be the technical editor for this book. You can blame any errors in the how to instructions on him. Just kidding! Paul's attention to detail has prevented more errors than I can count.

Friends, family, colleagues and clients all cut me some slack while I was meeting deadlines for this book. Thanks go to Matt Gardner, my parents and sister, my mother-in-law Pat Smith, and my sister-in-law Virginia Smith, all of whom got to witness a little stress-induced behavior.

And thank you, reader, for giving me your time and attention. I hope this book is everything you need it to be.

Shane: Thanks to Susannah for giving me the opportunity to collaborate with her on this book. It was an amazing experience and one I hope to repeat.

I appreciate the love and support of my friends and family. I especially want to thank Ken Driediger who keeps me focused and on track when stress gets the better of me and to A. Traviss Corry of *The New Wrinkle* video podcast who reminds me that once in a while fun and silly behavior just must be had. Thanks also to Scott Petersen, Anita Bleick, Nicole Morisette, Travis Smith, David Kelch, Aaron Mok, Sue McCarthy, Robin Thompson, Jennifer Chin, Gillian Gunson, and to my mother — who bought me my first TRS-80 computer, when I really wanted a Coleco video game console.

And most of all, thank you to my partner Allyson. She was very supportive in helping to proofread, listening to me report on all the latest blog technologies, and most of all walking our pug Serendipity when I was focused on getting the next paragraph just right.

Publisher's Acknowledgments

We're proud of this book; please send us your comments through our online registration form located at www.dummies.com/register/.

Some of the people who helped bring this book to market include the following:

Acquisitions and Editorial

Project Editor: Rebecca Senninger

Acquisitions Editors: Melody Layne, Tiffany Ma

Copy Editor: Virginia Sanders

Technical Editor: Paul Chaney

Editorial Manager: Leah Cameron

Editorial Assistant: Amanda Foxworth

Sr. Editorial Assistant: Cherie Case

Cartoons: Rich Tennant
  (www.the5thwave.com)

Composition Services

Project Coordinator: Patrick Redmond

Layout and Graphics: Reuben W. Davis, Melissa K. Jester, Stephanie D. Jumper, Barbara Moore, Christine Williams

Proofreaders: John Greenough, Evelyn W. Still

Indexer: Valerie Haynes Perry

Anniversary Logo Design: Richard Pacifico

Publishing and Editorial for Technology Dummies

  Richard Swadley, Vice President and Executive Group Publisher

  Andy Cummings, Vice President and Publisher

 Mary Bednarek, Executive Acquisitions Director

  Mary C. Corder, Editorial Director

Publishing for Consumer Dummies

  Diane Graves Steele, Vice President and Publisher

  Joyce Pepple, Acquisitions Director

Composition Services

  Gerry Fahey, Vice President of Production Services

  Debbie Stailey, Director of Composition Service

Contents at a Glance

Table of Contents

Introduction

Allow me to be the first to welcome you to the *blogosphere,* an exciting and energetic space online that people are using to reach out, build communities, and express themselves. *Blogging For Dummies,* 2nd Edition is designed to take you through the process of starting a blog quickly, and it gives you the tools you need to make the most of your experience in the blogosphere.

This book is designed to be useful for all kinds of bloggers, whether you're the CEO of a major corporation or a hobbyist with a passion for communicating. I focus on what makes a blog work — and how a blog can work for you. Also, I realize that not everyone has the technical skills necessary to start a blog themselves, so I provide options for all levels of experience.

This book will be useful to you whether you're taking part in the conversations in the world of blogs or becoming a blogger yourself. I cover everything from technology to legal issues, so you can go forward knowing you have a resource that covers every aspect of this new and exciting medium.

About This Book

The fact that you're holding this book very likely means you have some ideas about starting a blog — and I want to get you started right away! You don't have to memorize this book or even read it in order. Feel free to skip straight to the chapter with the information you need and come back to the beginning later. Each chapter is designed to give you easy answers and guidance, accompanied by step-by-step instructions for specific tasks.

The first part of the book gets you blogging quickly and safely. Chapter 1 introduces you to blogging, Chapter 2 shows you how to get started, and Chapter 3 helps you know what the consequences of your blog might be.

Even if you don't read anything else in the book, the first three chapters of this book can give you enough information to start blogging *today.*

If you want to create a more customized blog or want to choose blog software and set up Web hosting, you can go directly to the chapter that relates to your situation. Want to find just how real people are using blogs in their lives? The examples and figures in this book focus on real blogs using the technologies and techniques I describe.

Blogs, sidebars, blogrolls, RSS — this medium has more jargon that you can shake a stick at. Watch for my definitions so that you know what's going on when you start blogging. Don't let a few acronyms keep you from enjoying the blogosphere! And of course, you can always consult the glossary at the back of this book.

Conventions Used in This Book

Keeping things consistent makes them easier to understand. In this book, those consistent elements are *conventions*. Notice how the word *conventions* is in italics? That's a convention I use frequently. I put new terms in italics and then define them so that you know what they mean.

URLs (Web addresses) or e-mail addresses in text look like this: `www.buzz marketingwithblogs.com`. Sometimes, however, I use the full URL, like this: `http://traction.tractionsoftware.com/traction` because the URL is unusual or lacks the `www` prefix.

Most Web browsers today don't require the introductory `http://` for Web addresses, though, so you don't have to type it in.

What You're Not to Read

To make this book work for you, you don't need to sit down and start with Chapter 1. Go right to the information you need most and get to work. If you're new to blogs, skim through the chapters to get an overview and then go back and read in greater detail what's most relevant to your project. Whether you're building a blog as a rank beginner or redesigning an existing blog to make it better, you can find everything you need in these pages.

The chapters are written to give you the basics you need to get the job done, and although I've included sidebars that give you more information, you don't need to read those sidebars if you're short ontime. Technical Stuff icons also indicate helpful extras that you can come back to when you have more time.

Foolish Assumptions

Just because blogs have a funny name doesn't mean they have to be written by funny people — or even humorous ones! If you can write an e-mail, you can write a blog. Have confidence in yourself and realize that this is an informal medium that forgives mistakes unless you try to hide them. In keeping with the philosophy behind the *For Dummies* series, this book is an easy-to-use guide designed for readers with a wide range of experience. Being interested in blogs is all that I expect from you.

If you're new to blogs, this book gets you started and walks you step by step through all the skills and elements you need to create a successful Web log. If you've been reading and using blogs for some time now, this book is an ideal reference that will ensure you're doing the best job possible with any blog you start or manage.

I do expect that you aren't tackling starting a blog without having some basic computer knowledge under your belt, not to mention a computer on your desk. If you're still learning how to use your computer or don't have access to an Internet connection, keep this book for a time when you're more able to put your computer and the Internet to work for you.

Having said that, you don't need to know much more than how to use a Web browser, open and create files on your computer, and get connected to the Internet, so it's not necessary to be a computer genius, either.

How This Book Is Organized

To ease you through the process of building a blog, I organized this book to be a handy reference. This section provides a breakdown of the parts of the book and what you can find in each one. Each chapter walks you through a different aspect of blogging, providing tips and helping you understand the vocabulary of Web logs.

Part 1: Getting Started with Blogs

This part introduces you to the general concepts of blogging, including actually starting a blog today. In Chapter 1, I show you some good blogs and give you some background about this young industry. You find out what's involved in creating a blog and take a quick tour of what works in a blog and what doesn't.

In Chapter 2, you can jump right into a real blog and start a Blogger blog. Sign up in ten minutes and have some fun putting up text, links, and images.

While reading Chapter 3, you can get some guidance on how your friends, family, and business colleagues might react to your new blog. If you're interested in blogging frankly, you might want to read this chapter before you start criticizing your boss.

Part II: Setting Up Your Blog

In Chapter 4, you make a big decision: what blogging software you'll use. I explain what your options are and how to find blog software with the features and extras you need.

Chapter 5 takes you through some of the HTML you might need to do common text formatting in your blog — from links to lists. You even find out how to add a YouTube video to your blog!

Chapter 6 is for the dedicated geek: Get yourself a domain name and some Web hosting so that you can install your own blog software and control every aspect of the blogging experience.

In Chapter 7, if you haven't gotten enough geekiness yet, you can check out how to get into the guts of your blog software, customizing the design to suit your style.

Part III: Fitting In and Feeling Good

Part III is dedicated to making sure you know how to get the most out of your blog while meeting the needs of your audience. In Chapter 8, you can work on figuring out just what your topic is and how best to produce content around your subject. I even give you some good tips on dealing with writer's block.

In Chapter 9, you define your audience and work on targeting your blog to reach that group most effectively — and keep readers coming back for more.

Chapter 10 helps you avoid a common blog problem: spam. Discover the tricks every blogger must know to keep Viagra ads from dominating their comment areas.

Part IV: Adding Bells and Whistles

In Part IV, you find a series of chapters that help you dress up your blog with style and neat technological tools. In Chapter 11, you find out what the heck RSS is and how you can use it to build traffic to your blog. Not only that, you can use RSS yourself to read other blogs quickly and find out what others are saying about you.

In Chapter 12, you get to add some of the snazziest technology on the Internet today to your blog's sidebars. Use Flickr photos, polls, shopping recommendations, and more to really let your readers know where you're coming from.

In Chapter 13, you find out how to make the most of photos and other graphics in your blog. Did you know that adding a photo to your blog post will make more people read it? It's true!

Finally, if you can't say it with a photo, say it with your mouth by creating a podcast in Chapter 14. This is an exciting new area of technology that's being used by everyone from the newest blogger to the seasoned professional to make themselves heard.

Part V: Marketing and Promoting Your Blog

Make your blog known on the Internet and in the blogosphere by using the tools in Part V. Chapter 15 helps you use statistics and traffic-tracking tools to discover more about your audience members and how they're using your blog.

If you've ever thought that you ought to be able to make a little money with your blog, then Chapter 16 is for you. Find out how to put ads on your blog, form relationships with sponsors, and use affiliate programs to make a buck.

If you are a corporate CEO, then Chapter 17 is a must-read. In this chapter I show you how businesses, nonprofit groups, and other organizations are making use of blogs to form relationships with clients and customers.

Part VI: The Part of Tens

In The Part of Tens, you discover ten ways increase the community interaction on your blog, ten cool tools that can make your blog even snazzier, and, best of all, ten outstanding blogs making the most of technology and the Internet.

Glossary

The glossary defines all those weird blog terms that have sprung up in recent years.

Icons Used in This Book

Here's a rundown of the icons I use in this book:

The Remember icon reminds you of an important concept or procedure that you'll want to store away in your memory bank for future use.

The Technical Stuff icon signals technical stuff that you might find informative and interesting but which isn't essential for you to know to develop the Web sites described in this book. Feel free to skip over these sections if you don't like the techy stuff.

Tips indicate a trick or technique that can save you time and money — or possibly a headache.

The Warning icon warns you of any potential pitfalls — and gives you the all-important information on how to avoid them.

Where to Go from Here

Turn to Chapter 1 to dive in and get started with an intro to blogs and an overview of why this new medium is so exciting for so many people. If you just want to get started blogging today, read over Chapter 2. Otherwise, spend some time thinking about the best blog software solution for your situation — which you can read more about in Chapter 4. Don't forget to send me your efforts — I can't wait to see your brand new blog! Drop me an e-mail at susie@hopstudios.com.

Part I
Getting Started with Blogs

The 5th Wave   By Rich Tennant

"Tell the boss you-know-who is talking smack in his blog again."

In this part . . .

Part I is your crash course in blogging, from finding out what the heck this new format is all about to actually getting started posting to a blog. It's an exciting section, and you won't want to miss a word! In Chapter 1, you find out why people are bothering to post their most personal thoughts on the Web and why even some businesses are getting involved. In Chapter 2, you start a blog by using a great tool called Blogger. And in Chapter 3, you discover the tips and tricks to blogging safely.

Chapter 1

Discovering Blog Basics

*U*nless you live under a rock, you've heard the word *blog* used sometime in the last couple of years — journalists, in particular, are fascinated by this new type of Web site. And bloggers, in turn, are showing up as commentators and experts in news stories and on television. At the same time, you might have a son or daughter who has a blog, or perhaps you've been told about a blog your company is starting. What exactly is it that all these people mean when they say they have a blog? And how can such different organizations be using the same technology to communicate?

Don't be too hard on yourself if you aren't exactly sure what a blog is. The word *blog* is actually a mashup of two other words — Web and log — so if it sounds made up, that's because it is. A *blog* is a chronologically ordered series of Web site updates, written and organized much like a traditional diary right down to the informal style of writing that characterizes personal communication.

In this chapter, you find out just what makes a blog bloggy and why so many people are jumping on board with this trend. (Hint: It's isn't just that we're all narcissists!) You get some ideas that you can use to start your own blog and become part of the *blogoshere* (the community of blogs and bloggers around the world).

No matter what your teenager tells you, there is absolutely no requirement that you must write your blog while wearing your pajamas. Also, you are allowed to use a spellchecker.

Making Yourself Comfortable with Blogs

I talk to lots of people about blogs, many of whom know that you can find a blog on the World Wide Web, but who also have the impression that all blogs are written by navel-gazing cranks with an axe to grind or by 12-year-old girls. It's true that some blogs really are diaries in which the minutiae of day-to-day life are recorded, but blogs can be much more than that and are written by all kinds of people.

One of my favorite blogs falls into the personal diary category: Mimi Smartypants (`http://smartypants.diaryland.com`). This humorous blog is written by a woman living in Chicago who records her thoughts and activities with such hilarious prose that I find myself laughing out loud.

For contrast, visit Mäni's Bakery Blog Café (`www.manisbakery.com/blogcafe`), a blog written by the staff of Mäni's Bakery in Los Angeles for its customers (shown in Figure 1-1). Mäni's uses the blog to announce menu changes and weekly specials, offer coupons, and describes changes going on in the restaurant (like the recent addition of an ATM).

Figure 1-1: The Mäni's Bakery blog does a great job of keeping customers updated.

Think of a blog this way: It's a kind of Web site. All blogs are Web sites (the opposite isn't true, though), and what makes them blogs isn't the content or creator — it's the presentation. A blog can be many things: diary, news source, photo gallery, even a corporate marketing tool. Blog content can be text, photos, audio, and even video, and bloggers talk about nearly any subject you can imagine.

One of the reasons blogs have become such a popular way of publishing a Web site is because they are particularly good at generating high search engine rankings. With a blog, you're more likely to come up high in lists of search results for the topics you discuss, because your posts are fresh and current. Search engines give an extra boost to Web pages that have the most recently updated or created content on the keywords being searched. And better search engine listings mean more visitors, more readers, more comments, and a more vibrant community. Individuals and companies have been quick to take advantage of the medium to reach out to Web users.

How blogs are being used

With millions of blogs in the world — the blog search engine Technorati was tracking more than 133 million around the world in September 2008 — it's obvious that blogging is a popular and successful format for publishing a Web site. But just what are people doing with blogs? They can't all be people talking about their cats!

And they aren't. Bloggers are using the blog format to communicate effectively in all kinds of information spheres, from the personal to the professional. In fact, many blogs serve multiple purposes at once, mixing posts about activities at home with news pertaining to work. Your blog can serve many purposes in your life.

Documenting your life

Lots of folks use blogs for the same reason they might keep a diary — to chronicle their life and activities. This urge to communicate is expressed in all kinds of mediums, from scrapbooking to taking digital photographs, and if you're interested in sharing these personal details with others, a blog is a fast, efficient way to do so.

If you send Christmas newsletters every year or e-mail a group of friends and family to let them know about exciting events in your life, you'll find a blog to be a lot of fun. You can blog as often as you like, and your readers visit when they're ready to get more information. Best of all, each blog post gives your friends and family a quick way to respond to you without having to find the stamps; all they have to do is leave a comment on your blog post. You might find you're talking more to your family than ever before!

You don't have to find the stamps either, so keeping in touch is inexpensive and less time-consuming (no more envelopes to lick).

Of course, not all lives come up roses every day; it can't all be wedding and travel blogs. Personal blogs can be intense when they document rough times. Derek Miller (www.penmachine.com), a Vancouver-based writer, has used his blog to document his experiences with cancer. He posted this on June 26, 2007:

> "To boil it down: my cancer has grown and spread. My goals now are to see the Winter Olympics come to Vancouver in 2010, and beyond that to renew my driver's license when it expires again in five years. But while my medical team and I will do everything to try to make that happen, there is a significant chance I might not live that long, that I might be dead before five years are up.

> "It's a heavy day. I have cried, and laughed, and shared a drink and nachos with my friend Simon, and hugged my wife and my children and my parents. And I will fight on. It's a fine line between acknowledging and accepting what could happen and denying it. I'm naturally an optimistic guy, but I can't pretend that everything will be just fine, because it already isn't. The future, even the near future, is a mystery, and I must walk into it."

Figure 1-2 shows Derek's blog.

Figure 1-2: Derek Miller blogs about everything in his life, from chemotherapy to Apple's new operating system.

Don't forget, in your eagerness to let your friends know about what you're up to, that a blog (unlike a real diary or scrapbook) is available to anyone in the world, now and in the future. Don't publish anything you might find embarrassing in the future, and have the same consideration when talking about others or in using photographs.

Exploring a hobby or passion

If you have a passion or hobby you just love to talk about, consider doing so in a blog. Anyone who shares your interest is a potential reader and is bound to be looking for more information wherever they can find it.

You can detail your own experience, offer advice to others, drum up support for whatever you like to do, or just talk about what you love. Best of all, you might be able to make connections with others who share your infatuation, making friends and finding ways to get involved with your hobby more deeply.

Cybele May runs a blog about something she loves: candy. Candy Blog (www.candyblog.net) is her personal labor of love and a great excuse to buy lots of candy! Cybele reviews candies, writing extensive descriptions of taste, texture, and ingredients for fellow sugar-enthusiasts. And they respond! A post about Dots garnered 18 comments from fans and critics of the chewy movie theater favorite. Check out Candy Blog in Figure 1-3.

Figure 1-3:
Candy Blog
is a sweet
labor of love
for Cybele
May.

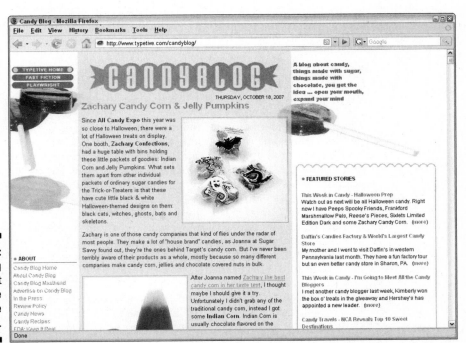

Sharing information

Sometimes a blog is all about sharing information. Journalists have used blogs to report on local, national, and international news; critics and commentators use the medium to state their opinions and predictions. Educators keep parents and students abreast of classroom happenings and dates. Co-workers let colleagues in geographically distant offices know what's going on with collaborative projects. The uses of the informational blog are really limitless.

The popular blog Boing Boing (www.boingboing.net) is a great example of an information-sharing blog. Self-described as a "directory of wonderful things," Boing Boing's several contributors are dedicated to keeping you up to date on all the weird and wonderful Web sites in the world. A selection of posts from July 2007 described a ceramics company that makes skull cake toppers, pointed out artistic vintage Polish movie posters, and explained why meerkats attack newcomers to their groups (and how to keep it from happening). This site is truly a random collection of news and links, perfect for the eclectic consumer of trivia.

Another popular information blog is Gizmodo (www.gizmodo.com). This gadget guide for the geek in all of us keeps you current on the latest Apple hardware releases, advises you about price drops in Xbox 360s, and explains how to insure your Apple iPhone against theft or damage. You might not find every post useful, but if you're trying to keep up with the breakneck pace of technological innovation you can fit in your purse, Gizmodo (shown in Figure 1-4) and blogs like it are an invaluable resource.

Making money

You spend a lot of time producing your blog, and a lot of people read it. Why not turn those eyes into dollars? That's a question many a popular blogger has asked, and there are several ways to make it happen.

The most common technique is to include advertising on your blog pages. Google Adsense is one provider of in-page advertising that is designed to match the content of your blog and therefore be of interest to your readers. Each time a visitor to your blog clicks one of these advertising links, you earn money from Google. I talk more about making money from advertising programs, affiliate links, sponsorships, and more in Chapter 16.

Of course, companies haven't missed out on the fact that blogs are a great way to drum up interest in their products and services or to inform and connect with consumers. Many companies have added blogs to their Web sites, and they've used the blogs to start conversations with their customers and potential customers. In many cases, taking on the informal voice of the blog medium has helped customers to understand that there are real people in these organizations. The result is better credibility for the company and often better recognition of the company and its values in the marketplace.

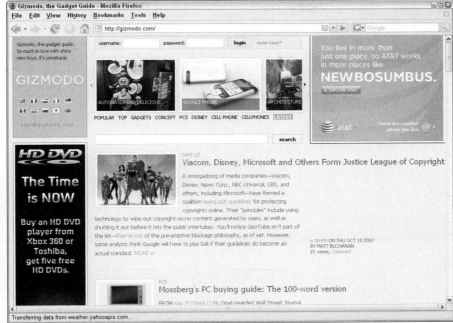

Figure 1-4:
Gizmodo
is your
source for
satisfying
your gadget
news
appetite.

General Motors, Google, and Sun Microsystems all have company blogs, but many smaller businesses, and even individuals, are also taking advantage of this new format, giving readers a peak inside the corporate culture of what might otherwise be fairly faceless monoliths.

Southwest has taken this approach (www.blogsouthwest.com). In the blog's "user guide," Southwest says, "Our goal with this blog is to give our readers the opportunity to take a look inside Southwest Airlines and to interact with us." Southwest tries to make sure that lots of voices inside the company are represented on the blog, from managers to captains — even the president of the company. As with personal blogs, the tone is light and conversational, making the company seem friendly and accessible.

Recognizing a blog

Chances are good that you've seen a blog online already. Because there's no requirement that the blogger put a big "This is a blog!" sticker at the top of the page, you might not have realized that you were seeing a blog at all. With a little practice and familiarity with standard blog elements, though, you can identify any blog in a snap.

Blogging through the ages

The concept behind a blog isn't new; after all, people have been keeping diaries and journals for as long as the written word has permitted it. Even on the Web, diary Web sites existed long before the word *blog* was first used.

No one really knows when the first true blog was created, but estimates put the date around 1994. The term *weblog* came into existence in 1997, and it was quickly shortened to the more colloquial *blog*. If you want to read more about the history of blogging, visit Wikipedia at `http://en.wikipedia.org/wiki/`

`Blog` and read author Rebecca Blood's essay on the early days of blogging online at `www.rebeccablood.net/essays/weblog_history.html`.

As of September 2008, the blog search engine Technorati (`www.technorati.com`) was tracking more than 133 million blogs from all over the world. Even if you discount some of that number as tests or short-lived experiments, the number of blogs is huge — and it's growing every month. In May 2007, for example, Technorati was tracking only 75 million blogs.

Regardless of what the blog is about or who writes it, every blog is characterized by

- ✔ **Frequent updates:** Most blogs are updated a few times a week; some are even updated a few times a day. There isn't a schedule for publishing; the blogger simply updates the blog when it seems appropriate.

- ✔ **Posts or entries:** Each time a blogger updates the blog, he or she creates a blog *post,* or entry, that is added to the blog.

- ✔ **Permalinks:** Each time a post is added to a blog, it's placed on the home page. At the same time, a *permalink* page is created to contain only that blog post and its comments. (The word *permalink* is short for "permanent link.") Permalink pages are a big part of why blogs do so well with search engines — every post adds a new page to your Web site and is another opportunity for your blog to come up as a search result.

- ✔ **Chronological order:** When a blogger writes a new blog post, it's displayed at the top of the blog's first page. The next time a post is written, it shows up at the top, and the older posts move down the page.

- ✔ **Comments:** Most (though not all) blogs allow readers to leave comments — short text messages — in response to blog posts. It is comments that really differentiate a blog from most Web sites, by encouraging interaction and conversation.

- ✔ **Archives:** Because a blog is updated so frequently, many blogs are sorted into a date-based archive so that readers can find older information easily.

- ✔ **Categories:** Blog posts can also be sorted by subject, or categories, allowing a blogger to blog about a number of different topics and readers to focus in on the topics that most interest them.

Blog anatomy: Dissecting a typical blog

In this section, I give you a tour of the usual blog elements using baker Rose Levy Beranbaum's blog, Real Baking with Rose (`www.realbakingwithrose.com`). This is an unusual blog because although Rose writes it herself, it's sponsored by Gold Medal Flour, who paid for the blog to be built and handles any maintenance costs associated with running it. It still has all the usual features that I discuss in this section, as shown in Figure 1-5.

Rose's sponsorship is unusual, but the format of her blog isn't. In fact, most blogs — no matter what topic they cover — look quite similar, because the elements of one blog are common to all blogs.

All blogs typically have the following common elements:

Sidebar material   Header   Most recent posts   Post information

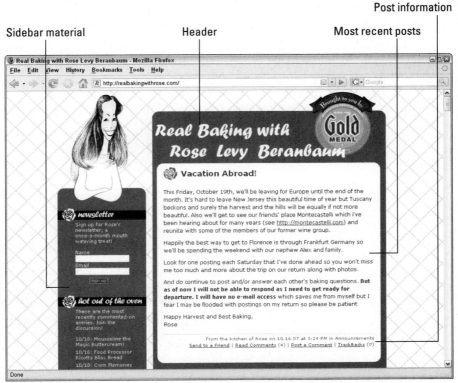

Figure 1-5: Real Baking with Rose is a sponsored blog written by a cookbook author.

Courtesy of Rose Levy Beranbaum, author of The Cake Bible

✔ **Branding/logo header:** A *header* at the top of the blog displays the name of the blog, often using a logo or other visual element. This header is visible on every page of the blog, identifying it even to a visitor who visits one of the interior pages without first going to the home page. In Figure 1-5, the header contains the name of the blog and also a caricature of Rose and the Gold Medal logo indicating the blog's sponsorship.

✔ **Most recent posts:** At the top of the blog's home page, the most recent post is displayed. As you scroll down the home page, you see the next most recent post, and the next most recent post, and so on. New posts are always at the top, making it easy to find the latest, freshest information when you visit. The number of recent blog posts displayed on the first page of the blog is usually around a dozen, and to read older posts readers can visit the archives.

✔ **Post information:** Along with each entry, blog software displays information *about* the post. This sort of post information is typical — but not mandated. A blog might be missing an element or two that I list, or have others I don't mention:

  • The date and time the post was published.

  • The name of the post's author. On blogs with multiple authors, this info is especially important to the visitor.

  • The number of comments on the post. In Figure 1-5, you can see the first post has two comments.

  • A link to the permalink page, usually labeled Permalink. Sometimes, as in Figure 1-5, the link to the permalink page is labeled Post a Comment because you can both read and post comments on the permalink page.

  • The category in which the post has been placed. In Figure 1-5, the category of the top post is Announcements.

  • Other links to bells and whistles unique to the blog, like the links to Trackbacks or Send to a Friend (that allow you to quickly e-mail the post to a friend) in Figure 1-5.

✔ **Sidebar material:** Most blogs are laid out in two or three columns, with the most real estate given to the column containing the blog posts themselves. The second and/or third columns display organizational material for the blog, and peripheral information. Some blogs don't have sidebars at all, and on some blogs you may see elements I don't mention in this list of typical sidebar components:

  • *Date-based archives:* Nearly every blog is archived as it's published, by date and by category. In the sidebar of a blog, you can usually access both archive methods. Figure 1-6 shows the date-based archives of Rose's blog, broken down by month. Date-based archives can also show weeks and years.

Figure 1-6:
A date-based archive.

Courtesy of Rose Levy Beranbaum, author of The Cake Bible

- *Categorized archives:* Figure 1-7 shows the category archives of Real Baking with Rose. By sorting each post into a category at the time it is published, Rose creates an archive organized by subject, making it easy for you to find the posts you're most interested in. Clicking a category link displays only the posts in that subject area, in reverse chronological order.

Figure 1-7:
A categorized archive.

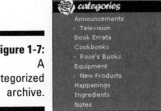

Courtesy of Rose Levy Beranbaum, author of The Cake Bible

- *Blogroll:* A blogroll is a list of blogs that you find interesting or useful. By including the blogs and Web sites Rose likes to read on her blog, she can direct her readers to other interesting Web sites (see Figure 1-8). And who knows, those sites may return the favor, sending their visitors to her site.

Figure 1-8:
A blogroll.

Courtesy of Rose Levy Beranbaum, author of The Cake Bible

- *Information about the author:* Because blogs are so personal, sometimes you want to know more about who's writing them. Many bloggers know their readers are curious and put together short bios and other information for readers. This information is sometimes displayed in the sidebar, or linked to as in Figure 1-9.

Figure 1-9:
An about
the author
section.

Courtesy of Rose Levy Beranbaum, author of The Cake Bible

- *RSS feed link:* RSS, or Really Simple Syndication, is a way readers can subscribe to your blog by using a newsreader such as Google Reader. After a reader subscribes via RSS, she can read the latest updates via the newsreader rather than visiting your blog. This is helpful because it means your readers don't have to visit your blog several times a day to see whether you've updated it. A blog often includes an RSS link near the bottom of the sidebar identified by a small orange icon, as shown in Figure 1-10. I talk more about RSS in Chapter 11.

Figure 1-10:
A links to an
RSS feed.

Courtesy of Rose Levy Beranbaum, author of The Cake Bible

Getting a Blog Started

One of the reasons that so many blogs exist is that they're so easy to set up and publish. The early days of the Internet were full of heady talk about the democratization of publishing; there was a lot of discussion about absolutely anyone having the power to publish thanks to the prevalence of personal computers. In fact, that wasn't strictly true. It's true that a writer no longer needed a printing press and a distribution method to be read, but specialized skills and technology were still required.

Unless the would-be publisher spent time learning HTML, had a computer with an Internet connection, and understood how to put files onto a Web server, he was still pretty much in the same boat he had always been in. Acquiring those skills and the tools to publish wasn't impossible, but it wasn't terribly easy, either.

The answer, as it turns out, comes down to technology, and specifically to software. I believe blogging goes a long way toward making that initial promise of the Web come true. If you can write an e-mail, you can figure out how to use the simple interface of blogging software without any of the muss or deal with HTML, FTP, or any of those other awful Web acronyms everyone is supposed to understand these days.

Figure 1-11 shows the publishing interface of my favorite blogging software, ExpressionEngine. When I want to write a blog post, I simply log in to my blogging software and fill in the blanks for a new post. When I'm done, I click Save and the post is published to my blog. It's that simple.

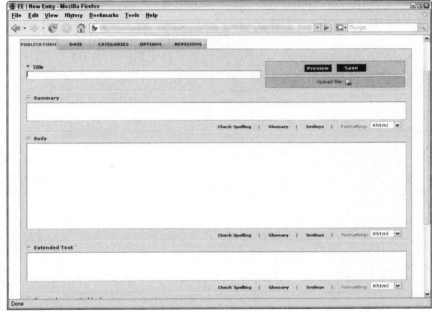

Figure 1-11: Publishing a blog is as simple as filling in a few form fields and clicking Save.

Different blog software offers different feature sets. As with all software, the tricky part is finding the right one to use for your situation and needs, but be reassured: blogging software comes in all shapes, sizes and price ranges. In Chapter 4, I talk extensively about choosing the right software solution for your blog. And Chapter 2 shows you how to start a blog with Blogger (popular blog software) in about 10 minutes.

Choosing What to Blog About

Blog topics are all over the map. If you haven't already read a blog, follow these simple steps to finding one and reading it — it's the best possible way to become familiar with the medium:

1. **Open your Web browser and go to www.technorati.com.**

2. **Type any search term you're interested in reading about into the search box at the top of the page.**

   For example, you might enjoy reading a blog written by someone with whom you share a hobby, like knitting or parasailing. Or, try a search term that describes what you do for a living; if you're an accountant, for example, you might search for "tax regulations." Or, search for something that can help you accomplish a task, like buying a house or learning to paint.

3. **Click Search.**

   Technorati returns a list of recent blog posts that used your search term. When I searched for "knitting," for example, Technorati showed me blog posts by someone who just bought some new yarn for making socks, a recipe for a knitting-themed birthday cake, and another post by someone who was frustrated with a pattern.

4. **Choose a blog post that looks interesting and click the title to visit the blog and read more.**

5. **Repeat as needed until you find a blog you enjoy!**

There are blogs on so many topics you won't be able to keep from finding something interesting, whether it engages you professionally or personally. I read blogs on all kinds of topics that interest me, from (surprise) knitting to the arts to real estate.

The blog format is exceptionally well-suited to letting you explore an idea, a hobby, or a project, but don't let that stop you from using it for other things. There have been blogs created to pass along marketing expertise, sell shoes, cover the latest celebrity gossip, raise funds for bike rides, and even to write books. The topic or topics you write about should excite you and hold your interest, and they can be about absolutely anything.

Having that much freedom can be a little scary, and if you're like me, leave you with an absolute blank in your mind. No problem; you can start a blog today about one topic, and when you actually figure out what you want to write about, change directions and go down another road. It's a very flexible format!

Think about these things when you start a blog:

- ✔ **Choose a subject that genuinely interests you.** Don't choose a topic that you think looks good to be interested in or will attract a lot a readers. You're the one who will have to do the writing for the blog, and it really helps if you're enthusiastic about your subject. That passion will shine through to your readers and keep them coming back.

- ✔ **Decide whether any topics are off limits.** Bloggers who keep personal diaries for their friends and families might decide to keep certain subjects out of the public forum of the Internet. For example, do you really want your boyfriend reading a frank account of last night's make-out session? How about your mom or your boss?

 ✔ **Think about your potential readers.** Who are they? How can you appeal to them and get them to keep reading your blog? Do you even care about how many readers you have? If you do, what do you have to show or teach or ask them?

Creating a Successful Blog

Blogs are so quick and easy to set up that it's very easy to start one without having much of a plan in place for what you'll blog about, why you're blogging, or what you're trying to accomplish. Some people thrive on this kind of wide-open playing field, but others will quickly become bored (or boring!).

To get your blog started on the right foot, you have to do some serious thinking about why you're blogging and then make a commitment to attaining your goals somehow. Don't get me wrong — this isn't a job! But, just as you wouldn't expect good results from a dinner prepared without paying any attention to ingredients, you can't start your blog without having a recipe for success.

Here's my recipe for a good blog:

1. Preheat the oven by setting goals.
2. Measure out several cups of good writing.
3. Mix well with frequent updates.
4. Sprinkle in lots of interaction with your readers.

One way to get ideas for how you'll be successful is to observe other blogs and bloggers. Keep track of how the blogs you enjoy are keeping you interested: Take note of how often the blog is updated, the writing style, and which posts are the most engaging and get you to leave a comment. Watching how someone else blogs is a great way of finding out how to be successful yourself!

Setting goals

Just as you have many different ways to approach a blog, you have many ways to be successful with your blog. *Don't* forget that your goals and plans might not be the same as another blogger's. *Do* think about what your goals are and keep those in mind as you start your blog.

Here are some ways you might define a successful blog:

- ✔ **Numbers:** Many bloggers are eager to attract a lot of readers to their blogs, and they define success by the number people who visit every day.

- ✔ **Comments:** For some bloggers, the interaction with readers in the comment area of the blog is very gratifying. For these bloggers, getting a comment every day or on every post might mean they're being successful.

- ✔ **Results:** Many bloggers start their blog in order to accomplish a task, like raising money for a charity, or to sell a product, or even to get a book contract (there have been blogs that have done all these things). When the goal is met, they know they've succeeded!

When you start your blog, spend some time thinking about how *you* will define success. Do you want to help your entire family keep in touch? Do you want to let your friends back home know more about your college experience? Are you starting a company and trying to get attention in the media? Consider writing your goals into your very first blog post and then returning to that post every few months to see whether your goals have changed and to remind yourself of what you're trying to accomplish.

Writing well

Blogs are frequently characterized as being poorly written, misspelled, and full of grammatical no-nos like incomplete sentences. Most criticism has at least some basis in reality, and this case is no different. Many blogs *are* written very casually, with only cursory attention paid to spelling and grammar.

For many, this is part of the charm of the format. The colloquial, conversational tone is accessible and easy to read, and bloggers who write informally seem very approachable and friendly.

This isn't an excuse, however, for ignoring all the rules of writing. Blogs that are well-written and spelled correctly are just as likely (perhaps more so) to be read as those that aren't. You can develop a friendly, personal way of writing without losing touch with the dictionary. I encourage the use of spellchecking, even for very informal blogs intended for friends and family.

For a professional blog, don't even consider writing without paying attention to spelling and grammar. Your readers will run the other way, and your competitors will get a good snicker out of it.

Most importantly, however, is to think through your writing and consider your reader. Take the time to practice and develop a voice that sounds personal and conversational while still qualifying as good, engaging writing. Don't let the chatty style of a blog fool you — the best bloggers spend just as much time writing a casual blog post as they would a work memo.

You can find tips on how to develop your voice in Chapter 8.

Posting frequently

Commit yourself to writing new posts on your blog *frequently*. Ah, "frequently." Such a deceptive little word — because really, what does it mean?

For some people, frequently is every day. For others, it's three times a day. For the purposes of having a blog that doesn't eat up every spare moment in your life and that's still updated enough to keep people interested, define the word *frequently* as at least two or three times a week. (If you want to blog more often than that, go to town.) This number of updates strikes a good balance for most blogs.

 Many bloggers use a little trick to account for periods of writers block or for when they go on vacation: They write posts ahead of time and then save them for later. Some blog software even allows you to schedule a date and time for a post to go live, making it possible for you keep your readers entertained even while you're having your appendix removed or sitting on a beach in Hawaii.

Pacing yourself is also important. In the first heady days of having a blog, the posts flow freely and easily, but after a few months, you might find it difficult to be creative.

Interacting with comments

Comments are what make blogs really different from a Web site; the opportunity to interact and converse with the creator of a Web site and with other readers is almost unique to blogs. Bulletin boards offer one way to engage in online conversation on the Web, but they aren't as directed as blogs.

Visitors to a blog have the opportunity to leave a comment on each post. Sometimes that comment is in reaction to what they read; sometimes it might be a suggestion or question. Because any reader can leave a comment, sometimes comments are even left about other comments!

Blog posts often include a link directly underneath each post indicating how many comments have been left. Clicking this link takes you to a page that displays the post, any comments that have been left on it, and a form you can use to leave your own comment.

After a comment has been made, it is displayed in the comments area, usually labeled with the comment writer's name, along with the date and time the comment was left. On some popular blogs, readers compete to see who can leave the first comment on a new blog post.

In Rose Levy Beranbaum's blog Real Baking with Rose (`www.realbaking withrose.com`), Rose often responds in the comments on her blogs posts to answer questions. Rose's comments have a shaded background that other comments don't have (see Figure 1-12).

Not every blog allows comments. Many popular bloggers find that they're overwhelmed by the sheer volume of responses they get and must turn off comments because they can't keep up with them. We should all be so lucky to have that problem. For most bloggers, comments are an important way of developing a dialogue with readers.

I recommend you keep comments turned on in your blog. They're an easy way to involve your audience in your topic and to get valuable feedback about what you're doing with your blog.

Unfortunately, spammers are able to take advantage of comments as easily as they are of sending you unwanted e-mail. If you keep comments turned on, you'll get unwanted comments with commercial messages. Some might even be offensive, just as spam e-mail sometimes is. If you decide to allow comments on your blog, be sure to read them and delete inappropriate messages. Your readers will thank you. In Chapter 10, I talk at length about how to cut down on spam comments.

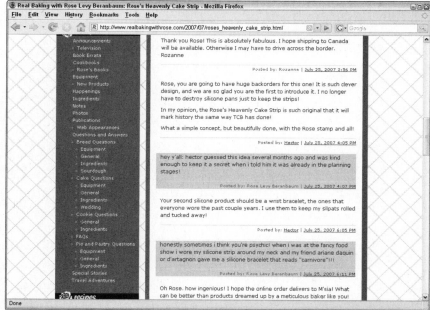

Figure 1-12: The Real Baking with Rose blog allows readers to leave comments and questions for the blog's author.

Courtesy of Rose Levy Beranbaum, author of The Cake Bible

Chapter 2

Starting a Blog

· ·

In This Chapter

▶ Signing up with Blogger to get started

▶ Writing your first blog post

▶ Managing your blog settings

▶ Customizing the template to match your style

· ·

*E*nough chitchat. It's time to start blogging! Part of the beauty of a blog is how quickly and easily you can get going — you can go from zero to blog in about 10 minutes with good blog software. (Of course, the medium's detractors say this convenience is responsible for a lot of self-indulgent navel-gazing, but I'm sure you have great plans for your little piece of the Internet.)

The first question is what kind of blogging software to use. Many bloggers, no matter what software they ultimately choose, find it useful to begin a test blog where they can experiment and figure out how to use the medium. There's no better way to do this than with what's called a hosted blog software solution.

Hosted blog software is a blogging tool that lives on the Web server of a company that provides blogging services. When you use hosted blogging software, you use that company's Web server to post to your blog, and the company provides you with a Web address. You don't need any of the resources that a normal Web site requires — a domain name, Web site hosting, HTML or FTP software — to create a blog. Best of all, many hosted blog software solutions are free . . . at least at the basic level. (If you want service upgrades, be prepared to fork over some cash.)

The alternative to hosted blog software is *server-based blog software* that you install on a Web server. Most professional bloggers and companies ultimately choose to go this route for the added control and customization they allow. To read more about the pros and cons of these two kinds of blog software and decide which is right for you, jump to Chapter 4.

In this chapter, you get started with a test blog. I show you how to set up a blog with Blogger, one of the Web's oldest and most well-known blogging companies.

Starting a Blog with Blogger

There's no better place to get introduced to blogging than Blogger (`www.blogger.com`). It's free, fast, and easy to use. Because getting started is so easy, Blogger is a good place to play with code and discover how blogging works without having to invest a lot of time and energy in Web servers and complicated installation processes.

Blogger (shown in Figure 2-1) promises to get you blogging in three steps: creating an account, naming your blog, and choosing a template.

Each hosted blog software platform has a different process for getting started, but each one requires the same kind of information: contact information for you and a name for your blog.

Blogger was acquired by the popular search engine company Google in 2002. Besides being a search engine, Google offers a number of popular Web-based software tools that you might already use, such as Gmail. Remember that because Google is improving the Blogger service all the time, you may see differences between what is printed here and how it works today.

Figure 2-1: Get a free, easy-to-use blog set up quickly with Blogger.

Creating an account

Before signing up with Blogger, you need login information (a username and password) that you can get in several ways:

- ✔ **Through a Google account:** If you have an account with one of Google's services, such as Gmail, you can log in to Blogger by using that account information.

- ✔ **Through Blogger:** If you don't have a Google account, you get one when you sign up with Blogger.

- ✔ **Through a pre-Google Blogger account:** If you started an account with Blogger before Google acquired it, click the Claim Your Old Blogger Account link at the top of the Blogger home page (refer to Figure 2-1).

To sign up for Blogger when you don't have a Google account, here's what you do:

1. **Click the Create Your Blog Now button on the Blogger home page.**

2. **Type your e-mail address in the Email Address field.**

3. **Choose a password and type it in the Enter a Password field.**

   As you type your password, Blogger indicates whether you need to increase the strength — that is, how difficult it would be for someone to guess your password — of your password. Click the Password Strength link to read about creating a more secure password.

4. **Retype the password in the Retype Password field.**

5. **Type the word shown as an image in the Word Verification field.**

6. **Select the Acceptance of Terms check box.**

   You can read the Terms of Service to see what you're agreeing to by clicking the Terms of Service link.

7. **Click Continue and move on to the "Naming your blog" section.**

To sign up for Blogger with an existing Google account, follow these steps:

1. **Click the Create Your Blog Now button on the Blogger home page.**

   You see the Sign up for Blogger page.

2. **Type your Google account password into the password field and select the Acceptance of Terms check box.**

   You can read the Terms of Service to see what you're agreeing to by clicking the Terms of Service link.

3. **Fill out the Display name field with the name you want to use on your blog.**

4. **Click Continue and move on to the "Naming your blog" section.**

Naming your blog

When you have a Blogger account set up, you choose a name for your blog. If you're creating a blog you really plan to use (rather than just test), you should give a lot of thought to choosing a name that will portray your tone and content well. I talk more about naming your blog in Chapter 3. If you plan to use this blog as a test space, don't worry too much about choosing a name with meaning, but be sure you choose something you can remember!

To name your blog:

1. **Type the name of the blog in the Blog Title field.**

   You can type about 50 characters in this field.

2. **Decide what phrase to use in your *URL* and type it in the Blog Address field.**

   A *URL* (uniform resource locator) is better known as a Web address. Visitors to your blog will type this address into the address bar of their Web browsers. You can use anything you like as a URL as long as it isn't being used by someone else, but it's a good idea to keep it short, sweet, and memorable. You cannot use spaces or punctuation, except dashes.

   You can type about 35 characters in this field.

3. **Click the Check Availability link to see whether the Web address you want to use is available. If it isn't, type a new phrase into the Blog address field and try again.**

   It might take several tries to find an available blog address — Blogger is popular!

4. **Click Continue.**

   You can now proceed to the Choose a Template phase of this operation, covered in the following section.

Choosing a template

One of the fun features of Blogger is that you can choose from a number of templates to use for your blog. The template determines both the look and feel of your blog, and also how the blog elements are laid out on the page. Blogger has some very fun templates to choose from, and don't forget that you can change the template later if your first choice no longer looks as fresh in six months. (For more info, see the "Choosing a new template" section, later in this chapter.)

To choose a template during the initial setup of your blog, follow these steps:

1. **Use the scroll bar to scroll through the available templates in the Choose a Template screen (see Figure 2-2).**

   The previews shown here give you an idea of how your blog would look in the various templates.

2. **When you find something intriguing, click the preview template link below the thumbnail.**

   A larger image of the template opens in a new browser window so you can take a closer look. Close the window with the preview when you finish.

   You can preview as many or as few templates as you like by using the corresponding preview template links.

3. **After you've decided on a template, select the radio button below the template of your choice.**

4. **Click Continue.**

   Blogger displays a Congratulations screen confirming that your blog has been created, and a Start Posting link you can use to add an entry to your blog.

After you've completed this setup process, you won't need to repeat it when you want to add a post to your blog. The next time you come to Blogger, simply use the login boxes in the top-right corner of the home page (refer to Figure 2-1) to log in and get started posting to your blog.

Figure 2-2:
You can preview the Blogger templates when you start a new blog.

Writing a Post

This is the moment when you join the blogosphere by writing your very first blog post, an *entry,* for your new blog. (The *blogosphere,* by the way, is the semi-ironic way that bloggers refer to themselves, their blogs, and the phenomenon that is blogging today. You're a member of the blogosphere when you have a blog, whether or not you think it's the dumbest word you've heard this year.)

The mechanics of writing a blog post aren't much different from writing an e-mail. Most posts are quite short and are written directly and conversationally. Of course, you might decide to use your blog to write the next Great American Novel, in which case your posts might be quite a bit longer than what's standard! That's fine, too. Every blog takes on a personality and life of its own. If you want to find your own narrative voice for your blog, go to Chapter 8.

If you've used a Web-based e-mail service like Gmail, Hotmail, or MSN, blog software feels very familiar. Creating the post is simply a matter of filling in the appropriate fields in a form, formatting some text, and then sending it off to its destination — in this case, to your blog, rather than a friend's inbox.

Here's how to write a blog post:

1. **Go to the publishing screen.**

   If you just finished signing up for your blog as described in the earlier part of this chapter, click the Start Posting link to start a blog post; the publishing screen appears, as shown in Figure 2-3.

   If you took a break and are coming back to Blogger, log in. Once you are in, Blogger takes you to the Dashboard — a kind of control panel showing you the blogs you have set up, and giving you access to tools like posting, help resources, or even creating another blog. Click the New Post link on the Dashboard to get to the Publishing screen shown in Figure 2-3.

2. **Enter a title for your post in the Title field.**

   Titles are a lot like newspaper headlines: They should be catchy and informative, and they should encourage visitors to your blog to continue reading the rest of the post.

3. **Write your post in the large field.**

   Consider writing your blog posts in a standard word-processing program such as Notepad or Microsoft Word — and saving it. Too many bloggers have spent hours composing right in the entry field of their blog software only to find that their Internet connection has failed or another technical problem has occurred — which results in a lost post. You don't want to lose all your carefully considered prose just because your cat pulled the cable modem out of the wall! Blogger does have an Auto Save feature installed, but it's still safer to compose offline, and simply copy and paste the text into the blog software.

Font Face drop-down list

Font Size drop-down list   Numbered List   Blockquote

Bold   Link   Check Spelling

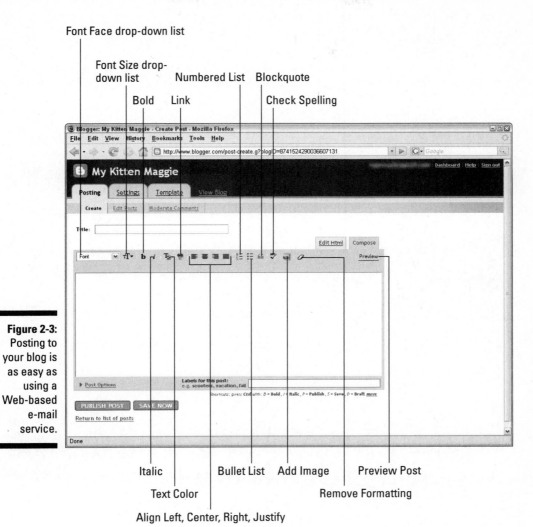

Figure 2-3:
Posting to
your blog is
as easy as
using a
Web-based
e-mail
service.

Italic   Bullet List   Add Image   Preview Post

Text Color   Remove Formatting

Align Left, Center, Right, Justify

4. **Format your post.**

   Blogger's entry field includes icons across the top that let you change the
   font and font size, apply bold and italics to text, and create common formatting styles like lists. To use these features, select the text in the field
   that you want to modify by clicking and dragging over the text; then click
   the appropriate icon or select an option from the desired drop-down list.

If you know how to write HTML code, you can also try composing your post
in the Edit HTML mode. Click the Edit HTML tab and include HTML tags in
your text as needed. If you want to find out more about coding HTML, I discuss common tags in Chapter 5.

Adding a link

One of the icons that deserves special attention is the Link icon — the small globe icon with a link of chain on top of it (refer to Figure 2-3). Use this option whenever you want to link to another blog, a news story, that embarrassing Web site your best friend just created, or any other Web site.

When you want to create a clickable link in your blog post, follow these steps:

1. **Highlight the text you want to make clickable by clicking and dragging.**

2. **Click the Link icon.**

   A pop-up window appears, as shown in Figure 2-4.

3. **Enter the URL of the Web site you want to link to and click OK.**

   Include the full URL of the Web page in this field. You need to keep the `http://` that is prefilled in the form for you. The URL you use should look like this:

   ```
   http://en.wikipedia.org/wiki/Abyssinian_(cat)
   ```

   And not this:

   ```
   en.wikipedia.org/wiki/Abyssinian_(cat)
   ```

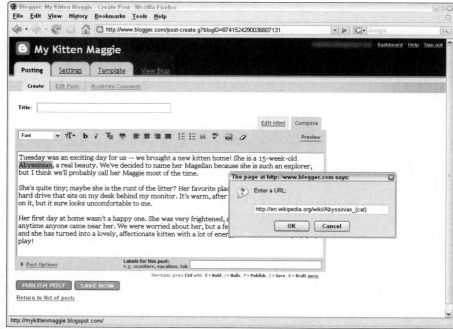

Figure 2-4: Using the Link icon to create clickable text in your blog post.

The easiest way to make sure you have the right link is to go to the Web page you want to link to, copy the URL from the address bar (press Ctrl+C to copy and then Ctrl+V to paste; on a Mac, use ⌘ instead of Ctrl).

After you click OK, the linked text appears in underlined blue text. It isn't clickable until you publish it.

Don't forget that if you know HTML and would prefer to create the link manually using HTML code, you can do so from the Edit HTML tab.

Spellchecking your text

Blogger provides a handy tool for anyone who needs some help with spelling (and who doesn't?). After you finish writing your post, click the Check Spelling icon. It's the icon showing the letters ABC with a check mark underneath (refer to Figure 2-3).

Incorrectly spelled words are highlighted in yellow. Click any misspelled word to see a list of suggested alternatives, as shown in Figure 2-5. Select any suggestion from the list or simply type your own correction.

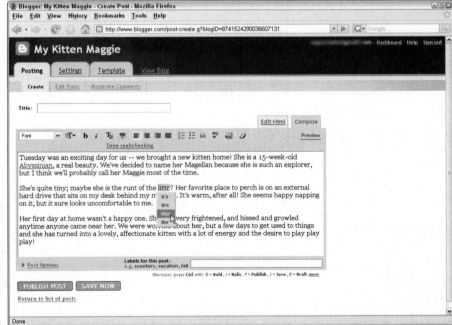

Figure 2-5:
Blogs don't have to be full of misspellings (they just often are).

Including an image

One way to make your blog post more appealing is to include an image. Longtime bloggers will tell you that adding a photo or a piece of artwork is a great way to get visitors to read more of the text that surrounds it. And of course everyone knows how many words that photo is worth!

Blogger has some good built-in tools for uploading an image that's already the right size and format for displaying on the Web. If you need help formatting photographs from a digital camera or another source, Chapter 13 shows you how to make the most of some of the great photo software options available today.

Here's how to upload an image from your computer to add it to your blog post:

1. **Click the Add Image icon.**

   It looks like a photograph (refer to Figure 2-3).

   The Upload Images window opens.

   Some Web browsers have begun to include functionality that blocks pop-up browser windows from opening. If you click the Add Image icon and nothing happens, go into your browser settings to turn off this protection. In some browsers, it's possible to do this for certain Web sites rather than for all of them, so you can choose to allow Blogger to open a pop-up window without subjecting yourself to other annoying pop-ups. Consult your browser's Help menu if you need assistance doing this.

2. **Click the Browse button in the Add an Image from Your Computer section of the page.**

   A File Upload dialog box opens, as shown in Figure 2-6.

3. **Locate the image you want to upload from your computer and select it.**

4. **Click Open.**

   The location of the image is inserted into the image field.

5. **Choose a layout and image size from the options:**

   • *Layout* determines how text will wrap around the image. You can choose None, Left, Center, or Right.

   • *Image size* determines what size the image will be shown in your blog post, regardless of how big the source image is. You can choose Small, Medium, or Large.

6. **Click to accept the Terms of Service.**

7. **Click the Upload Image button.**

   Your image is uploaded and inserted into your blog post.

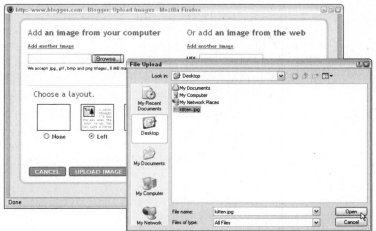

Figure 2-6:
Using
Blogger, you
can upload
an image
from your
desktop and
display it in
your blog
post.

8. Click Done.

The Upload Images window closes, and your image is visible in your blog post field.

You can also add an image to your post from another Web site. As long as you have permission to use the image, or it is in the public domain (read more about copyright in Chapter 9), you can do so easily using Blogger. Here's how:

1. Find an image or photo on the Web that you want to use.

Make sure you are allowed to use it by checking copyright permission, or asking the creator.

2. Right-click the image and select Copy Image Location from the menu that opens.

Phrasing of this option may differ in different browsers. If you don't see anything that looks right, choose Properties from the menu. A window opens that shows you the URL address, which you can then click and drag to highlight. Press Ctrl+C to copy the address; on a Mac, use ⌘ instead of Ctrl.

3. Head back to Blogger and start a new post, or open one that you have already created.

4. Click the Add Image icon.

It looks like a photograph (refer to Figure 2-3).

The Upload Images window opens.

5. Press Ctrl+V (⌘+V on the Mac) to paste the image address into the URL field on the right of the window.

6. **Choose a layout and image size from the options:**

    - *Layout* determines how text will wrap around the image. You can choose None, Left, Center, or Right.

    - *Image size* determines what size the image will be shown in your blog post, regardless of how big the source image is. You can choose Small, Medium, or Large.

7. **Click to accept the Terms of Service.**

8. **Click the Upload Image button.**

    Your image is uploaded and inserted into your blog post.

9. **Click Done.**

    The Upload Images window closes, and your image is visible in your blog post field.

Publishing Your Post

When you're satisfied with your blog post, you can publish it so that the world can admire your erudition. This isn't hard: Click the orange Publish Post button at the bottom of the page. Your post is published on your blog, making it available for others to read.

Before you publish, you can take advantage of three areas of the Blogger publish page that I find very helpful: previewing, saving as a draft, and post options.

Previewing your post

Before you publish, you can preview what you've created by clicking the Preview link found on the far right of the editing icons. This preview is WYSI-WYG (what you see is what you get), which means that it shows you the post exactly as you formatted it, with links, text colors, embedded images, and so on.

I like to preview my post before I publish because I find it's easier to read for meaning and content at this point. Think of this as a last chance to catch grammar problems or even to think twice about what you're posting if it's controversial. Of course, you can also see how the text and content flows around any images you have added.

If you see changes you want to make, simply click the Hide Preview link to go back to the editing screen.

Saving as a draft

Many bloggers like to create posts in advance of when they plan to publish them. For example, if you're planning a vacation, you can write several posts before you leave. When you put them into Blogger, click the Save button instead of the Publish button. This sets the status of the post to draft, and even though it is accessible via the Blogger Dashboard, it won't be visible on your blog until you go back into the post and click the Publish Post button.

When you create a post, Blogger automatically saves it once a minute, so you may not have to click Save if you want to keep a post as a draft. Clicking the Save button, however, ensures that the saved version is the latest one. If you want to keep the post as a draft until later, simply click the Return to List of Posts link when you are finished.

Setting post options

Below the entry text and just above the Publish Post button, you see a Post Options link. Click this link to open a menu. You can choose whether you want readers to be able to comment on your blog post by selecting the Allow or Don't Allow radio button.

The decision to turn off comments is one you can make at any time, so if you decide later that you don't want to receive further comments, you can always edit the entry and turn this option off then. Most of the time, allowing comments is a good idea; after all, part of what makes a blog exciting to read is the opportunity to interact with the blogger. Sometimes, though, you might write an entry that you don't want to hear discussion on, perhaps because you don't want to start a long argument or because the entry has become a target of spammers. You can find more about interacting with your reading community and preventing spam in Chapter 10.

The other option you can set is the publication date and time that appears on the post. By default, Blogger sets the publication date and time of the entry to the same date and time you began writing it. However, you have the power to alter the date and time. Setting the date in the future tells Blogger to hold your post until that date, making it easy for you to schedule blog posts for times when you're traveling, working, or otherwise unavailable.

Why might you choose to change the date or time?

✔ **Social or professional reasons.**

- Create a blog post for a friend's birthday and make the date match the time your friend was born.

- If you're blogging at work, it might be a good idea to set your date and time to a period when you weren't supposed to also be at your desk (ahem) *working*.

✔ **To work around your schedule.**

- If you take a long time to write a post, by the time you're ready to publish it, you might need to put a more realistic time on the entry.

- If you save your post as a draft and publish it later, you can update the date and time to accurately reflect the real publication date.

Changing the date and/or time is as easy as typing the new figures in the same format.

Viewing Your Blog Post

After you publish, you can see how your post looks on the blog. This is a rewarding step to take and an important one not to skip. Even if you preview your post before publishing, you haven't seen your post as your readers see it. You can do that only by actually going to your blog in the Web browser and taking a look.

Viewing your post is important for another reason, too: Computers can still make errors or fail between the moment you click Publish and when the entry shows up on the blog. I like to look at my blog every time I post a new entry to make sure it actually looks right on the page, and that it was processed successfully by the blog software.

When you click the Publish button with Blogger, the system provides you with a handy link to view your blog. Click View Blog to head over to your blog and see your handiwork.

Of course, if you prefer taking the long way, you can always type the Web address you chose when you set up your blog into the Web browser and get to your blog without going through the Blogger Dashboard.

While you look at your blog, make sure the formatting, images, and text look the way you want them to, and click on any links you created. If anything doesn't work quite right, go back into Blogger and make changes to your entry.

Setting the Dashboard Settings

Blog software, as a rule, is quite customizable. As the owner of the blog, you can decide a number of things about the way your blog looks and works, and you can control those elements from the control panel — called the Dashboard in Blogger — of your blog software.

Most blog software packages work quite similarly, and if you know how Blogger works, you can make the most of any other software.

Blogger divides its settings into several areas: Basic, Publishing, Formatting, Comments, Archiving, Site Feed, Email, and Permissions. I cover some important highlights from each area in this section.

You access all the Blogger settings via the Blogger Dashboard. (In other blog software packages, this area is called the control panel, the admin panel, and so on.) To reach the Dashboard, just log in to the Blogger Web site. If you're already logged in, look for a link to the Dashboard in the upper-right corner of any page and click it. My Dashboard is shown in Figure 2-7.

The Dashboard shows all the blogs you have started with Blogger. For each blog, you can quickly start a new post, or jump into editing older posts. As well, a click takes you into the blog settings or to the template or layout you are using.

If you make changes to any of the settings pages, be sure to click the Save Settings button at the bottom of each page to save your new settings.

Figure 2-7:
The Blogger Dashboard gives you quick access to layout and posting tools.

Making basic changes

On the Basic Settings tab of the Dashboard, you can change the name of your blog (Blogger refers to this as the blog title) and also give it a short description. Most of the Blogger templates display the description near the top of the page.

Here's how:

1. **From the Dashboard, click the Settings link for the blog you want to edit.**

   You go directly to the Basic Settings tab shown in Figure 2-8.

2. **Edit the Title and/or Description.**

3. **Scroll to the bottom of the screen and click Save Settings.**

   Blogger reloads the screen with a confirmation message that your settings were saved at the top of the page.

The most interesting setting on the Basic Settings tab is Show Email Post Links. Setting this option to Yes adds a small e-mail icon to each of the blog posts on your blog. This setting permits your blog visitors to e-mail the post to a friend or colleague who might find it interesting. This is a nice little service for your readers that might gain you a few more visitors.

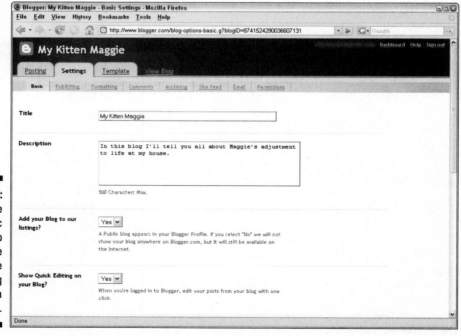

Figure 2-8:
Using the Basic Settings tab to change the name or your blog or add a description.

At the bottom of the Basic Settings tab is a dangerous but important button: Delete This Blog. If you ever decide to remove your immortal words from the Web entirely, this button removes your blog — all your posts, images, and other files — from Blogger and from the Web.

Making publishing changes

The Publishing tab of the Dashboard is small but mighty! The most important setting here is the blog address setting. If you aren't happy with the Web address for your blog, you can edit the address here. For instance, if you start a blog called "My New Kitten Maggie" and your cat grows up (they do that, I hear), you might want to edit both the name and the location of your blog. (The name change must be made on the Basic Settings tab, as I describe in the preceding section.) Use the Publishing tab to change the URL, for example

```
http://mynewkittenmaggie.blogspot.com
```

into

```
http://mygrownupcatmaggie.blogspot.com
```

You can only change your address to one that isn't already in use by another Blogger member, so it make take several tries to find one that is available.

Blogger has great tool that allows you to export your blog as HTML pages to your own Web server so that you can display them as part of a larger Web site. To configure Blogger to perform this function, look for information on how to get started on the Publishing tab.

Making formatting changes

On the Formatting tab of the Dashboard, you can customize how your blog is presented, from the format of the date and time to the number of posts on your blog home page. You can also set the language of your blog.

My favorite setting in this tab, however, is the Post Template setting at the bottom of the page. Many blogs follow a standard format. For instance, if you start a movie-review blog, you might choose to follow a similar way of reviewing each movie, perhaps by giving the name of the movie, the director, the lead actors' names, a short review, and a numeric rating. No matter what movie you review, you provide the same information and use the same format each time your write a blog post.

The Post Template allows you to set up standard HTML code that formats your blog post. After you set up a Post Template, every time you start a blog post, that code is automatically placed in the entry, and formatting your post is as easy as putting the information in the right spots.

I can't cover this feature in depth because I don't know just what kind of standard formatting you want to use, but the process of implementing a standard template works like this:

1. **From the Dashboard, click the Settings link for the blog you want to edit.**

    You go directly to the Basic Settings tab (refer to Figure 2-8).

2. **Click the Formatting option in the Settings area.**

    The Formatting tab opens, as shown in Figure 2-9.

3. **Scroll to the bottom of the screen and type or paste the text or HTML code you want to use in every blog post into the Post Template field.**

4. **Click Save Settings.**

    Blogger reloads the screen with a confirmation message that your settings were saved at the top of the page.

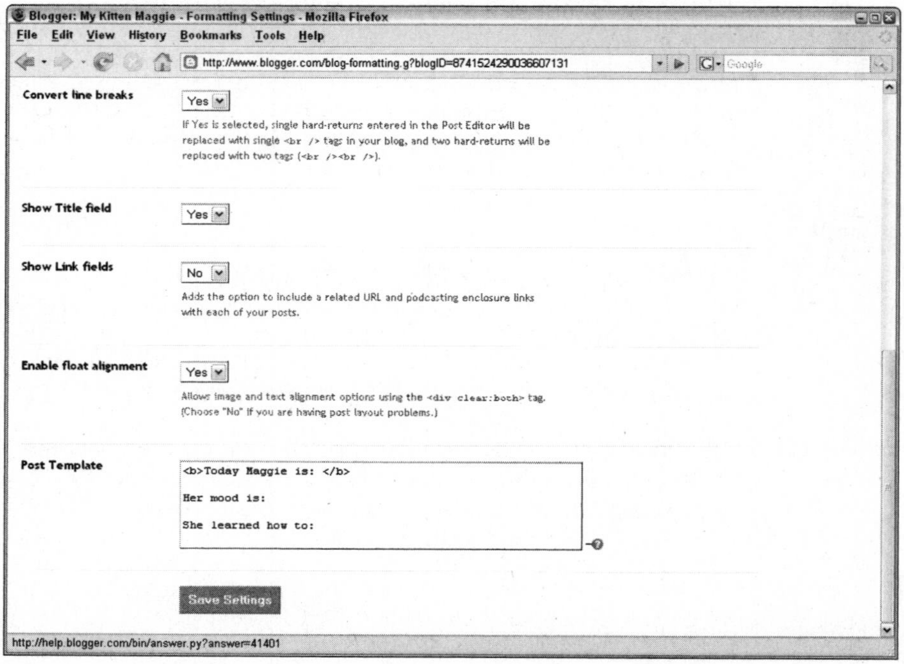

Figure 2-9:
Text or code put into the Post Template field is automatically included in every new blog post.

Making comment changes

Comments are both a strength and a weakness of the blog medium. The ability to leave a comment and interact or converse with a blogger is imminently attractive to readers. This interaction is very valuable to bloggers, as well.

Commenting has a downside: The technology has been discovered by spammers as well. Just as with e-mail, you can expect some commenters to tell you about fabulous mortgage opportunities, Mexican pharmaceuticals, and other fabulous even less savory possibilities — information neither you nor your readers want.

The Comments Settings tab of the Dashboard provides settings that can help to cut down on the amount of spam found on your blog. One of the best ways to accomplish this is to set who can comment on your blog. From the Comments Settings tab, use the Who Can Comment pull-down menu to select:

- ✔ **Anyone:** This option allows the widest possible audience, with no limitations on who is allowed to comment. It provides no spam prevention but imposes no barriers to leaving a comment to genuine commenters.

- ✔ **Only registered users:** Set your blog to accept comments only from registered members of Blogger to cut down on some spam. Don't forget that not everyone has a Blogger account, or wants one, so you might lose some real comments.

- ✔ **Only members of your blog:** Disallow anyone who isn't a member of your blog from leaving a comment. No one you haven't personally authorized as a member will be able to leave a comment. This is a lot of overhead for you, but you won't get any spam.

You can add members to your blog to your blog from the Permissions settings tab.

There are two other important Comment settings you can implement if you have spam problems. From the Comments Settings tab of the blog:

- ✔ **Comment moderation:** Change the Enable comment moderation setting to Yes. Turning on comment moderation prevents anyone from being able to post a comment you haven't approved. When someone leaves a comment, you get an e-mail letting you know about the comment. From the Dashboard, you can authorize or reject the publication of the comment. You can also moderate comments via e-mail.

   Moderating comments is a lot of work for you, but it improves the quality and readability of comments on your blog for your readers, and it discourages spammers in the future.

- ✔ **Word verification:** Change the Show word verification for comments to Yes. People who want to comment on blogs with word verification turned on must type a word displayed in an image in order to submit a comment. Because many spammers use automated scripts to post spam on blogs, and only humans can read the text in an image, this verification cuts down significantly on the amount of spam — or at least guarantees that the spam you receive is from a real human rather than a machine.

At the bottom of the Comment Settings tab, you can enter an e-mail address in the Comment Notification Address field at which you would like to receive notification when a comment is left on your blog. This is a great way to keep track of comments left on your blog, especially when you have a lot of old posts you might not see comments on when you view your blog.

Making e-mail changes

On the Email Settings tab of the Dashboard, you can turn on a cool feature that allows you to post to your blog by sending an e-mail message. When configured, you can simply send an e-mail to the address from any device capable of sending e-mail (like your phone!). The subject of the e-mail becomes the title of the blog post, and the text of the e-mail is the entry body. It's a very quick, easy way to publish to your blog, great for when you're traveling.

To set up a Mail-to-Blogger Address, visit the Email Settings tab and fill out the address field. Be sure to save the settings and test to make sure it works!

Making permission changes

On the Permissions tab of the Dashboard, you can add authors to your blog — people who can also contribute blog posts, creating a group blog. To add someone as an author, you simply need that person's e-mail address. If the person you're adding has a Blogger or Google account, I recommend using that address so that all his or her Blogger and Google account services are tied together.

To add an author:

1. **From the Dashboard, click the Settings link for the blog you want to edit.**

   You go directly to the Basic Settings tab (refer to Figure 2-8).

2. **Click the Permissions option in the Settings area.**

   The Permissions tab appears.

3. **Click the Add Authors button.**

   A field for e-mail addresses appears.

4. **Type or paste the e-mail addresses of the authors you want to invite to post on your blog in the field.**

Editing templates old-skool: Using code

If you're a Web designer or coder and want to sink your teeth into the Blogger template itself, you can still do so. To get to the code from the Blogger Dashboard, choose Template➪Edit HTML. You can edit the template in two ways:

✔ **Edit the HTML template directly within the Blogger Dashboard,** previewing and saving the Template as you go.

✔ **Download the template to your computer,** edit it in your chosen HTML editor, and then upload the new template.

Both approaches require you to be proficient with HTML and CSS and to know a certain amount of Blogger's own coding language to be successful.

5. **Click Invite.**

    Blogger reloads the screen, and displays the information for the invited author.

You can also decide whether anyone can view the blog, or you can chose to restrict viewers only to people you invite or the authors of the blog. If you want to blog only for your family, use the Permissions tab to invite them as readers, and others are blocked from even seeing the blog (much less leaving a comment!).

From the Permissions tab, you can select who can view your blog in the Blog Readers section by choosing between: Anybody, Only people I choose, or Only blog authors.

Customizing Your Template

The layout you picked when you started your blog might look great to you, but many bloggers want to tweak and customize the look and feel of their blogs — I know I did when I started working on my blog. The words and pictures were personal, and I wanted to make the rest of the site look more like my own Web site rather than a Blogger design.

There are three ways of going about customizing the design of a Blogger blog; you can accomplish all three by going to the Dashboard and clicking the Layout link next to the blog you want to customize.

Upgrading to templates

If the first item on the Template tab isn't Page Elements, you might need to upgrade your template to the current format. This is pretty simple to do:

1. **Click the Customize Design tab.**

2. **Click Upgrade Your Template.**

3. **Select a template to use.**

   If you're already using one of the existing Blogger designs, it is pre-selected for you, and you can go to Step 4.

To pick a new template, preview any template by clicking the Preview Template link below the corresponding thumbnail. A larger image of the template opens in a new browser window so you can take a closer look. Close the window with the preview when you're finished with it. When you've found a template you want to use, select it.

4. **Click the Save Template button.**

   The template is implemented in the latest format, which allows you to add or arrange layout elements on the next screen.

If you see the word "Template" instead of "Layout" next to your blog information in the Dashboard, you probably are using a blog that was set up before Blogger added the Layout features. You need to upgrade your blog in order to use the new features. To do so, read the "Upgrading your template" sidebar in this chapter. It's extra confusing because the Dashboard refers to Layout, but the tab for the same features is called Template.

In Blogger, the layout and design of the blog are controlled by a single template — a document that controls everything from the size of the text to the color of the background. Changing the templates changes the design. In the past, changing the template required a fairly extensive knowledge of HTML and Blogger code, but recent changes put more control at your fingertips.

Editing page elements

When you click on the Layout link, the Page Elements tab opens by default. The Page Elements tab (see Figure 2-10) of Blogger is a ground-breaking tool for bloggers that gives you finer control over the layout and look of your blog without requiring you to become an HTML guru and stay up late learning the intricacies of Web publishing. It reflects the growing do-it-yourself attitude found in the blogosphere — bloggers want sites that reflect their own sensibilities, but not everyone has the time to become an expert or the budget to hire one.

It also reflects the growing expertise of many computer users who are able to edit photographs and create graphics, and it gives them the ability to make the most use of those skills.

In the Page Elements tab (see Figure 2-10), you see a wireframe of your blog template. A *wireframe* is a visual representation of the template layout using only outlines, or boxes, of the elements.

Using this tool, you can:

- Click **Edit** for any page element already being used and change its formatting. In most layouts, this means you can customize the navigation bar, blog header, blog posts, and sidebar elements like About Me and the Archive.

- Click **Add a New Page Elements** to place polls, images, lists, advertising, and more, from a library of Blogger-provided elements in your sidebar:

  - Poll
  - List
  - Link List
  - Picture
  - Google AdSense (see Chapter 16)
  - Text
  - HTML/third-party functionality (see Chapter 12 for third-party tools you might enjoy)

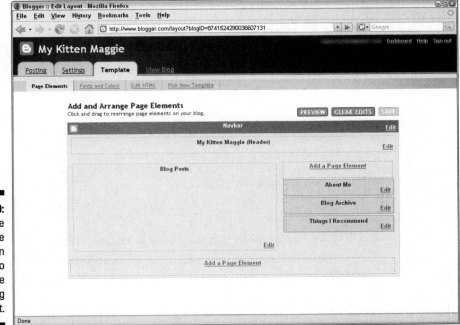

Figure 2-10:
Use the Template tab in Blogger to customize your blog layout.

- RSS or Atom feed (more about RSS in Chapter 11)
- Video clips
- Logos
- Your profile
- Headlines

✔ **Move page elements** around by clicking and dragging them to a new position.

✔ **Preview edits you have made** before saving them to your blog by making a change and then clicking the Preview button.

✔ **Revert** to the original version of your template by clicking the Clear Edits button.

Editing fonts and colors

If you like the customization possibilities in the preceding section, I think you'll like what you can do in the Fonts and Colors section of the Template tab as well.

This screen gives you fine control over the colors of the

✔ Text

✔ Page header

✔ Dates

✔ Blog entry titles and footers

✔ Sidebar background, text, and titles

✔ Link color

You can also edit the fonts being used for the text elements of the blog, as well as control the size of those text elements. If all the colors of the rainbow get to be too much, click the Revert to Template Default link and start over with the template designer's choices.

To edit a font color:

1. **Click the Fonts and Colors tab of the Template area.**

2. **Select the item you want to edit from the scrollable menu in the top left of the page.**

   In Figure 2-11, I selected the Post Title Color.

Figure 2-11:
Use Fonts
and Colors
to change
the text
colors on
your blog.

3. **Use any of the palettes on the right to choose a new color, by clicking the color box you want to use. You can choose from these palettes:**

- *Colors from your blog:* This palette shows the other colors you are using in your layout.

- *Colors that match your blog:* This palette shows colors that Blogger thinks fit in well with the colors already in use.

- *More colors:* This palette shows a selection of other colors you can play with.

- *Edit color hex code:* If you know the hexadecimal code for the color you want to use, you can type it here. *Hexadecimal code* is a code containing letters and numbers that equate to a color, and is used primarily by graphic and Web designers.

When you click a color, Blogger shows a preview of how it looks on your blog in the lower half of the screen.

4. **Once you have made your edits, click Save Changes.**

Blogger reloads a page with a confirmation that your edits have been saved.

Choosing a new template

When you want a fresh new look, sometimes no amount of tweaking is enough — you need an entirely new template design to work with. At any time, you can visit the Pick New Template section on the Template tab and look through the available Blogger templates, preview them, and select a new one to use on your blog. Click the Save Template button when you've selected a new template.

If you customize your template using the Fonts and Colors section and then pick a new template, all your edits and tweaks are lost. If you want to be able to implement those tweaks sometime in the future, print a copy of your blog and make notes about what colors you used for each element. Then put your paper template in a safe place!

As you look through the available templates, you see that some of them have multiple versions listed. The template designer has created variations on the main template that you might enjoy. To see the variation, simply select the radio button for one of the versions. The thumbnail loads, and when you preview the template, you can see a larger view.

Don't forget that you can customize your new template by using the Page Elements and the Fonts and Colors sections.

Chapter 3

Entering the Blogosphere

*I*f you put something on your blog, *anyone* can read it. Blogs, like all Web sites, are accessible anywhere in the world, anytime, and are readable by anyone who can access a computer and understand the language the blog is written in. (Some blog software does allow privacy settings or password protection — and if you're using these options you have more assurance of privacy.)

And, like all Web sites, blog posts can be printed, duplicated, faxed, posted on lamp posts, or distributed to a class. A reader of your blog can even copy and paste the text of your blog posts into a text editor or e-mail message, sending them buzzing around the world in the blink of an eye.

You can't know who is reading your blog, or why, or what they might do with what you post. I often talk to bloggers who say, "Well, my only readers are my friends and family, so I don't worry too much about what I write." Your friends and family may very well be reading (in fact, I hope they do or they'll miss you!) but they may not be the only readers. Don't make the mistake of assuming you know who is reading your blog! It isn't that your readers *aren't* "only your friends and family," but that you can't know that for sure.

Some blogs are hosted by sites that require you to register in order to use them, such as MySpace, and so by definition have a smaller potential audience. Those blogs can't be read by just anyone with a computer and an Internet connection; they can be read by anyone with a computer, an Internet connection, and an account on that service. They might be somewhat more private, but generally the barriers to registering for a service like MySpace are very low: You just need an e-mail address. The blogs might as well be public.

In rare instances, an entire blog is password-protected and therefore readable only by visitors who know the login information for the site. As long as that login information stays private, the blog is private.

In this chapter, I drive home the point that you shouldn't post anything to your blog that you don't want anyone in the world to read, and yes, that includes your best friend, your significant other, your mother, your co-workers, your boss, your landlord, your neighbor . . . you get the idea.

Understanding What Happens When You Publish

Blogging is a very immediate medium — when you publish a post, it goes live on your blog right away. In fact, several things happen the moment you click the publish button:

- ✔ The post appears at the top of your blog's home page.
- ✔ The post is added to your blog's archive, usually by both date and subject.
- ✔ An e-mail is sent to anyone who signed up for e-mail notifications.
- ✔ The post is added to your RSS feed, which is updated in newsreaders.
- ✔ If your blog software pings blog search engines and services, they receive a notice that your blog has been updated. (A *ping* is simply an electronic notification.)
- ✔ The post is indexed the next time a search engine crawler visits your blog.

All this happens whether you think about it or not. It's part of the beauty and effectiveness of this format that blog posts are quickly distributed with a minimum of effort on the part of the blogger. Blog software and services are designed to deliver your content quickly.

Of course, you can edit your blog posts after you post them, and many bloggers do this when necessary (see the "Making mistakes" section later in this chapter for some suggestions about doing this appropriately), but the fact is that the original post might be read or e-mailed before you make your edits. Editing after you post is a pretty ineffective way to control your message.

Publishing a blog or Web page can have a few other unintended effects as well:

- ✔ Other bloggers might quote your post and expand on it on their blogs, creating partial copies of your deathless prose.
- ✔ Your blog post might be pointed to from blog services and even partially excerpted.

✔ Search engines might cache or otherwise archive the content temporarily or permanently.

✔ Your blog post might get included in an Internet archive such as the Wayback Machine (`www.archive.org`).

These effects are demonstrated in Figure 3-1; a Google search for the phrase *what happens when you drink coke* turns up not only a blog post, but several references to that same post on other blogs and Web sites, and on the news-sharing site Digg. Google links to the original blog post, and a cached version archived by Google is also available.

I don't want to scare you — after all, publishing to your blog is a good thing! You want each of these processes to happen; each process is designed to bring readers to you and to present your content to your readers. But it's best to be sure about what you're posting before you do so.

If your blog includes controversial, emotional, personal, political, or other sensitive topics, read what you've written twice before you publish!

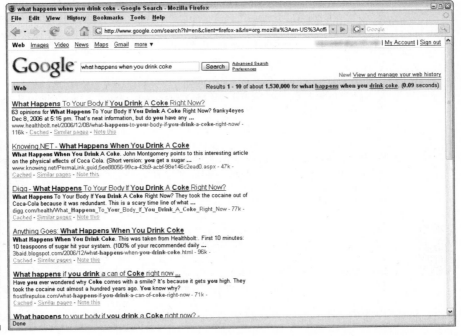

Figure 3-1: Searching for the topic of a post turns up the post, references to it, and links to the search engine's cached version.

Blogging Ethically

The best defense, as they say, is a good offense. As a blogger, you should think about what you write before you publish it as well as afterwards.

What I'm about to say might shock you, so prepare yourself: Bloggers have a code of ethics.

Okay, what I really mean is that *some* bloggers have a code of ethics. As blogs emerged as a new Web medium, they became associated with some styles of writing and types of content, and then a loose set of ethics and standards emerged that an ideal blogger adheres to.

For most old-school bloggers, the word to think about is *transparency.* This word is used as shorthand for a whole range of ideas:

- **Truth-telling and honesty:** In keeping with the diary format of a blog, being transparent on your blog has a lot to do with telling the truth about who you are, why you're blogging, and what you want to accomplish with your blog. The communication on a blog is about being open and honest, dealing straightforwardly with your topics and ideas, and with your readers. Blogging traditionalists think blogs shouldn't be used as corporate marketing mechanisms, at least not in the usual sense.

- **Admit mistakes:** No one is perfect, and you'll eventually make a mistake. Whether you post something you heard that turns out not to be true or you blog angry, the real test is how you respond to making a mistake. In the blogosphere, it's all about owning up to your words, apologizing if you need to, and making corrections when they're needed.

- **Dialogue:** A good blogger is aware of, and responsive to, his or her readers via the comments that they leave on blog posts. A blog isn't created in a vacuum. In fact, many bloggers will tell you that a blog is a great tool for building real relationships with people.

The idea that you can use a blog for meaningful interaction is revolutionary for this format. At the core, blogging is about real people talking with each other and sharing real knowledge and experiences.

Of course, that doesn't mean a blog is going to be great literature — and that's fine. But the ideas that being transparent represent are worthy ones, especially if you plan to blog about personal and sensitive topics.

Telling the truth

Being honest on your blog is an interesting concept, especially when you think about the number of people who choose to be anonymous. For many bloggers, telling the truth is first about emotional honesty and second — or perhaps not at all — about revealing who you are.

What it comes down to is this: The blogosphere doesn't like poseurs. If you choose to blog about your life and do so anonymously, be prepared to be challenged about whether you're a real person. If you're a CEO writing a blog, be prepared to defend your writing as your own.

Some blog hoaxes demonstrate the kind of thing I'm talking about. Perhaps the most famous occurred in 2001, when bloggers revealed that the blog of a young teenager who had just died of leukemia was a hoax. In fact, the life and death of Kaycee Nicole was the product of imagination, even though bloggers all over the world followed her blog, chatted with her online, even spoke with her on the phone during her illness. Bloggers tracked down evidence in the real world that she not only hadn't died, but hadn't even existed.

It isn't all about literary hoaxes, however. Bloggers have been slammed for blogging about products and services for money and not revealing that they were being paid. A blog scandal in 2003 put Dr Pepper into the public eye for soliciting blog posts from a group of teenagers about a new product called Raging Cow. The teens were given trips, samples of the product, and gift certificates, and asked to promote the drink on what were essentially personal blogs. Many did so without revealing that they were basically being paid to promote the product, and when the arrangement was discovered, it prompted a blogosphere boycott of the company and a lot of anger against the bloggers.

Interestingly, Dr Pepper also started a blog for the product written, ostensibly, by the Raging Cow herself during her travels around the country, as shown in Figure 3-2. This blog was roundly criticized at the time (for being fake, of course), but the idea of creating fictional characters that blog has stuck around and been used successfully since then. The format is still controversial, but it is also highly effective!

In general, you should follow these rules about honesty in your blogging:

- Explain who you are and why you're blogging.
- If you need to hide your identity or those of people you mention, indicate that you are doing so and why.
- If you start a fake blog, make sure you disclose somewhere on the site that it is, in fact, fake. (One would think it's pretty obvious that a blog that appears to be written by a cow is fake, but it doesn't hurt to say so, either.)
- If you're making money from your blog posts, explain the arrangement and how you're allowing it to influence (or not influence) what you write.
- If you mention a fact or story that you got from someone else, explain who. If you can link to it, do.
- Take responsibility for what's on your blog, no matter where else you might have heard or read about what you write about.

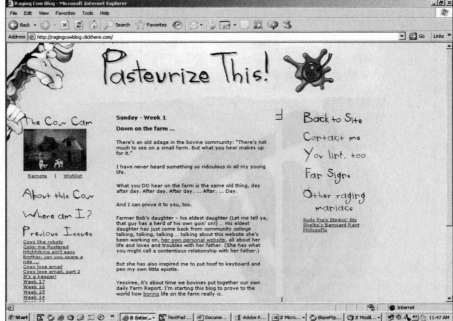

Figure 3-2:
The Raging
Cow blog
was an
early
example of
a fake blog
written by a
fictional
character.

Making mistakes

If you make a mistake on your blog, admit it. Apologize, if necessary. Above all, don't try to deny it or hide it.

Mistakes, big and little, are inevitable. And, of course, mistakes upset people, but you can do a great deal to help yourself and your credibility in how you handle the mistake after it's discovered.

In general, most bloggers try to avoid editing posts after they've been published — this is part of the transparency I talked about earlier in the chapter. Sometimes, however, you need to correct the original post when you've made a factual or grammatical error.

Fortunately, bloggers have evolved some ways of indicating corrections in blog posts that you can benefit from.

Many bloggers make corrections by using strikethrough text on the original error and following it with the correction, like this:

```
President Bill Clinton played his ~~trumpet~~ saxophone on The
Arsenio Hall Show.
```

Blogger Darren Barefoot uses this technique on his blog (www.darren barefoot.com) in Figure 3-3, where he corrects a grammatical error that changes the meaning of a sentence.

Other bloggers use italics, bold, or make notes at the top or the bottom of the blog post to make these kinds of corrections. The strikethrough style, however, has the advantage of letting you indicate the original error clearly.

Making a correction while retaining the error is best (unless it was libelous or is causing legal trouble) rather than simply changing the text as if it was never there.

You can handle updates that you want to make to a blog post in two ways:

✔ **Expand on your original post:** If you change your mind about something, or simply need to expand on what you first said, it's sometimes better to do so in the original blog post rather than starting a new one. Updating the original blog post ensures that your first words are associated with the update and also that people are likely to read the update along with the original post.

Figure 3-3:
On his blog, Darren Barefoot uses strikethrough text to cross out and correct an error.

Darren Barefoot has two styles for updates. For very important updates that change the intention or meaning of a post, he posts the update at the end of the original post labeled UPDATE. For updates that expand on the original post or for new resources that have come to light, he posts a labeled update at the bottom of the post, as shown in Figure 3-4. Some bloggers preface the new content with the acronym ETA (Edited to Add).

Figure 3-4:
When he has new information to add to a blog post, Darren Barefoot adds an update to the bottom of the original post.

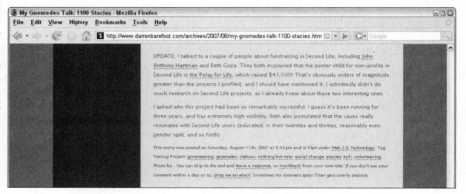

✔ **Start a new post:** When you really mess things up, you might also choose to post a new blog post explaining what went wrong and how you might be able to avoid similar mistakes in the future (assuming that's possible!) or just clarifying the whole situation. This isn't always necessary, but if it helps clear the air, why not? Plus, it's a great way to apologize if you need to.

If you start a new post to explain a mistake, it's a good idea to link to the old post, and to go into the old post to create a link to the new one, just so all your readers get a chance to see all the details.

Handling dialogue

One of the biggest areas of controversy on a blog is in the comments, both in the content of comments that are left and in how the blogger handles them.

Comments are an important part of your blog, and deserve your time, attention, and — when warranted — response. A blogger that neglects to read comments and respond to them quickly loses the community of people leaving comments, who then can get frustrated and leave.

Be sure to read your comments regularly, especially if you have an active blog that receives lots of response. Think of what you are reading as you would a conversation and respond to those comments that ask questions, make you think, or just intrigue you.

You can respond to a comment by leaving a comment yourself. Or, if a comment inspires you to write another blog post, you can mention the comment in your new blog post. Whatever technique you use, don't ignore your commenters.

Unfortunately, not all your comments will be fun to read, or are even remarks that should stay on your blog. When it comes right down to it, you control what comments appear on your blog, whether you moderate them ahead of time or afterward. Moderating is entirely necessary because quite a few comments come from spammers and add nothing to the conversation. But sometimes you'll need to delete comments that are from real people and are even on topic. Every blogger has to make a choice about what kinds of comments need to be deleted.

Bloggers choose to delete comments for these kinds of reasons:

- ✔ Comments that are off-topic for the post they're attached to (a common issue with spam comments).
- ✔ Comments that are personal attacks on the blogger or other readers. For example, many bloggers draw the line on comments that contain racial slurs, name-calling, hate language, or speculation on things such as sexual orientation. People who leave these types of comments are often called *trolls*.
- ✔ Comments left anonymously or with a fake name/e-mail.
- ✔ Comments that include a URL that appears to be included for marketing purposes.
- ✔ Comments that are libelous.
- ✔ Comments that are obscene.
- ✔ Comments that contain private information that shouldn't be public.
- ✔ Comments that contain plagiarized material.

Deleting comments is quite a personal decision, and it's one that any good blogger runs into — after all, you want to get people talking, so you need to have opinions that will start dialogue. A milquetoast approach doesn't make an interesting blog even if it does keep the comments from being offensive.

Most blog readers can accept that it's your blog and you get to make the decisions about which comments stay and which get the heave ho. Nobody likes to have their comments deleted, however, and often bloggers are criticized when they delete comments, especially when it isn't clear why they've done so.

Some bloggers have chosen to institute a blog comment policy that outlines for readers (and for the blogger!) what kinds of comments will be removed. Figure 3-5 shows the blog comment policy written by Kathryn Lord, who blogs about online dating and relationships on her Web site Find-A-Sweetheart (www.find-a-sweetheart.com).

For Kathryn, it all comes down to having common courtesy for her and for other readers — mud-slinging comments are history.

On Greg Mankiw's blog for economics students, he asks his readers to simply treat each other with respect: "Please approach this blog with the civility you would bring to a college seminar. Don't post anything here that you wouldn't say to a fellow seminar participant face to face." You can read Greg's full blog comment policy at http://gregmankiw.blogspot.com/2006/09/comments-policy.html.

If you're thinking about writing a blog comment policy, take a look at what other bloggers have done. A quick search on Google for *"blog comment policy"* turns up some well-done policies that might give you ideas. And remember, you can add a blog comment policy at any time and amend your policy as needed.

Figure 3-5:
Kathryn
Lord makes
it clear
in her
blog policy
that she
maintains
the
appropriate
level of
courtesy.

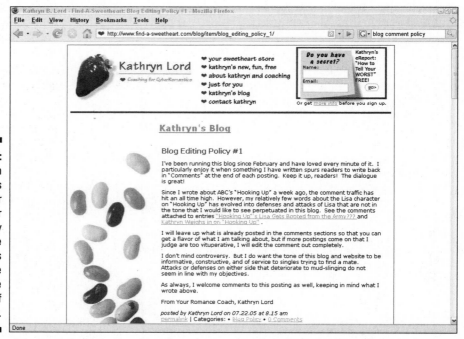

Blogging — and Keeping Your Job

You can blog about anything you want. You spend a lot of time at work. So maybe you're blogging about work. Work is certainly a great source of stories and jokes. In fact, at my office the other day, my partner did the stupidest thing. . . .

Ahem.

Anyway, blogging about work can get you in trouble. Your colleagues and your boss might not appreciate that you repeat water cooler gossip on your blog, complain about the most boring meeting ever, or talk about how you photo-copied inappropriate body parts when you were "working" late on Thursday.

If you choose to discuss people you work with on your blog and they are identifiable even if not by name, you can get yourself in hot water with both the folks you work with and with your boss.

And that's all before you reveal trade secrets or stock information!

Some bloggers identify both themselves and their employers on their per-sonal blogs. It's certainly transparent to do so — after all, work is a big part of who you are — but it isn't necessarily wise. For one thing, if you blog about your work place and you name your employer, you might be perceived as blogging on *behalf* of your employer.

This isn't fair, but it's true. After all, if you blog on your own time (and you do blog on your own time, right?) and don't use company blogging software, how can you be considered a spokesman for your company? The truth is that most people won't think you're a mouthpiece for your company, but they might associate your thoughts and opinions with your employer, and gener-ally speaking, employers don't really want to be identified by the political agendas, family relationships, or dating habits of their employees.

All kinds of bloggers have been fired for blogging about work, or for identify-ing themselves as employees of a particular organization, or for posting pho-tographs taken at work or in work uniforms.

Flight attendant Ellen Simonetti was fired from Delta Air Lines in 2004 over "inappropriate pictures in uniform" that were on her personal blog *Queen of Sky* (http://queenofsky.journalspace.com). She turned the experi-ence into a book called *Diary of a Dysfunctional Flight Attendant: The Queen of Sky Blog* that was published in 2006.

Blogging institution Heather Armstrong writes the blog Dooce (www.dooce.com). In 2002, she was fired from her Web design job for blogging about her workplace, colleagues, and boss. Some bloggers now refer to being fired for blogging as being *dooced*. Her advice:

"Never write about work on the internet unless your boss knows and sanctions the fact that YOU ARE WRITING ABOUT WORK ON THE INTERNET. If you are the boss, however, you should be aware that when you order Prada online and then talk about it out loud that you are making it very hard for those around you to take you seriously."

Most employers today are aware that blogs exist and are fully capable of typing your name, their name, or the company name into a search engine and finding blogs that talk about them or their company. Blogging anonymously — although a good idea if you want to criticize your employer — isn't a real guarantee that you won't be caught, particularly if other people in your office know about your blog.

Employers who regard their employees as representatives of their businesses might even institute a company blogging policy that dictates whether you can identify your employer on your personal blog or even requesting that you not blog at all. This is especially true for certain types of employees — those, for example, that are the visible face of an organization or who speak for that company in other situations.

I encourage you to blog about whatever floats your boat, but if you want to blog about work, you need to do so safely. Here are a few tips you can use to protect yourself:

- ✔ **Regardless of what you blog about, don't blog at work.** Using company time and resources to write a personal blog is a clear violation of most employment contracts and will get you disciplined or fired even if all you do on your blog is sing your boss's praises.

- ✔ **Find out whether your workplace has a blogging policy.** If your boss doesn't know, consult with the HR department. In some cases, a policy might be in place that makes certain requests of your blogging behavior, and complying with them might be your choice. Give some thought to complying with them and have good reasons if you choose not to.

- ✔ **Ask questions about your employer's blogging policy if it's unclear or incomplete.** Find out whether you simply can't discuss certain subjects and whether you can identify yourself as an employee.

- ✔ **Be smart about what you choose to say about your work and your colleagues.** If you wouldn't feel comfortable saying what you write in public, don't put it on your blog. (Go back to the beginning of this chapter if you're unclear on the idea that the Web is a public place.)

- ✔ **Don't reveal trade secrets.** This includes confidential information about how your employer does business that will impact revenue or reputation. If you aren't sure whether something is bloggable, ask whether you can blog about it or run it by your boss first.

↳ **Review other rules and regulations that might impact what you can blog about.** For example, some employers have policies about taking photographs of the workplace or revealing addresses or buildings that seem unrelated to blogging — until you put those photos or information on your blog.

↳ **Consider including a disclosure statement on your blog that makes it clear that you're blogging for personal expression and not as a representative of your employer.** Thomas Duff does this in his very thorough disclosure statement on Duffbert's Random Musings (`www.twduff.com`), which is shown in Figure 3-6.

Figure 3-6: Disclosure statements like Thomas Duff's go a long way to making it clear that you blog for yourself and not for your company.

Blogging without Embarrassing Your Mother or Losing Friends

It goes almost without saying that if you can lose your job over opinions you express on your blog, you can also damage your personal relationships with friends and family. I'm saying it anyway.

Many bloggers have gotten caught up in the confessional mood and posted content that they later regretted, though perhaps not as much as a friend or relative regretted it.

Successful blogger Heather Armstrong alienated her family early in her blogging career when she posted her views on the religion in which she was raised, and the post was read by the parents who were still firm believers in that religion. The post also hurt her extended family and the community they lived in. (I'm sure she also received plenty of e-mail from people outside of family who also felt strongly about their religion, too.) Heather calls herself a poster child for what not to do on a blog, though in fact the process has resulted in Dooce (www.dooce.com), a blog that is one both well-known and profitable online today.

Nonetheless, in an interview with Rebecca Blood (who studies blogs), Heather cautions that criticizing others might make great posts, but the chances are good that they will read what you've written and be hurt:

> "I started out thinking that I could say anything in my space and that everyone else needed to get over it, including my family and friends. Of course, I ended up alienating my family and losing my job and pissing off my friends, and it took WAY TOO LONG for me to figure out that while there is great power in personal publishing, there is also great danger. My supposed right to say anything I wanted got me into hot water in so many facets of my life that I finally realized that it wasn't worth it.

> "My boundaries are constantly changing as more people read my site, as my daughter gets older, as neighbors walk up to me and say, 'Saw you in the paper! Funny stuff!' Do I really want my neighbors to know how constipated I am? I guess I really don't care, but I never thought I'd have to ask myself that question. I would say that now I am much more conscious about how what I write is going to affect the people in my life."

You can read the full interview on Rebecca Blood's Web site at www.rebecca blood.net/bloggerson/heatherarmstrong.html.

Even if you never criticize others, you might possibly reveal information about others — their conversations with you, the date you had last night, the disappointing sexual encounter — that your friends and family will find disturbing.

Call it the Mom test: Will your blog post get you in trouble with your mom? Sure, you're an adult, and so is she, but she's the most likely person to call you on an inappropriate blog post. Your co-workers might be appalled when they read about your love life, but they probably won't ever tell you that your blog is a problem. Your mom will.

In some ways, all this is common sense:

 ↳ Don't blog about topics you think will hurt others.

 ↳ Don't blog about others without their permission, even about topics you consider inconsequential. Don't identify friends and lovers by name without their permission.

 ↳ Remember that your blog is archived, so what you say today might be read later. Your report on an unsuccessful relationship might be read by the next person you want to date.

Before you hit the publish button, stop for a second and put yourself in the shoes of your reader: Are you writing for the reader, or are you writing for yourself? If the answer is the latter, you might be better off keeping a real diary in a format that isn't publicly accessible to the entire world.

Protecting Your Privacy and Reputation

Your blog might not reflect your employer's viewpoints or your family's, but it certainly reflects your own. Don't lose sight that what you put on your blog today might stick around for a long time to come, and that the reader might not always have your best interests at heart.

Never put any personal identifying information online that exposes you to possible identity theft or physical confrontation: Don't post your Social Security Number, home address, birth date or place, mother's maiden name, passwords, bank account numbers, or any information you use as password reminders or identifying information with financial institutions. Most bloggers prefer to keep phone numbers private as well. Don't reveal this information about other people either.

Many bloggers solve the issues discussed in this chapter by choosing to blog anonymously or by using a *handle* — a phrase or moniker that doesn't identify the writer.

Don't forget that many of your online identities are linked or are easily linked. For example, if you use a nickname when leaving comments on other blogs and then use that same nickname on a bulletin board or when signing up for a social networking service, it won't be hard for people to connect the dots. In fact, many of these services already work together.

For example, on one of my blogs, I display my Flickr photo stream, my blogroll maintained with Bloglines, and my latest Twitter messages. My FaceBook profile pulls in my Amazon wish list, my music playlists, and my horoscope. The point is that if you've identified yourself on any of these sites or tools and then tied them together in some way, it won't be hard for others to follow the trail back to you.

Anonymity is a great way to protect yourself on your own blog, but it won't keep you from showing up in other people's blogs or Flickr photo streams. If your friends and family have blogs, consider setting some ground rules with them about situations and topics you want excluded as subjects on their blogs. Be willing to accept the same kinds of requests about your own blog writing.

One of the best ways to take charge of your own online identity is to start a Web site or blog yourself. If other people are mentioning you online, having an "official" Web site with the right information on it can help supplant or downplay less desirable material.

If you want to find out more about controlling your online identity or protecting your privacy, I suggest you review some of these great online resources available:

✔ Visit the Electronic Frontier Foundation's (EFF) guide "How to Blog Safely (About Work or Anything Else)" for advice on blogging anonymously. www.eff.org/Privacy/Anonymity/blog-anonymously.php

✔ The EFF's Legal Guide for Bloggers (shown in Figure 3-7) is a great resource on a number of issues, including defamation, privacy rights, and legal liability. www.eff.org/bloggers/lg

Figure 3-7:
Read the Electronic Frontier Foundation's Legal Guide for Bloggers to know your rights and responsibilities.

✔ Get a good overview of online identity issues in Wikipedia's comprehensive coverage of the topic. `http://en.wikipedia.org/wiki/Online_identity`

✔ Anil Dash's take on taking control of your own digital identity. `www.dashes.com/anil/2002/12/privacy-through.html`

Part II
Setting Up
Your Blog

The 5th Wave   By Rich Tennant

"We have no problem funding your blog,
Frank. Of all the chicken farmers operating
blogs, yours has the most impressive
cluck-through rates."

In this part . . .

You extend your blogging skills and expertise into the realms of custom code and YouTube videos in Part II. This part of the book is designed to let you poke around in the guts of your blogging software, right after you choose some! Chapter 4 shows you the ins and outs of several blogging software applications and guides you through picking the right solution for you. That done, move on to Chapter 5 to make the most of your blog posts using code, photos, and video. In Chapter 6, you discover what you need to install blog software on a Web server. Finally, find out how to take your blog to the next level by exploring templates in Chapter 7.

Chapter 4

Choicing Blog Software

. . . .

In This Chapter

▶ Figuring out how to pick blog software

▶ Deciding between hosted and nonhosted software

▶ Knowing what you absolutely have to have

▶ Looking at the software available today

. . . .

*T*he first three chapters covered what blogs are, why people blog, how bloggers choose their topics, and how to set up a basic blog. In this chapter, you move on to the gritty details. Prepare yourself for strange new technology jargon as you take the next step towards what makes blogging exciting, frustrating, confusing, and rewarding — blogging software.

No matter where you take your blog, it all starts with one crucial decision: what blog software you'll use. Choose wisely, grasshopper, and watch your blog software grow as you add more bells and whistles. Pick poorly, and be faced with the ultimate chore: migrating your blog from one blog software package to a better one. It can be done, but it isn't pretty. Spend the time finding out about the available blogging tools and the functionality they provide now so you can save yourself a lot of headaches later.

In this chapter, you take a look at what the blogging software market has to offer. Making these decisions carefully is important if you want to retain your sanity. You find out about the differences between some of the most popular software packages and touch on the benefits and disadvantages of the major blogging platforms.

Deciding on the Right Blogging Software

The first thing to recognize about blogging platforms is that they aren't all created equal. Of course, blogging software packages, whether they're managed by you or by paid Web-hosting technical staff, all share the same or similar functionality needed for a typical blog. Yet, each software package was designed with very different goals in mind.

Unlike software that you install on a desktop or laptop, blogging software requires a server environment to function. What a challenge, for a nontechnical blogger who just wants to start posting, to make a good decision about Web servers!

Two kinds of blogging platforms are available for bloggers:

✔ **Hosted blogs:** *Hosted* blog services provide a unique situation where you don't need to worry about the software technology at all. You can concentrate on worrying about what your next blog post will be about rather than how to configure a Web server. To use hosted blogging software, you log in to the editing tool, write a post, click the publish button, and log out.

There's no need to think about *how* the software is managed, just as long as it's there the next time you want to post something. Many bloggers consider this setup the deal of the century. Sustainablog (`sustain ablog.blogspot.com`) is an example of a blog run entirely on Blogger's hosted blogging software (see Figure 4-1).

✔ **Nonhosted blogs:** You might want to run your own blogging system right from the beginning. This type of setup is known as *nonhosted* blogging software. By installing blog software on your own Web server, you take on all responsibilities related to maintaining the blogging software and the data created when you blog. Strictly from a technical point of view, this type of setup for a new blog might be a little on the difficult side and cause more stress — especially for the nontechnical folks who are figuring things out as they go — but you ultimately get more flexibility with a nonhosted setup. FC Now (`blog.fastcompany.com`), the blog of business magazine Fast Company, is run using Movable Type, a blogging solution you install on your own server.

Okay, I lied. Hosting your own blog is a lot more difficult compared with the point-and-click solution of hosted software. If you love a challenge or want all the bells and whistles, however, it's the best possible choice.

That brings you full circle back to just how to make this choice. As important as all the technical stuff is, you don't base your choice on types of Web servers, the functionality of different blogging software, or even how much each of these services costs. Instead, consider what you want to accomplish with your blog. In the following sections, I discuss some fundamental elements of this decision process to help you make the best possible choice for your situation. I know that this isn't the sexy part; it's the meat and potatoes of planning any new project. Perseverance will pay off later, when your blog software can grow with you.

In order to get you up and running as quickly as possible, check out a very cool Web site called CMS Matrix (`www.cmsmatrix.org`). It is a site that has been designed to help people compare different Web software packages. Select the software you're interested in and then compare their functionality and features side by side.

Figure 4-1:
Sustainablog
is run using
Blogger, a
hosted blog
software
service.

Establishing concrete goals for your blog

Any productivity guru will tell you that individuals looking for advice think with their short-term brain. When you start a new project, you rarely think beyond the end of the calendar year — and even that could be a somewhat generous assumption. New bloggers aren't any different.

Think about where you want the blog to be in five years. Will the blog be active, or is this "blogging thing" something that will last a few days, weeks, or months? Recognizing your level of commitment helps establish a clear vision about the resources you should put into the blog, and in turn, helps determine the right blogging platform for the job.

Making decisions about the future of a blog can be a tricky business, but here are a few questions to write down and answer (maybe in your new blog!) about where your blog will take you:

✔ **What level of commitment are you willing to put towards your blog?**

Take a moment to visualize your level of commitment. If you're wondering why the heck you thought you might want to blog in the first place, maybe the blogging thing isn't for you. On the other hand, if you're thinking about how many ways you can use your blog to enhance your business visibility or to keep your family up to date about what you're doing, blogging is something you might want to try.

You can view commitment in an assortment of ways — some methods might work for your blogging style; some won't. The best starting point in determining your commitment is how many posts you're planning to write per day or week. Many popular blogs tend to post more than once per day, but at that stage, they're usually making a little money, or the bloggers already have an established business, and the blog is mainly a supplemental outlet for them. A posting of once per week works for most personal blogs.

✔ **Do you like writing? How's your typing?**

Being able to write is one skill, but being able to write and make your writing interesting and fun is entirely different. Blogging isn't something you can pick up overnight; it's something you must learn to do. If you have any distaste for writing or aren't sure whether the medium will work for you, you don't need to invest a lot of time and money until you know the answers to these questions.

Knowing how to type is an important skill that some new bloggers might not be very good at. This kind of issue can kill a blog right from the start because if blogging isn't fun, you won't do it. If you don't like to type, consider a podcast or videoblog. I talk about those formats in Chapter 14.

✔ **What will the blog be about? Is your blog personal or professional?**

If you think of your blog as a personal space, hosted services are definitely the place to start. If you've already decided that the blog will serve a business purpose or promote your professional acumen, don't mess around with low-end solutions: Go for a nonhosted setup on your own server.

Design is also important. A company or consultancy needs to present a polished, professional image online, ideally one that's integrated with any existing branding and logos. Typically, nonhosted services provide much more design flexibility. Of course, you also need the skills necessary to implement a custom design; you can find more on this subject in Chapter 7.

✔ **Do you think your new blog might grow into a new career, lead to new clients and business, or help build connections with peers and colleagues?**

Web sites are terrific at making connections (just like joining social networks and finding old classmates) and presumably part of why you're starting a blog is to reach out to a community. If the community is a professional one or a group whose respect you must earn, your blog can send unspoken messages about who you are and what you stand for. This doesn't mean you need to get all corporate!

Most popular bloggers have developed careers based on their blogs unintentionally, all thanks to the quality of the blog. Bloggers have used blogs as starting points for book deals, television shows, and even direct sources of revenue. Think about the needs of your audience members and how to appeal to them even when considering software. If you want to build an empire, choose the software with the bells and whistles necessary to make that possible.

✔ **How comfortable are you with sharing information about yourself or about your business or industry?**

The Internet is a public space. Don't forget that what you reveal about yourself on your blog is available to anyone, not just the people you're trying to reach. Thanks to *caching systems* — computer systems that save copies of Web sites and Internet-based files for archival purposes on search engines and Internet archives — you might find that your prose is around for your entire life. Occasionally, bloggers find themselves the recipients of unwanted attention and discover they need to blog more anonymously than they had planned.

If anonymity is a priority, a hosted blog solution might give you the ability to be a little more private than one you install on your own Web server.

Budgeting for software

Many of the hosted services available to new bloggers tend to be free to you, at least at the basic level of service. A great number of the nonhosted blogging software packages are also free, but the Web server you need to install them on most definitely isn't. Deciding on how much money you can commit to your new blog is another good indicator of what platform you should acquire.

Consider for a moment how much financial commitment you want to dedicate to your new blogging life. Costs can be associated with

✔ **Blogging software:** Some packages are free; others aren't. In some cases, the blogging software might be free for personal use but can cost money if you use it for commercial purposes.

✔ **Upgrades:** When you choose a software package with a price tag, be sure to note the costs for upgrading that software down the line. Blog software is in flux, and there will be updates!

✔ **A domain name:** Regardless of whether you choose a hosted or non-hosted solution, you can buy a domain name (also called a *Web address*) and point it at your blog.

✔ **Web hosting:** If you choose a blogging software package that needs to be installed on a Web server, you need to find Web hosting.

- **Support costs:** If you have questions about your blog software or Web hosting, it might cost money to get answers. Find out what the support policies are for both software and hosting before you buy.

- **Web designers:** If you need to hire a Web designer or developer to produce a design, install the software, and get things started, you'll have to pay those folks.

- **Special bells and whistles:** You might find that you can purchase and use extra add-ons with your blog, from cool functionality to exciting designs.

Getting geeky

Being a nerd has its advantages in the world of blogging. Not every blogger is a geek, but those that are have a distinct leg up! If you've given up a social life to play more World of Warcraft, congratulations! For you, blog software might be the most fun since sliced bread.

If you still have a social life and want to keep it, think about choosing a hosted blog software solution or getting a good geek buddy to help you out. For you, playing with software and tinkering with technology might give you a headache before it gives you results. (Incidentally, I'm not slamming geeks. After all, I am one.)

Some Web-hosting companies do provide the ability to conduct automatic installations of some blogging software or even install the software for you, but as with any online or Web-hosted software, you need to manage and update that software yourself.

It might be prudent to seek out some technological help to get the ball rolling on your new site. Getting a hand from a nerd friend might go a long way toward letting you keep your sanity while maintaining some level of control over your new blog.

Making sure you get the basics

Each blogging package has a great number of options to choose from. Some are designed to trick out your ride, making your blog into a thing of beauty and delight. Some are must-haves.

Obviously, all blogging software should give you easy access to a publishing/posting tool. If you install some software and can't find something like that, you've probably installed the latest copy of some popular icon smiles program.

Good blogging software *must* have the following:

- ✔ **A usable publishing interface or control panel:** Check out how the control panel looks before you commit yourself. A good user interface is important, and if you can't make sense of what you see, chances are good that you won't enjoy using the software.

- ✔ **Comments:** A blog isn't a blog unless your readers can leave comments on your posts. You don't have to use the comments, but blogging software without comments takes away a vital element of blogging — allowing your readers to cultivate discussions.

- ✔ **Spam deterrents:** Spam comments are a part of every blog, but that doesn't mean you have to live with them. Like e-mail spam, comment spam tends to be an automated process that posts useless information with links to all kinds of other sites on your blog posts. Look for blogging software that has functionalities in place to help you moderate and block spam.

- ✔ **Pinging:** A blog software package that uses pinging services is a great idea. *Pinging* is an automated notification system for search engines and newsreaders, letting those services know that your blog has been updated. And if search engines know you have new content, more people can find your blog.

- ✔ **RSS feeds:** If your blog software doesn't have an RSS feed, move on to different blog software. If you are at all interested in building traffic to your blog, an RSS feed is the single best built-in software feature you can have to meet that goal. An *RSS feed* is a computer-readable version of your blog, standardized so that it can be displayed in newsreaders and on Web sites and blogs. You can get the icons online at www.feedicons.com.

I highly recommend two other features, although not all bloggers use them:

- ✔ **Categories:** Blogs often jump from topic to topic, and categorizing your posts gives your readers a quick and easy way to sort through your content, focusing on what most interests them. The Modern & Contemporary Design Blog — MoCo Loco — at www.mocoloco.com uses categories to sort blog posts; Figure 4-2 shows them in the sidebar to the right.

- ✔ **Tags:** A *tag* is a term associated with a blog post. (For example, when I write a blog post about my new cat Maggie, I tag that entry "kitten.") Tagging is a newer technology, but it has proven to be one of the best ways to sort through blog data quickly. The Cool Hunting blog (www.coolhunting.com) uses tags in the left column, shown in Figure 4-3.

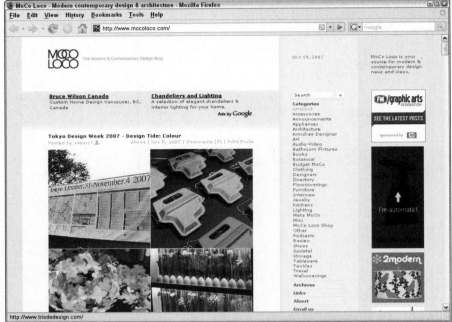

Figure 4-2:
MoCo Loco
sorts
reviews of
modern
design using
categories.

Upgrading with bells and whistles

You can implement a number of cool toys on your blog:

- **Trackbacks:** Trackbacks are a useful technology that allows bloggers to link to blog posts on related topics. If your blog software is trackback-enabled, you can link to another blog simply by using the URL of the original posting. This is an automatic process in which your blog software lets another blogger's software know that a post has been referenced, so that a link can be created on the original post.

  Trackbacks can also be a source of spam, and as a result, are decreasing in importance in the blogosphere. So, although they're nice to have, if the blog software package you want to use doesn't offer trackbacks, it shouldn't eliminate that software from consideration.

- **News aggregation:** One of the handiest features of blogging software is the ability to aggregate news by using RSS feeds. Having a news aggregator included with your blog package allows your site to pull in information from another blog. You can then provide this information to your readers, offering them content from other sources.

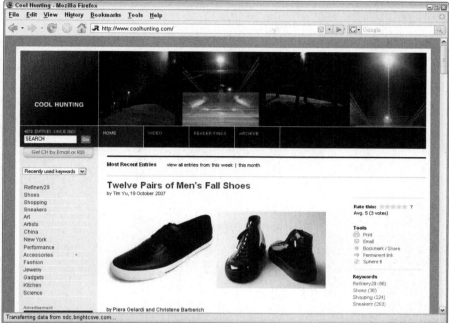

Figure 4-3:
The Cool Hunting blog uses tags to organize content — they are displayed in the left column.

✔ **Spam blacklist:** Most blogging packages have some kind of blacklist protection against spam comments. These blacklists are often centralized lists of e-mail addresses, URLs, and IP addresses used by spammers which are then forbidden in any blog post on your blog. With an up-to-date blacklist, a lot of spam is stopped before it becomes a comment.

✔ **Spam whitelist:** Some blogging software includes the ability to use a whitelist where you pre-select the users that can comment. This type of system, however, is being quickly replaced by spam filtering systems and blog user accounts.

✔ **CAPTCHAs:** *CAPTCHAs* are images that display letters and/or numbers that a person can read but a machine can't. When a comment is left on a post, these letter/number combinations must be typed into a comment field correctly. This proves to the blog software that the commenter is indeed a human and not a computer spam system, blocking out the comment spam and letting through the valuable feedback. Variations on CAPTCHAs include simple math problems that a user needs to solve in order to post a comment. Robin Rauzi's Slow-Motion Tourist blog (slomotourist.com) uses CAPTCHAs, as shown in Figure 4-4.

Figure 4-4:
You must fill
out a
CAPTCHA
form to
leave a
comment on
Slow-
Motion
Tourist.

Understanding Hosted Blog Software

Hosted services take a whole lot of responsibility off the blogger. The blog
software company manages the data, software, and Web hosting; the blogger
manages the content. Some services such as Blogger do it all for free,
whereas other services such as TypePad charge a monthly fee to run your
blog. Yet other services, such as Wordpress, offer a level of free service with
the option to upgrade when your blogging requires a little more power. But,
being able to rely on and allow someone else to take on the entire gauntlet of
technical things that don't excite you is great way to go.

Seasoned blogging veterans recommend that new bloggers start by using a
hosted service that provides services for free. The reason is simple. If you find
the idea of having a blog appealing but haven't ever tried blogging or played
with blogging software, the reality might not be all that much fun. So an
expert — say, the one writing this book — tells newbie bloggers to take a free
blogging service for a test drive before committing a lot of time or money.

After all, actually sitting down and running a full- or part-time blog is a whole
lot of work. If writing turns out not be your cup of tea, using a free service for

a while means you haven't poured much money down the drain in to find that out. If you're interested in installing your own blog software, I talk about doing that in Chapter 6.

Reaping the benefits

An upfront cost of zero is very attractive to new bloggers. If you want access to blog technology and have a limited budget (not to mention all those other annoying budget commitments like food and rent), free looks just about perfect. Not all hosted software is free, but costs are generally quite reasonable. A hosted blog that charges a monthly fee is still cheaper than most monthly cell phone charges, about on par with a newspaper subscription.

But free or inexpensive isn't the only upside to hosted blog services. The best thing about them is that they really take the complication out of starting a blog. For the technophobe, a hosted solution is ideal.

Hosted services take care of

- ✔ Web domains
- ✔ Software maintenance and updates
- ✔ Data storage and back up
- ✔ Template design and management

Besides being free or inexpensive and removing quite a few technical headaches, hosted solutions are also generally quicker to set up, so you can start blogging sooner when you choose one of these solutions.

Updates are generally free, and the software is available to the end-user 24 hours a day and seven days a week. Sounds like a really good deal, huh?

Living with the limitations

Before you sign yourself up, be sure you understand the tradeoffs that are part of using a hosted blog service. The first limitation is that, ultimately, you don't control your own blog. If the company goes out of business, takes servers down for maintenance, or decides to change its offerings, you're pretty much stuck with the results.

A free hosted solution, for example, might suddenly decide it should start charging; one that already charges can always raise its rates.

Most hosted solutions let users make some modifications and tweaks, but you can't install your own plug-ins and extras; in many cases, the level of customization is quite limited. With hosted blog software, that ubiquitous WYSIWYG (what you see is what you get) acronym is a double-edged sword: You can't actually do more with less.

If you blog on behalf of a company or business, you might want to cross a hosted solution off your list for a couple of reasons. Your blog probably needs to be part of an existing Web site, integrated into the look and feel of the company brand; hosted blogs don't allow this customization or integration. Also, control of the data is important. Putting the blog on your own server removes any doubts about security or data ownership.

Following the rules

One thing you should consider when thinking about a hosted solution is that because you are using their service, make sure you are familiar with the terms of service of that host. Some hosts reserve the right to cancel or remove your blog or blog posts.

Make sure to read all the fine print for the host you want to use! You don't want to run into legal restrictions that mean you can't actually use your blog the way you want to, or suddenly find your blog missing if the hosted software company decides you're in violation of its rules.

Choosing hosted software

In this section, you can take a look at some of the most popular hosted platforms to see which might be the best fit for you and your new blog. These blogging software packages have been around for quite a while and bloggers have used them for some time and are regarded as some of the best the blogging community has to offer.

Blogger
www.blogger.com

Blogger is the quintessential hosted blogging platform. Started in 1999 at Pyra Labs, Blogger weathered the rough Internet waters at the turn of the century to become the most well-known hosted blogging platform. The Blogger service became incredibly popular and, eventually, was purchased and merged into the Google family. Since then, many new features have been introduced, and Blogger has remained one of the premier blogging platforms. Blogger has many features that allow bloggers to publish multiple blogs:

✔ All blogs are free and are hosted for you with no hassles and no mess.

✔ Blogger offers a wide variety of free templates to get you going, which you can customize in a number of ways.

✔ Google AdSense (a blog advertising program) and other neat elements such as polls and lists are now integrated into the publishing tool, allowing functionality to be added.

✔ If you don't want Blogger to host your files, you can save all your blogging files to another server.

I show you how to get Blogger set up in Chapter 2. Because it's so easy to use and quick to set up (and because it's free), I encourage all new bloggers to use Blogger as a learning tool, even if you plan to use other blog software for your real blog.

WordPress.com

    www.wordpress.com

In 2005, the popular WordPress blogging platform launched a hosted service in addition to software that you can install on your own server. WordPress.com, as shown in Figure 4-5, offers a clean, easy-to-use interface, and is regarded as more flexible than anything else on the market. With the addition of new functionality and additional themes, WordPress.com is also very quick to set up.

In short, WordPress.com

✔ Is free to use.

✔ Has many options for design templates, letting you choose a look that suits your content.

✔ Includes features like tags and categories, permitting easy organization of your posts.

✔ Offers spellchecking, rich-text editing, and photo uploading.

✔ Lets you measure your site traffic and statistics to help gauge your popularity.

✔ Integrates an excellent spam-fighting tool, Akismet.

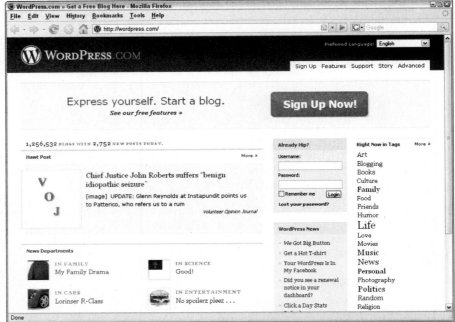

Figure 4-5:
WordPress.
com is a
great place
to get a free
but powerful
blog.

TypePad

www.typepad.com

TypePad (shown in Figure 4-6) was launched in 2003 to great fanfare. TypePad allows you to do more than just blog; it was one of the first blogging platforms to offer the ability to create static content pages. TypePad pricing starts at $4.95 a month and ranges upward depending on the services you want to include.

TypePad offers

- ✔ WYSIWYG (what you see is what you get) posting and editing environment, which means you don't need to know HTML.
- ✔ Quick tools for inserting photos into your posts quickly, automatic resizing and thumbnails.
- ✔ Equally quick tools for placing videos and podcasts into your blog posts.

Figure 4-6:
TypePad
offers levels
of service to
meet the
needs of
most
bloggers.

Understanding Blog Software You Install on Your Own Server

Hosted solutions are good, but nonhosted blogging packages can be a better choice for bloggers who require more flexibility. Configuring software to your own tastes and requirements can really improve the overall quality of your blog, making it more attractive to readers and ultimately more successful.

Flexibility is awesome. It can make or break your blog. If you can afford it and have the skills to make it happen, installing your own blog software is the right solution for nearly every blog.

Choosing a nonhosted blog doesn't mean you can install some software on your computer and start blogging away. Unfortunately, choosing to install blog software rather than use a hosted service opens a whole bunch of other technical services you need to make it all work.

Reaping the benefits

Being in full control means you can do just about anything to the software after you've installed it. A few areas of your blog that benefit are

- ✔ **Design personalization:** Depending on your ability with Web design stand-alone blogs generally are very adaptable. Some blogs have incredibly diverse and clever designs, many created by the author of the blog to match the style and topic of the blog. Installing the software on your Web server gives you access to every part of the blog software's innards, from templates to graphics, so you can make your blog as pretty as a picture. Or tough. Very tough.

- ✔ **Customization:** A lot of the blogging software available is *open source* (meaning the code for the software package is available to developers to manipulate). Programmers can add, remove, update, and improve functionality for each package. Some packages offer many different options, and independent programmers might also offer additional functionality — plug-ins — either for free or a low cost.

- ✔ **Looking smart:** The blogging world has social divisions just like any other, and at the top of the heap you find geeks. If you want to play with the cool nerds, installing your own blog software is a must. Technical bloggers will recognize your prowess and give you props.

Living with the limitations

The first stumbling block you discover with installing your own blogging software, is . . . installing your own blogging software. Somehow you have to get the software files onto your server, run the scripts, modify the code, and generally muck about in the ugly innards of the software. This process can either be simple or a complete nightmare, depending on just how technically savvy you are and how complex the blog software package you choose is.

You can shortcut this issue by choosing a Web-hosting company that offers blogging software. Most blogging companies provide a list of Web hosts who have in-house expertise in handling their software; just browse around on the blogging company's Web site to find it. Your other option is to have the blogging company install the software for you. For a fairly reasonable fee, you can put that job into the hands of an expert. This solution makes sense for one big reason: You need to install the software only once. If you don't already know how to do it yourself, you don't have to spend hours beating your head against a wall for knowledge you'll never need again.

Of course, all software requires some level of maintenance, and most Web hosts don't handle software upgrades and tweaks; be prepared to handle those requirements as they come up, by doing them yourself or finding an expert who can handle them for you.

You have some other downsides to consider as well:

- ✔ **Design personalization and code customization:** Making your blog look pretty sounds great, but a cornucopia of associated skills is needed to make that happen — everything from graphic design to HTML coding. If you don't have these skills yourself or access to someone who does, the ability to customize your blog doesn't do you much good.

- ✔ **Domain registration and Web hosting:** Unlike the hosted systems, there's no way to avoid spending money to host your own blog software. Several costs automatically kick in, such as registering a *Web domain* (Web site address) and Web hosting.

- ✔ **Technical support:** Even if you pay to get the blog software installed for you or sign up with a Web host that does it automatically, if the software breaks (and doesn't all software break at some point?), many Web hosts won't want to fix it or won't be able to.

- ✔ **Backing up:** If you install your own software, you're responsible for making sure that the software and data gets backed up or for finding a Web host that includes backups as part of the hosting package.

Choosing nonhosted blogging software

If you're ready to make the leap into the deep end of the blogging pool, this section is for you: Read on to get recommendations for a range of well-respected non-hosted blogging tools.

Movable Type

www.movabletype.com

Movable Type is the grandfather of all installable blogging platforms. Released in 2001, it quickly became one of the most popular blogging software packages for geeks and pundits alike. Movable Type, as shown in Figure 4-7, was the first blogging software that permitted contributions by multiple authors, and is highly regarded for the many ways it can be leveraged to create easily updateable Web sites and blogs.

If you're serious about looking at hosting your own installation, Movable Type is a strong contender. Movable Type offers

- A WYSIWYG (what you see is what you get) editing environment that saves you time and effort.
- Easy tools for categorizing your posts, inserting photos and multimedia, and spellchecking.
- Automatic generation of RSS feeds to give your blog longevity.
- Search, tags, and other cool tools.
- A range of licensing options for personal, commercial, and education use.

You might be interested in a free personal license of Movable Type but it lacks support from Six Apart and is limited to non-commericial bloggers. If you want to have advertising on your blog, you must use the commercial version. Pricing varies, but the basic commercial installation is $395.95, and permits five users to blog.

Figure 4-7:
Movable Type is highly regarded as one of the premier blogging platforms available.

WordPress

www.wordpress.org

Since 2003, WordPress, as shown in Figure 4-8, has provided a solid platform for new and experienced bloggers who want the control of installing blog software on their own computer. WordPress is reputed to be the easiest blogging platform (aside from hosted blogging software) to set up and configure.

The interface acts exactly the way the hosted WordPress.com system works, so if you're considering using it, sign up for a test blog on WordPress.com to get a good preview of how WordPress works.

Here are some of the highlights; WordPress

- ✔ Is free!
- ✔ Offers many, many user-submitted and prepared designs, ready for use.
- ✔ Includes tags and categories, allowing you to organize your posts easily.
- ✔ Has editing tools (such as spellchecking), offers common text styles, and gives you easy ways to include photos, videos, and other media.
- ✔ Displays statistics about your visitors, to help you judge traffic to your blog.
- ✔ Fights spam with a range of antispam tools.

Figure 4-8: WordPress is free to use and is an open source blogging platform.

ExpressionEngine

`www.expressionengine.com`

Back in 2001, a company called pMachine released a blogging software package called pMachine Pro. pMachine Pro quietly hatched a following based on pMachine's clean interface, solid performance, and flexibility with both design and layout. From that success, pMachine built the content management system and blogging software ExpressionEngine (see Figure 4-9), an exceptionally powerful platform.

Today, pMachine (now known as EllisLab) supports all kinds of sites with ExpressionEngine, which is offered in both commercial and personal flavors. Like Movable Type, ExpressionEngine is highly regarded by Web developers because it offers great blogging tools, but it's flexible enough to be used to develop all kinds of Web sites and not just blogs.

ExpressionEngine users enjoy

- The ability to run multiple blogs with many contributors
- A powerful templating engine
- Additional modules and community plug-in, including mailing lists, forums, and photo galleries

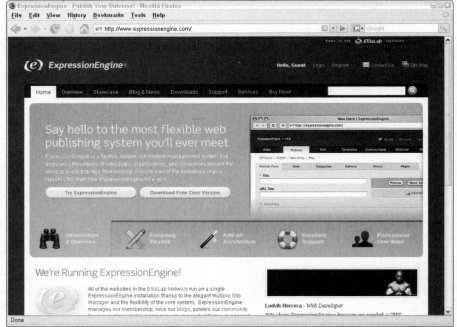

Figure 4-9: Get more than just blogging software with EllisLab's Expression-Engine.

Blogging on social networks

Social networks allow you to connect with current friends and make new ones while sharing photos, videos, and text. They've exploded in popularity in the last few years and many of them have added a blogging tool. From MySpace to Facebook, these tools are proliferating, and their quality is improving. It can be quite stressful to choose which social networks to belong to, but a good rule is to find out which ones your friends and family are using. Don't forget to consider which ones have the coolest designs and best functionalities, either.

In general, social networks with blogging tools are good for, well, social networking. These aren't appropriate blogging tools if you're starting a business or professional blog — unless you're trying to appeal to a very young, hip audience. Many bands have gained a lot of success and followers by creating MySpace pages because the informality of these services suits a band.

If you decide to blog using a social networking site, it's a good idea to use the blog tool of only one of them. Even if you sign up for several social networks, having multiple blogs on each system is confusing for you and for anyone trying to keep track of your blogging efforts.

Facebook (www.facebook.com) and MySpace (www.myspace.com) are two sites where you can explore blogging within a social community.

✔ Strong comment moderation and prevention tools

✔ Different levels of user access, allowing administrators to control what blogs and templates users can edit

ExpressionEngine's commercial license runs you $249.95, the nonprofit version is $99.95, and the free version can be used for personal use.

Chapter 5

Dropping Code into Your Skill Set

In This Chapter
▶ Showing off some HTML code skills
▶ Putting Flickr photos into your blog
▶ Embedding YouTube videos in your posts

*I*f you've ever thought about learning some geeky things or trying out some fancy new code on your blog, this chapter is for you. Knowing some HTML code lets you make your posts look better, and even do some nifty tricks like adding video to you blog. A few code basics can make you a better blogger, and it can do wonders for increasing your readership.

This chapter shows you that code isn't necessarily a digital monster just waiting to sneak up and bite you. If you follow some simple rules, you can make some great layout changes, so don't be afraid to experiment. Making a few small changes or tweaks to your blogging code can make all the difference to search engines, readers, and the overall quality of your blog.

Coding Your Blog with Style

On a blog, *code* can mean many things. It can refer to the complicated programming that makes up the software that runs your blog, or it can mean simple styles that make written words look cool when displayed on your blog. In this section, you find out how to make the text in your blog posts look like a million bucks. You can leave the blogging software code to the experts.

The first thing to know is that you're working with code inside a given blog post; it's the blog software itself that builds the blog pages. This means you don't have to know very many pieces of code — just those commonly used to format text and photos or to insert video files.

In fact, most of the code you need is actually HTML (HyperText Markup Language).

What is HTML?

HTML documents are really nothing but text, designed to be read and then displayed by your Internet browser. HTML tells your browser all kinds of things. For instance, it has instructions for all Internet browsers about where to find images that should be displayed, how the text on the screen is supposed to be aligned, and what text is linked to what Web page. It can also have instructions about how audio or video are to be displayed on the screen.

Using HTML is easy. Each bit of code, or tag, with few exceptions, has opening and closing tags to surround the element you want to affect. A few tags are standalone elements that are inserted in only one spot. The basic idea with HTML is that it is used to "mark up" text, photos, and other elements.

Adding headings, paragraphs, and line breaks

Long blocks of text generally benefit from being broken up, maybe even given labels here and there. Styling headers, adding line breaks, and making sure you use paragraphs can really improve the flow of your posts.

Headings

HTML has six levels of headings. H1 is the most important, H2 is slightly less important, and so on. The final heading is H6, and it's rarely used because it produces very small text. For most cases, first- and second-level headers do the job, giving you text larger than the main body text, and they are also usually bold. You can implement header tags like this:

```
<h1>The most important heading ever</h1>
```

Like a light switch, the tag is turned on before the first letter of your header and turned off after the last character.

All headers are implemented the same way — just substitute the number 1 with a 2, 3, 4, 5 or 6:

```
<h2>The second most important heading ever</h2>
```

Figure 5-1 shows each of the header tags as the browser interprets and displays them.

Headers are interesting because they have more than just an effect on how your text looks: Search engines understand that text defined by a header tag is important, so words and phrases you enclose in a header will be marked as especially relevant to your site.

Figure 5-1:
Headers
from the
largest to
the smallest.

Paragraphs

To create paragraph breaks, you need to start the new paragraph with a <p> tag. The closing </p> is placed at the end of the paragraph after the text, like this (see Figure 5-2 for how the browser displays this code):

```
<p>Paragraph one has amazing text in it.</p>
<p>Paragraph two has amazing text in it too.</p>
<p>Paragraph three is being neglected by the first and
             second paragraphs.</p>
```

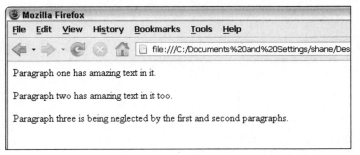

Figure 5-2:
Text
paragraphs,
displayed
by a Web
browser.

Most blogging software makes provision for paragraph breaks automatically, but if you ever end up looking at the code, you'll be able to recognize these fundamentally important tags. On most Web sites, paragraph breaks actually produce the effect of two line breaks, so that paragraphs are spaced out from each other in the same way they are in this book.

Line breaks

You can end a line of text and start the next word on a new line by using a `<br>` tag. These are standalone tags that you need to insert only once — which makes sense! To create a line break, here's what you do:

```
Break your line of text<br>
and start again on the next line.
```

Emphasizing text

Dress up your text by using italics, underlining, bold, or even strikethrough code. These are on/off tags, so you place the first tag at the start of the text you want to affect, and follow the text with the closing tag. Figure 5-3 shows how each of the following code examples is displayed in the browser.

Here are the codes for each:

✔ **Bold:** `<b>` or `<strong>`

```
<b>Some of this text</b> is going to be bold.
```

✔ *Italics:* `<i>` or `<em>`

```
<i>Some of this text</i> is going to be italicized.
```

✔ Underline: `<u>`

```
Add punch with an <u>underline</u>.
```

✔ ~~Strikethrough~~: `<strike>`

```
Correct an error <strike>by striking it out</strike>.
```

Even though I just showed you how to create underlines in your blog posts, I don't actually recommend that you use this style. As you know, underlining is a common way of indicating links online, so it can be very confusing for your readers to see underlined text that isn't also a link.

Figure 5-3:
Use bold, italics, underlining, and strike-through in your HTML to make your text pop.

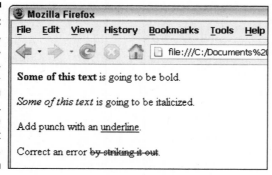

Linking up

As a blogger, you'll be doing all kinds of reading. A bunch of what you should be reading is other blogs. When reading other blogs, you're bound to want to comment on or quote other people's blog posts. You might also run across some news article that you want to tell other people about.

Links make the Web what it is — an interlocking canvas of information that bounces visitors from one Web site to another. Used judiciously, you can add enormous value to your blog posts with links by informing readers, linking to more detail, pointing out a great news article, or sending them to another page on your own blog or Web site.

In HTML, links are defined with the <a> tag (the *a* stands for anchor). But that's not all! This special tag gets what's called an *attribute* and a *value* to go along with the basic tag. The attribute is `href`, and it indicates to the browser that what comes next is a hypertext reference — in this case, a Web page. The value is the actual Web page that's being linked to, enclosed in quotation marks. Here's how all that looks in action:

```
This link goes to <a href="http://www.google.com">Google</a>.
```

When the preceding line is posted in a blog, the word *Google* is a clickable link that leads to the Google Web site.

Make sure you use the full URL when you create a link. That means you need to include the `http://`! Unless you include that prefix, the browser won't understand that it needs to find another Web site, but it will instead look for a document on your Web site called `www.google.com`.

Also note that when you turn off the tag, you need to turn off only the main tag, not the attribute or value. Those are turned off automatically simply by using the closing </a> tag.

You can also use this tag around an image to make the image clickable to a Web page. Simply place the tag around your image code, like so:

```
<a href="http://www.google.com"><img src="googlelogo.gif"></a>
```

Read more about putting an image into your blog posts later in this chapter, in the section "Adding images."

Making lists

Lists are a great way to let people know about your favorite kinds of candy, music, or whatever. With a little help from your friendly HTML you can create three types of lists: unordered lists, ordered lists, and definition lists.

All lists, no matter the flavor, are created using a series of HTML tags. This makes them more complicated to implement, so pay close attention to those closing tags — they're easy to forget.

Creating unordered lists

An unordered list is a series of bulleted items and is used for lists that do not require numbering. For example, if you want to create a list of cat breeds, you don't need to list them in any particular order. But if you were ranking the breeds from 1 through 5, you would want to make sure the number one breed is at the top. Unordered lists use the `<ul>` and `<li>` tags. Set up the code as I do in this list of kinds of chocolate:

```
<ul>
<li>Milk.</li>
<li>Dark.</li>
<li>White.</li>
</ul>
```

The `<ul>` tag stands for unordered list, and is turned on at the beginning of the list, and turned off following the last item in the list. The `<li>` tag stands for list item; it gets turned on at the beginning of each new item and turned off at the end of that item. Figure 5-4 shows an unordered list.

Figure 5-4:
Use unordered lists to bullet items.

Creating ordered lists

An ordered list contains items that are ranked, or must be listed in a particular order, like a list of ranks or preferences. It may also indicate a list of steps for the reader to follow. Format an ordered list just the way you format an unordered list, substituting the `<ol>` tag for the `<ul>` tag (see Figure 5-5):

```
<ol>
<li>Get a graham cracker.</li>
<li>Lay on a piece of chocolate.</li>
<li>Add a toasted marshmallow.</li>
<li>Add a second graham cracker on top, squish
        marshmallow, and eat.</li>
</ol>
```

Customizing bullets and numbers

With a little more code, you can customize the kind of bullets that are used in your unordered lists, or use Roman numerals or letters instead of numbers in your ordered lists. To do this, you need to add an attribute and value to the code you're already using. For example, you can change the bullets shown in your unordered lists to squares like this:

```
<ul type="square">
<li>Milk.</li>
<li>Dark.</li>
<li>White.</li>
</ul>
```

Experiment with setting the type to circle, as well.

To use letters instead of numbers in an ordered list:

```
<ol type="a">
<li>Get a graham cracker.</li>
<li>Lay on a piece of chocolate.</li>
<li>Add a toasted marshmallow.</li>
<li>Add a second graham cracker on top, squish marshmallow,
    and eat.</li>
</ol>
```

Using a capital A if you want your list to be shown with capital letters instead of lowercase. To use Roman numerals, set the type to be i or I.

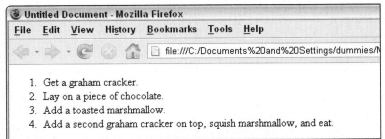

Figure 5-5:
Ordered
lists work
well for
instructions.

Always make sure you're closing the lists with the appropriate closing tag.

Creating definition lists

The third type of HTML list is the *definition list*. This type of list gives a term and then its definition and has built-in spacing to lay those elements out properly. Each list starts with a `<dl>` tag and closes with the `</dl>` tag. Each term starts with a `<dt>` tag and each definition starts with a `<dd>`. Sound confusing? Well, it is, a little. This is definitely one of the most complicated HTML tags:

```
<dl>
<dt>Milk chocolate.</dt>
<dd>Makes a standard smore; a workmanlike choice.</dd>
<dt>Dark chocolate.</dt>
<dd>Makes a designer smore; clearly the superior
          choice.</dd>
<dt>White chocolate.</dt>
<dd>Pretends to be chocolate, but isn't; a poor
          choice.</dd>
</dl>
```

Figure 5-6 shows how a definition list looks in a Web browser. Pretty neat, huh?

Make sure to close each of the tags with their matching tags. The end tags `</dt>` and `</dd>` shouldn't be left off.

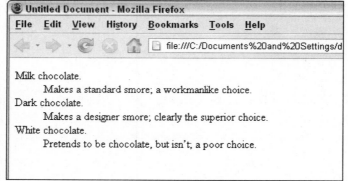

Figure 5-6: Definition lists are used for glossaries.

Putting lists into your lists

You can embed a list inside another list. In fact, you can even embed a different kind of list into a list. Each time you embed a new list, additional indenting is creating, giving you a nice stair-stepped look in your final page.

Here's how you should format the code for placing an unordered sublist inside an ordered list in a s'more recipe:

```
<ol>
<li>Get a graham cracker.</li>
<li>Lay on a piece of chocolate. It can be:
   <ul>
   <li> Milk</li>
   <li> Dark</li>
   <li> White</li>
   </ul>
</li>
<li>Add a toasted marshmallow.</li>
```

```
<li>Add a second graham cracker on top, squish
        marshmallow, and eat.</li>
</ol>
```

Figure 5-7 shows how this list looks in a Web browser.

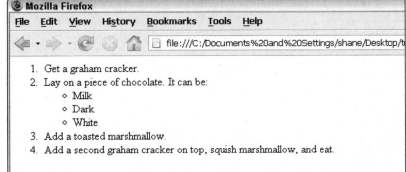

Figure 5-7:
Styled lists
embedded
within
another list.

Adding images

In Chapter 13, I talk about using the popular photo service Flickr to store your images so you can insert them into your blog posts, and give you some tips for getting code for inserting those images in your blog. In this section, though, you see the straight HTML code for inserting photos or other graphics in your blog posts.

Images can be used to make your blog unique — they're such a great way to add value to your blog, and readers really respond to photos.

The HTML for inserting an image is the same no matter whether you're putting up a photograph, a graphic, or even an animated GIF. Assume, for a moment, that you have a photograph image file called `mypugdog.jpg`. Getting it onto your blog takes two steps:

1. Get the file onto a Web server somewhere so that it is online.

   I recommend using Flickr, so check out Chapter 13 for more information on that.

2. Create the HTML the calls that file into your blog posts:

   ```
   <img src="http://www.mywebsite.com/mypugdog.jpg" width="400px"
           height="250px" alt="My Pug Dog" />
   ```

The `src` attribute tells the browser that an image is available at that URL location and filename. The `height` and `width` attributes are the pixel measurements of the image, and the `alt` attribute sets up a text description of the image that can be seen by search engines.

You can find images in any number of ways. For example, use a digital camera to take your own photographs or use some of the great stock photography resources on the Web to find photos others have taken. iStockphoto (`www.istockphoto.com`) is one terrific and inexpensive source of stock photos and illustrations.

If you want to find out more about digital cameras and photos, check out the current edition of *Digital Photography For Dummies,* by Julie Adair King, published by Wiley.

Featuring YouTube Videos

YouTube (`www.youtube.com`) is a video-sharing service that provides users with the ability to share their home movies and other videos with other members of the community. Using social networking techniques like comments, ratings, and simple sharing, YouTube videos litter the Internet, especially blogs.

YouTube, shown in Figure 5-8, went online at the beginning of 2005 and was a sensation within weeks. At the time, no one really understood the impact it would have, and now, some time later, bloggers everywhere are shooting video and posting video commentary on their blogs.

Video has proved to be a popular and dynamic Web format, and quite a few bloggers have moved from text to video: These video blogs are called *vlogs*, and the practice of video blogging is *vlogging*. Even bloggers who traditionally post text and photos sometimes indulge by posting a video they create themselves or one created by someone and shared via YouTube.

YouTube users can upload videos much in the way Flickr users can upload photos, and obtain similar sorts of results: Videos can be shared with friends, comments can be left, and the files can even be included in blog posts. When the video is uploaded, the YouTube system takes the video and formats it to stream through its video player technology. The format of your videos, after they're uploaded to YouTube, is accessible on most browsers without too many additional add-ons to the browser.

YouTube gets its share of videos that are actually copyrighted material, and when those are removed by YouTube's staff, they won't be accessible from blog posts or Web pages in which they're embedded.

Figure 5-8:
YouTube
videos can
while away
many a dull
hour.

Video production is too big a topic to get into in detail in this chapter, but if you're interested in exploring this exciting format, check out *Digital Video For Dummies,* by Keith Underdahl (published by Wiley). And for more on videoblogging, jump to Chapter 14.

To add a YouTube video to your blog, here's what you do:

1. **Find a video on YouTube you want to include in a post on your blog.**

2. **Find the Embed code on the video page, as shown in Figure 5-9.**

3. **Highlight the Embed HTML code and copy it (press Ctrl+C or choose Edit⇨Copy).**

4. **Paste (press Ctrl+V or choose Edit⇨Paste) the code into your blog entry and publish your blog post.**

5. **Check your blog to make sure the video is displaying properly.**

Every blog package treats text in its blog posts differently. Some protect blog posts by filtering out certain kinds of HTML code. If you paste the HTML embed tags into your blog software, it might remove them when you post the blog entry to the system. If this happens, look for a code view of your blog post interface, and refer to your blog software documentation.

Other video sharing Web sites

Don't like YouTube? Not a fan of Google Video? There are many different video solutions for bloggers.

Blip.tv: (www.blip.tv) Blip.tv says its goal is to take care of "the servers, the software, the advertising and the distribution" of putting video or a podcast online, so that you can spend your time being creative. Use blip.tv to share your videos using the online uploading process, and then post to your blog.

Revver: (www.revver.com) Revver is a video-sharing Web site that offers free and unlimited media sharing, and handles the advertising and technology for you. In fact, Revver splits ad revenue earned by ads placed on your videos with you.

Daily Motion: (www.dailymotion.com) Like Revver and Blip.tv, you can use Daily Motion to upload and share your videos. You can share them publicly or keep them private to your friends and family, and post them to your blog.

Do some research on video sharing services as some of them add restrictions and requirements in their terms of service documents that you need to be aware of. Some claim copyright on your videos while others claim the rights to resell your home movies, some without asking for your permission. Read all of the fine print before choosing your video hosting service.

Embed code

Figure 5-9:
You can embed a YouTube video into a blog.

Chapter 6

Hosting Your Blog

In This Chapter

▶ Buying Web domains and hosting

▶ Getting your blog software in place

*I*f you're serious about turning your blog into a visual masterpiece, you're likely to choose a blog software package that you install on your own Web server. Hosted solutions are great, but you run up against the limits of customization quite quickly.

In Chapter 4, you find information about choosing the right software for your situation. If you picked blog software that needs to be installed, the next step is to get yourself a domain name and some Web hosting where you can install your software.

Registering a Domain

The first things you need to do are choose a name for your blog and buy a Web domain that reflects that name.

A *domain* is the address or main URL, that people type in the browser to get to your Web site. Think of it like an address to your house. Each house on a street has an individual address in your town. When someone looks for you in the phone book, they can find your address. If you search for a Web site with your favorite search engine, you find the Web site address. For example:

```
www.google.com
```

Picking a domain name

The domain name you choose can be anything (assuming it isn't already being used by someone else). It can be a company name, a nickname, or your favorite food group. For years, professional Web designers and developers have been saying that all of the good domains are gone. This is far from the truth. After all, new Web sites and blogs are launched all the time, and many of them have great, memorable domains!

For an example of a great domain name, check out Vanessa Farquharson's blog Green As a Thistle (www.greenasathistle.com), which documents her effort to live a more sustainable lifestyle by doing something "green" everyday (see Figure 6-1).

Even if you end up using a hosted blog solution and therefore don't need to get Web hosting, you can buy a domain and forward the address to your blog. This is handy to do because it makes your blog's address easier to remember. After you register your domain, check the Help text of the registrar to find out how to forward the domain to your blog's Web address (URL). Instructions vary by registrar.

Thinking up a phrase or sentence that says something about you and your blog is always a great starting place. Write down your topic keywords onto sticky notes and then move them around and see whether you can stumble upon something great.

Figure 6-1:
Think creatively to find a blog name and domain, like Green As a Thistle.

What exactly does a domain do for you? Because you're doing this blog site on your own, you'll see a few advantages right away:

- ✔ It allows your site to be easily remembered by your readers. Your mom will be able to brag about you and send visitors easily.

- ✔ Having a domain of your own looks more professional; it's a huge benefit at a small cost.

- ✔ Having a domain means you can change Web hosts or hosted blog solutions with impunity, since your address is actually a separate service. If — or when — you move your blog, you simply point the address to the new location.

Your domain should represent your blog properly, although at the end of the day, there are no hard and fast rules. Here are a few quick guidelines you might want to follow. Try to choose a domain that

- ✔ Matches your blog name.
- ✔ Is based on your topic keywords.
- ✔ Is a play on words or slang based around your topic.
- ✔ Is humorous or memorable.

If you're having trouble coming up with a name idea, consider using your name. In fact, even if you ultimately want to use another domain for your blog address, owning the domain for your own name is a good idea. You can point several domains to the same Web site or blog, too, so it might help people find you in search engines.

Many online tools can help you choose a domain name if you're having trouble. Domain-name-choosing Web sites help by suggesting word combinations and coming up with some randomly generated choices. One good site to use for this purpose is Bust a Name (`www.bustaname.com`), which is shown in Figure 6-2.

Registering a domain

Registering a domain is a straightforward process. First, use a domain registrar to buy your name. After you've done that, all you need to do is "point" your new domain at your Web host.

You can use many domain registration services. The choice really comes down to the domain management interface — the tools that are provided to you in order to manage your domain. Some management screens are incredibly difficult to work with. Finding a host that has a clean and easy-to-use interface makes a world of difference when you're updating or making changes to your Web domain.

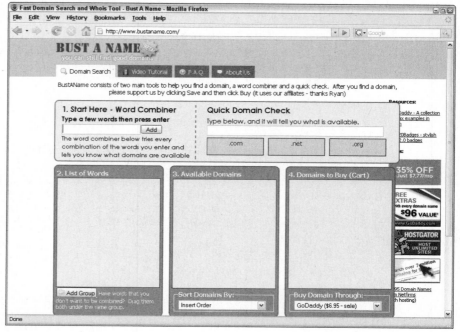

Figure 6-2:
Bust a
Name can
help you
brainstorm
name
possibilities
for your
domain.

Visit any of these domain registrars to check whether your domain is available and then register it. You can choose to register for your domain for a single year or for multiple years at a time. Typically, registering for multiple years earns you a small discount. If you choose to register for only a year, you need to renew the domain in a year (assuming you want to keep your Web site going). Many domain registration companies also offer Web-hosting and e-mail packages.

Make sure you keep your domain registration up to date. If you have any changes to your domain or contact information including your e-mail address, update your domain information immediately. If your information isn't current, you could lose access to your domain or even miss e-mail reminders to renew your domain. Make sure to print a copy of the login information and store it safely.

Go Daddy

www.godaddy.com

Go Daddy is a popular Web host and domain registrar that provides a long list of Web services from domain hosting, Web hosting, and e-mail address hosting. It has a decent reputation and is easy to contact should you require assistance. A .com domain is priced at $9.99 for a year's registration.

To register a domain with Go Daddy:

1. **Point to your Web browser to www.godaddy.com.**

2. **Type the domain you're interested in into the Domain Name Search box.**

3. **Choose the suffix you want to use from the drop-down menu, as shown in Figure 6-3.**

4. **Click the Go button.**

   Go Daddy returns a page indicating whether your domain is available or not.

5. **If your domain is available, and you want to complete your purchase, click the Continue button to add it to your shopping cart.**

   If your domain is unavailable, scroll down the page to the Search for Another Domain box, and try a new name.

6. **You can continue shopping on Go Daddy or follow the instructions for completing the credit card purchase of the domain.**

Figure 6-3:
Choose a suffix to use with your desired domain name.

Network Solutions

```
www.networksolutions.com
```

Network Solutions is one of the grand daddies of all registrars. At one time, it was one of the few places you could register a domain. Services are varied and flexible, but domains are a little pricier here. A .com domain is priced at $34.99 for one year of registration.

Domainsatcost.ca

```
www.domainsatcost.ca
```

This domain registrar located in Canada provides registrations for all major domains, including .com and .ca domains. They have a support number (long distance applies) but they do answer the telephone — something that is rare with domain hosts. Domainsatcost.ca is reasonably priced at $12.95 CDN (that's Canadian dollars!) a year.

Finding Web hosting

With a domain in hand, you can turn your attention to Web hosting.

If the domain is your address, *Web hosting* is your actual house on the Web. Web hosting provides the Web server where your software, graphics and other files live online. When people use your address — the domain — the Web server gives them the pages they want.

Doing your research

Your primary concern is to find a Web host that has everything your blog software needs to run. Because you want to use a blog software package, you might have more specific needs than are on offer for a typical Web site.

Spend a little time researching what's available before you commit to a particular Web host.

Most blog software uses a LAMP (Linux/Apache/MySQL/PHP) Web server, a mix of several kinds of Web server technology that are ideal for running dynamic Web sites like blogs:

- ✔ **Linux:** Linux is a very common Web server operating system. It's a very stable operating system and is considered a standard for Web servers. As a blogger, you won't be doing too much to the operating system, as long as it's in place for you.

- **Apache:** Apache is *Web-page-serving software,* which means it looks at what Web page is requested and then feeds the browser the appropriate file. It does most of the hard work of serving Web pages to visitors coming to your Web site.

- **MySQL:** MySQL is the most popular database software for blogs. For any blogging package, you need some kind of database system to store all your blog posts and run the other functionality of the blog software.

- **PHP:** PHP is the programming language that a lot of blogging and content management systems use. It sits between the blogging software and the database, making sure all the parts work together.

The preceding four technologies are considered the bare minimum that most blogging packages need to function. But, you should consider these requirements as well:

- **Disk space:** For blogging, disk space is important if you decide to store a lot of images on your blog, or to upload audio and video files. Uploading images is relatively easy to do, but you need the space to store those images. For the average blog with a few photos, you most likely want about 500MB. Blogs that have a lot of photos require several gigabytes (GB) of disk space. Video blogs need a whole lot more disk space (unless you are using an online video sharing service) and you want more than 10GB — those files do take up a lot of space!

  Running out of disk space is an easily solved problem, however: Most Web hosts allow you to add disk space as you go at an additional cost. Check with your Web host to make sure what costs you can expect in the long term.

- **E-mail management:** You'll want an e-mail address with your new domain. If you want to use your blog for business purposes, having an e-mail address that matches your domain is highly recommended. Strong e-mail offerings and management tools are signs of a good Web host.

- **Backups:** Consider how you'll be backing up your data (including your database content) and how the files on your Web-hosting account will be backed up. Knowing this information can save you from disaster and data loss in the future. Daily backups aren't a bad idea!

- **Bandwidth and CPU resources:** Computers and networks can take only so much load, and hosts usually set a quota on how much bandwidth you can use for the size Web-hosting package you buy. Ask about what happens if you exceed your monthly allowance of bandwidth. (Usually you have to pay for the extra resources.)

Buying Web hosting

After you purchase your domain, picking a Web host should be just as easy. But the truth is that Web hosts are all over the map in terms of what they offer. Unlike domain hosts, Web hosts are unregulated. The hosting company gets to choose which Web-hosting services are offered.

This complexity means that you need to do your research. Here's how I recommend you find the right Web host for you:

1. **Do a Web search for "Web hosting" and select ten different Web hosts to compare.**

2. **Compare their services and narrow your search to the ones that look right for you. Take into account the requirements of the blog software you have chosen.**

   Check the requirements of a good Web host from the previous section.

3. **Give the Web hosts a call and talk to their staff.**

   You can tell a lot about what the company is like by how friendly staff members are on the telephone. How are they on the phone? Are they friendly or noncommittal? If they offer customer service only by e-mail, e-mail them. How quickly do they respond? Are your questions actually answered?

   When comparing, always confirm the numbers provided in sales materials. Here are the top questions to ask a prospective Web host about its Web-hosting packages:

   • What is your reliability and uptime guarantee?

   • What is your data transfer limit and what are the charges for additional bandwidth?

   • How much disk space is the package, and what are charges for additional space?

   • What is the technical support like? What are your telephone hours? How is e-mail support handled?

4. **Look for online reviews for each company.**

5. **Seek out the Better Business Bureau and find out what kinds of problems the Web-hosting company might have run into and read about how it dealt with them.**

6. **Check in with other bloggers that use the software you plan to use and find out what hosts they use.**

When you find a Web host you are interested in, check out the packages on offer. Many Web hosts provide a handy comparison chart you can use to quickly compare pricing and features, as Nexcess.net does in Figure 6-4.

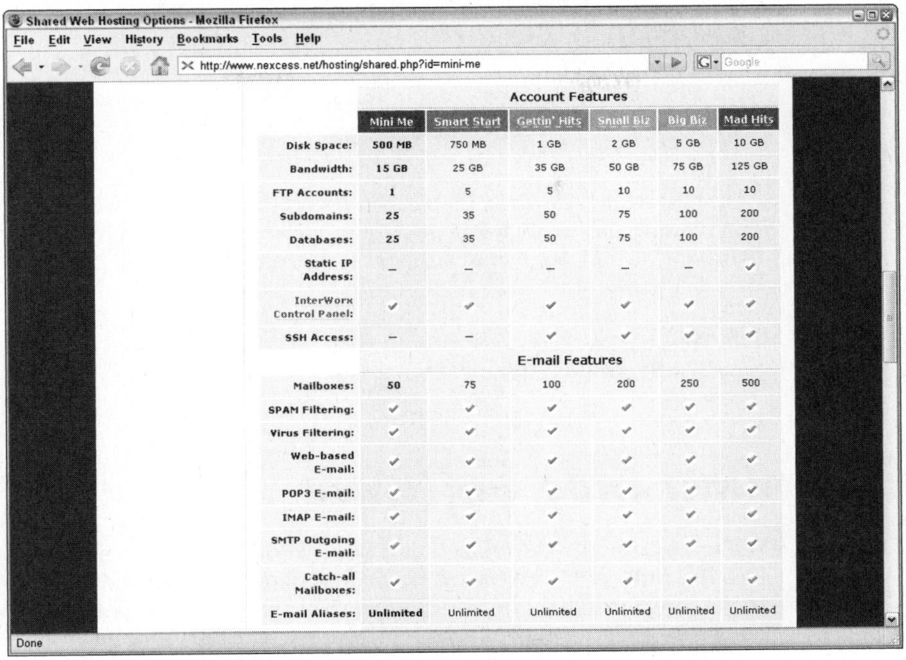

Shared Web Hosting Options - Mozilla Firefox

File   Edit   View   History   Bookmarks   Tools   Help

http://www.nexcess.net/hosting/shared.php?id=mini-me

Account Features	Mini Me	Smart Start	Gettin' Hits	Small Biz	Big Biz	Mad Hits
Disk Space:	500 MB	750 MB	1 GB	2 GB	5 GB	10 GB
Bandwidth:	15 GB	25 GB	35 GB	50 GB	75 GB	125 GB
FTP Accounts:	1	5	5	10	10	10
Subdomains:	25	35	50	75	100	200
Databases:	25	35	50	75	100	200
Static IP Address:	–	–	–	–	–	✓
InterWorx Control Panel:	✓	✓	✓	✓	✓	✓
SSH Access:	–	–	✓	✓	✓	✓
E-mail Features						
Mailboxes:	50	75	100	200	250	500
SPAM Filtering:	✓	✓	✓	✓	✓	✓
Virus Filtering:	✓	✓	✓	✓	✓	✓
Web-based E-mail:	✓	✓	✓	✓	✓	✓
POP3 E-mail:	✓	✓	✓	✓	✓	✓
IMAP E-mail:	✓	✓	✓	✓	✓	✓
SMTP Outgoing E-mail:	✓	✓	✓	✓	✓	✓
Catch-all Mailboxes:	✓	✓	✓	✓	✓	✓
E-mail Aliases:	Unlimited	Unlimited	Unlimited	Unlimited	Unlimited	Unlimited

Done

Figure 6-4:
Check the Web host for package comparison charts to help make your decision.

The next sections help you get started with your Web-hosting search with three top Web-hosting services.

Go Daddy

www.godaddy.com

Go Daddy is a popular Web host — and domain registrar — that provides a long list of Web services. It has a decent reputation and is easy to contact should you require assistance. Its smallest Web-hosting packages start at around $4.99 a month.

I recommend the Economy Plan, which includes 10GB of disk space, and 500GB of bandwidth, in addition to daily backups and 24-hour phone and email technical support. There are discounts for signing up for a year or more at a time.

Dot Easy

www.doteasy.com

Dot Easy is another host that offers a wide range of Web-hosting solutions for bloggers. Dot Easy offers 24-hour e-mail technical support. Blog-friendly Web-hosting options start at $7.95 a month with the Ultra Hosting package.

This package includes 1000MB of disk space, and 20GB of bandwidth per month.

Nexcess.net

```
www.nexcess.net
```

Nexcess.net is a popular Web-hosting company located in Ann Arbor, Michigan. It has quite a few packages and displays them in an easy-to-compare format. Its e-mail support is extremely fast and effective. Web packages start at $6.95 a month.

The Mini Me package sets you up with 500MB of disk space and 15GB of bandwidth, and includes daily backups.

Installing Blog Software

With your domain purchased and your Web hosting purchased, you can get into the nitty gritty technical tasks: installing your blog software. Get started by looking for instructions on doing the installation on your blog software company's Web site. Each blogging package has a set of instructions on doing the job yourself and details about getting them to do the job for you.

Keep in mind that installing blog software is a one-time task! When it's done, you won't ever need to do it again, and you're unlikely to need the skills necessary to install the software in order to use your blog.

Unfortunately, the steps needed to install each blog application vary dramatically from those used to install any other, so I can't give you step-by-step directions. Each blog software package has its own particular requirements for installation, but the general process goes something like this:

1. Download the latest version of your blogging software.

2. Uncompress the package, and upload it to your new Web host using FTP (file transfer protocol).

3. Execute the installation application associated with your application.

There are a few things to watch out for in order to make your installation experience as trouble free as possible. Here are some common problems that you may run into:

✔ **File location:** When you upload your blog package, make sure you upload it to the correct location. All Web hosts tell you where to place your Web files and software in order for it to be found by visitors. If you put your files in the wrong place, it won't be accessible to Web visitors.

✔ **Database requirements:** Sometimes you need to create a database prior to installing your blog software. This procedure is different from Web host to Web host, so if your installation instructions mention this requirement, consult the Web host documentation or support materials to find out how to set things up properly.

Sound like gibberish? The truth is that almost anyone can use blogging software, but only quite technically advanced computer users can install it themselves. If you're a Web designer or developer, installing the software yourself is a viable option. If you aren't technical but want to be, this is the chance you've been looking for to really get your hands dirty.

However, if tech stuff makes you cringe, you can investigate having someone else install the software — but my main advice is to find a professional:

✔ **Local bloggers:** If you have an active blogging community in your area, you might be able to pick the bloggers' brains for advice and information. There's no better resource to find out great information about blogging software than from those living in the trenches each day and actively blogging. Finding local bloggers is pretty easy; use a search engine to look for bloggers who talk about your city, or consult a community organizing site like Meetup.com to find folks who share your interest in blogging.

✔ **Consultants and professional bloggers:** Many professional bloggers have great online resources to help even the most timid of new bloggers make the right choices and avoid any installation pitfalls. Try a Web search for "professional blogging" and see if there are any blogging consultants in your area.

✔ **Web designers:** Many people who build Web sites for a living can help would-be bloggers get blogging software installed and running. Of course, you need to pay these folks for their time, so shop around for several quotes to get the best deal.

✔ **Blogging software companies:** The best blogging software companies offer inexpensive solutions to this problem: They install the software for you on your own Web site. Check with the blogging company to see whether it offers this service.

✔ **Web-hosting companies:** Some Web hosts install software for you upon request (and payment) and some even offer a one-click installation. These one-click installations can save bloggers from headaches, pain, and midnight crying sessions. You click a button to install the desired blogging software on your Web server. If this sounds appealing, check with the Web host before signing up and see whether it offers one-click blog software installations.

Many of the blogging companies have figured out that installing blog software is a real barrier to the nontechnical customer. As a result, you can often go to a blogging company's Web site and find a list of Web-hosting companies that offer one-click installation for a particular blogging platform. You can see this in action on WordPress.org (`www.wordpress.org`), which offers suggested Web hosting partners (see Figure 6-5).

Figure 6-5:
WordPress suggests Web hosts that they know can handle the WordPress software.

And, as a final reassuring note, keep in mind that you only have to install blog software once.

Chapter 7

Customizing Your Blog

· ·

· ·

*I*f you're not careful, customization of your blog can become an obsession. Granted, the obsession can be a pleasant one, but the relationship between a teenager and his first car is not unlike that of a blogger and his or her first blog. Hours upon hours are frittered away thinking about how to make your blog function better than the other guy's blog. It can become a time-consuming activity that, at times, can overshadow the real reason you started the blog in the first place. This chapter is all about this obsession and how you can give in to it without letting it take over your life.

The moment your blog software is up and running, right after you click the Save button on your first blog post, the desire to customize hits you. You look at your first blog post on your shiny new blog and start thinking "Maybe I should change the color of that header. . . ." and "How would it look if my blogroll came before my About Me link?"

These are all great questions and, of course, why wouldn't you want to make a few tweaks to your new blog? The real question is how you can turn your vision into reality. The best way is to follow the blog software's instructions on customization. Start your love affair with blog design by working within the areas where the blog software creator made customization easy.

Of course, I could be wrong. You might install your blog software, start using it, and never want to change a thing; writing and sharing information is enough to satisfy your creative urge. If that's the case, congratulations — you are the few and the proud.

Designing Your Blog

Blog design is a very personal experience. The decisions you make about how your blog looks are just as important as the technology you choose to run your blog and what you choose to put on it. Because the Web is an ever evolving medium, no solid rules exist that tell you what you should do or shouldn't do with your blog. But, you can follow guidelines to keep your best foot forward.

The blog you're starting is a reflection of you and your professional life. Even if your blog is for personal expression, it represents who you are. So, make sure that you have a good handle on how you want to present yourself to the world. If pink bunnies say everything you need, you should have pink bunnies. And if you need to look more corporate, you should avoid the pink bunnies — unless you sell Easter baskets and egg dye.

If you're blogging for business reasons, either on behalf of a company or to promote yourself, you most definitely want to make sure that both the writing and design demonstrate the proper tone. Seek out advice from bloggers in your community and find out from friends and family just how they think you should make your blog look. Take a look at other blogs, especially those who are doing something like what you are trying to accomplish. What does the design of those blogs say about the blogger and the blog content?

If you have your own blog designed for you or if you try to make the design yourself, seek ways to make your blog stand out from the rest. If you're a business, make sure your logo is on your blog. If this is a personal blog, try to incorporate some photos. Even if you use a default template, you may be able to put an identifying graphic or element on the site that differentiates you from other blogs.

Don't be afraid to start small and plan to redesign later. You can grow into your big ideas when you're sure you know what you want, so take the time to look at what other blogs are doing while you make your plans.

Let your readers be your guide: If your mom visits your site and says she can't read it, find out why. If your friends start talking more about the annoying background color than your latest blog post, you have a problem. Just as you do with your content, keep the design focused on the readers to keep them coming back for more.

Exploring blog layouts

The average blog has four very distinct areas in which to place and customize content: logos, headers, sidebars, and footers. In a blog, each of these has a very specific purpose. As more blogs have come into existence, these areas have developed in very specific ways that can help you organize your content.

Here's some more detail about each of these customizable areas:

- ✔ **Logos:** Getting a visitor's attention on the Internet is a science in itself, and clean, crisp logos can hold a visitor's attention long enough to get him interested in reading some of your blog. Typically, a logo is located near the top of each blog page. Many logos include an illustrated element and a special font treatment of the blog name. For an example, check out the logo on Jory Des Jardin's blog, Pause (`www.jorydes jardins.com`) in Figure 7-1.

- ✔ **Headers:** The header of any blog contains a few things. The first should be, of course, the name of your blog. The title should explain what your blog is about or who you are as the main writer of the blog. Other things you can throw into the header might be some form of navigation that help your visitors find their way around and provide them with quick links to special areas that you want highlighted on your site. On many blogs, the logo is also contained in the header. As the name suggests, headers are located at the top of blog pages. The Sensory Impact blog (`www.sensoryimpact.com`), which is shown in Figure 7-2, uses a header with a logo and site navigation in it.

Figure 7-1:
Jory Des Jardins uses a photo and a graphical text treatment for her blog's logo.

Image courtesy of Jesse Markman

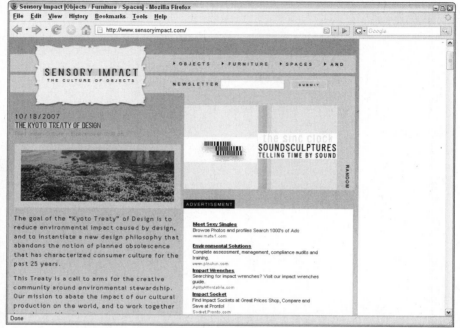

Figure 7-2:
The Sensory
Impact blog
header
includes
a logo,
navigation,
and a
newsletter
signup box.

✔ **Sidebars:** Sidebars usually become a major focus for the site. They are columns to the right or left (or both) of the main content area. Sidebars contain things like navigational links, special highlighting graphics that point to social networking sites, lists of blogs you read (*blogrolls*), archive links, or anything that you want to share with your visitors outside the context of a blog post. Sidebars are usually included on every page of your blog, and are consistent from page to page. I cover customizing your sidebar with fun applications and features in detail in Chapter 12.

✔ **Footers:** Footers live at the bottom of each blog page, and sometimes they do nothing more than feature a copyright message. More advanced bloggers have been expanding the use of footers to include a significant series of links to content within their sites. These links might be connections to comments on the blog or links to recent posts or posts you particularly want to highlight. The footer can be a place where you highlight things you want your visitors to have an easy time finding. Derek Powazek uses this kind of footer on his blog (www.powazek.com) shown in Figure 7-3.

Standards there might be, and hard and fast rules there are, but these are just basic guidelines. Many bloggers have come up with all kinds of interesting ways to reinvent basic layouts.

Figure 7-3:
Derek
Powazek
uses his
footer to
give
information
about
himself, sell
his book,
and link to
archives.

Customizing what you can

Customizing a blog is a challenge for some and a breeze for others. Some of the things you can customize are really easy, but some configurations require a much deeper understanding of what lies beneath the hood of the technologies you're playing with. And, knowing what's easy to do and what isn't can be tough.

Take a look at your blogging software documentation to find out what you can customize using the publishing interface for your blog. Most blog software offers some settings that you can customize — look for labels like "Settings," "Themes," "Templates," or even "Design," but remember that your blog software may use different words to describe an area that lets you customize the appearance of your blog. Settings you can customize in your publishing interface are the easiest things to change because often you can simply point and click to make your choices — no need to know how to do anything technical. Show off your geeky side and embrace simple upgrades whenever possible.

For example, the hosted blog software package Blogger (www.blogger.com) allows you to customize the text colors using the simple point and click interface shown in Figure 7-4.

Figure 7-4:
Blogger
offers some
simple
customiza-
tion tools
you can use
to change
the look of
your blog.

If design customization is important to you, you might even want to choose your blog software specifically for the customization features available in the control panel.

Here's a list of some of the items that blog software lets you tweak via the control panel:

✔ **Add some flare:** *Flare* is anything that people jam onto their blogs and Web sites that blinks, flashes, and attracts a reader's attention. I usually add flare to my site when it helps communicate something, like my support for a cause or my plans to attend a particular conference. Flare is typically placed in your blog's sidebar, and I talk extensively about building out your sidebars in Chapter 12.

Some flare is great, but avoid overwhelming your readers with too much. Including animated graphics just because they're cool isn't a good idea.

✔ **Play with color and spacing:** Some blog software allows you to change the background and text colors on your blog. Some also let you control the size of your text and the font that is used. These techniques for changing the personality of your blog are quick and easy — they don't require you to get a degree in Web design to use.

Keep an eye on your blog for readability, especially in the size and color of the text in your blog posts. Your blog posts should be the easiest text to read. Make sure the text appears clearly and doesn't blend in with the background of your blog design. Space out the text sufficiently to keep it readable and distinct from other elements on the page.

✔ **Add photos and clip art:** Graphics add visual interest to your blog. In fact, including a great photo with each blog post might be an easy substitute to redesigning your blog: Your visitors will remember the photos and probably won't pay much attention to the background color. Chapter 13 has a lot of information about acquiring and using photos and other graphics, so jump there if this interests you.

Photos should add value to your posts and be formatted attractively. Add a border around your images for even more impact.

✔ **Change your link colors:** Lots of blog software lets you set the color of your links in three different states: a link before it's clicked, as it's clicked, and after it's clicked. You can give your blog some funky personality by using a cool link color, but make sure that the color is recognizably different from other text colors and stands out. Some themes or designs might actually have links that look like the rest of the text because the designer wanted to hide the "unsightly" link underlines. The Internet is a beast made of links. Embrace links and always consider them to be foremost in any design you choose. Don't make people hunt; make them click!

Having said that, I just know you're going to go looking in your blog software and write to me saying, "I can't find where to change my link color!" Keep in mind that not all blog software allows design customization via the control panel, and even those that do might not include all of the possibilities.

Khoi Vinh's Subtraction blog (`www.subtraction.com`), shown in Figure 7-5. uses open space, bolded link text, columns and lines together to create a very attractive layout. If you haven't visited this blog, you might be surprised to know that there are no colors except black, white, and grey used in this design. While this blog has been highly customized, you may get ideas from looking at blogs you think are successfully designed, and adapting elements that you think work well to your own blog.

Feel free to experiment. You can always take the time to evaluate a new change on your site without too much damage to your blog's accessibility. Make sure to back up your site as you experiment — you can do this by noting the changes you make as you go, or even writing down the original settings.

Test what the printed version of your blog looks like because your visitors will want to print your valuable blog posts. The day of the paperless office is still years away, so you still have to worry about how your digital blog will look on cold, hard paper. If you keep your text clear and free from clutter, people will love you even more and share your thoughts with others beyond the screen.

Figure 7-5:
This blog uses different elements to create an attractive design.

Keeping it together

With all of these recommendations and warnings floating around in your head, you should keep in mind one thing: Content is always king. A site with little or poor content and the best design in the world will attract few readers. If you're writing some really good blog posts, the way they're presented definitely is secondary. Another reality is that you probably won't ever stop customizing the way your blog looks. You might find the perfection you seek in a combination of templates and tools.

The important thing is that you pay close attention to what you want to do. Don't pick some kind of cool customization that doesn't fit your vision. Following the crowd can fill your blogging days with more stress than you really need. Keep the vision for your blog clear, and reevaluate it from time to time.

Many people have tried to remain alive in the blogosphere by relying on HTML tricks or by promoting their site in all kinds of different ways, but a lot of them have lost sight of why they blog in the first place. Keep your content fresh and meaningful, and blog about what makes you happy.

Tiptoeing Through Templates

Blog design comes down to one thing: the templates you use to run your blog. In these templates, you find all the code and snazzy bells and whistles that make a blog look great. When you choose blog software, don't forget to take a peek at the default templates that come with your choice — a default option might be able to do exactly want you need.

One of the greatest things about blog software is the ability for it to provide you with a quick and easy way to get a Web site up and running with very little effort. A good template makes you look more professional, framing and setting off your blog content to its best advantage.

Usually, several free templates are available with the blog software you've chosen. Some blog software even makes it easy to switch between the available templates as the mood strikes you.

With any design, consider your content and readership: What do your visuals say about you, and what you have to say? If the theme doesn't answer some subtle questions about you as the blogger and who it is you're trying to attract, there will always be another blog template around that will fulfill your needs.

Start simple with a default template, and change your blog templates as your blog matures. Many new bloggers seek that ultimate design right from the beginning, but at that stage in the game, it probably serves you better to concentrate on generating quality content to fill out the template. A good blog with lots of traffic might even earn the money for some professional design help with ads or sponsorships, so don't be afraid to really concentrate on the content!

When you're ready to start customizing your templates, start by looking at the free templates available online.

Using free templates

If the default template doesn't do it for you, you still have several options, beginning with some of the free templates produced by other bloggers and blog designers. Of course, you can have your dream blog designed from the bottom up by a professional, but that might be cost prohibitive for you if you're just starting out. Using a free template and design might be the quickest route to a shiny, happy blog. But like most free things, you must understand some catches.

Not all templates are created with your blog software in mind. Many popular templates have been converted and changed to fit with different blog platforms — but not all. If you see a template you like, you might need to do a little coding to make it work with your blogging software.

A word about blog markup languages

Sorry, a blog markup *what*? Even if you have never made a Web page, you might have heard of HTML, but it's very unlikely you have ever come across any of the proprietary *markup* coding used by the different blog software applications.

If HTML is what makes your blog layout work, it's the blog's markup language that calls the right blog post into a page, permits comments, and handles all that neat functionality that makes a blog bloggy.

One of the coolest technical things you can do with your blog (should your blog permit said coolness) is play with some of the markup tags that are unique to your blog package. Sadly, each blogging system does it differently, and you can't use identical code in one blog program and try the same thing in the other. The codes are very different, so what works in one won't work in another.

However, if your inner geek has made itself known, you can explore blog markup languages. The place to start is with the documentation for your blogging software. Typically, you find a guide to all the tags used by the system that you can reference as you explore your blog's templates.

Most blog software communities have some form of a template that fits your budget, and some template providers might even be willing to help you convert the template you want to use. Check out community forums and see whether anyone is willing to help you out.

A lot of the free template designs have been around for some time, and the code definitely has a track record. Some blogging sites review common blog designs, let you know what kinds of problems you might run into, and give you advice about how to avoid those problems. If you see blog after blog using the same template, that's a good sign that the template is solid. Don't hesitate to contact a blogger for a review of the template he or she is using; bloggers love to talk blog!

The following sections describe a few Web sites that you might be interested in checking out. These sites don't have any particular blog template system in mind, but you can see the potential for having them converted into your blog software.

Open Source Web Design

`www.oswd.org`

This Web site is great and has a lot of different designers contributing to the site. The designs are fairly basic, but they cover a decent number of themes. You might find a few duds here and there that don't really look bloggy, but the majority are great.

The Open Design Community

```
www.opendesigns.org
```

On this site, the goal of the design community is to "make the Internet a prettier place." It has a decent number of blog templates, and all of them are of a high quality.

Open Web Design

```
www.openwebdesign.org
```

Open Web Design has much the same goal as the Open Design Community (almost the same name, too), but this design group has a much larger collection. It can take a while to look through all the options, but taking the time is worthwhile because you can find a series of good designs that any blogger can use.

Heading off free template problems

If you aren't that comfortable with either HTML or the blog software design elements that each blog package has, using free templates might be a big problem for you. Just because the templates are available on the Internet doesn't mean they'll work for your blog. All blog software has special code that needs to be inserted into any template you choose.

The design might be simple, and you might be able to work your way into setting up the special codes properly, but more advanced designs might not accommodate your blog software as readily as you'd like. Keeping this in mind, if you think you absolutely must have a free template that isn't available for your platform, see whether you can wrangle some assistance from a Web designer or geeky friend to get it installed on your blog.

Aside from needing to do a lot of the code work yourself if you choose a free template, watch out for a few common problems as you browse free templates:

- ✔ **Duplication:** Because the templates are freely available, you must understand that other blogs might use the same design you have. This might not be a problem for the casual blogger, but for those who want to build a blogging career, it can be jarring to come across a site that looks just like yours. It can also be jarring for your readers. Using a design also found on other blogs puts the pressure on your content to be fresh and meaningful to your blogging public.

- ✔ **Incompatibility:** Some blog software is unforgiving when it comes to the design of your blog. One of the best indicators of the quality of your blog software is in how the design elements are able to work with the rest of the package. Normally, there isn't any problem with this, but some packages out there still need software to work in one particular way and no other. This means that some designs might suffer from weird design flaws that might not be the design's fault. No one ever said programmers are perfect designers.

- ✔ **Bad code:** Another reality about templates is that even if the design looks great, it might not be using code that will benefit you or make it easy for your blog to function. With blogs, having your content accessible is always the first priority, and some poorly written code might prevent your blog from being the best it can be. Because blogs are a little more intensive in their requirements than standard Web sites, some of the free template code might actually hurt your blog ranking.

- ✔ **(In)Flexibility:** The fact is that free templates are designed for everyone and for no one. The template designer does his or her best to create an attractive and appealing design, but in the end, that template wasn't designed with you specifically in mind. This means that the template needs to be flexible enough to handle all kinds of Web sites and blogs — and ultimately, that means it might not suit any of them perfectly.

Even with all of these potential pitfalls, there really isn't anything wrong with using pre-made templates. Checking the layout and reviewing the code behind the layout are two good ways to make sure you have your bases covered.

Putting a Web Designer to Work

If you're thinking that maybe the whole technology side of blogging is not for you, don't forget plenty of people can help. (I'm one of them; hope you don't mind a little self-promotion!) Web designing services aren't free. If you're lucky, you can find a Web designer who might also know a thing or two about setting up blog software — in fact, I recommend you look for one who has some familiarity with the software you plan to use. Seek out the Web design professionals, check out Web sites and blogs, and don't be afraid to ask questions of the designers you're considering.

If you're really lucky, you might even know a designer already, but don't be afraid to ask other bloggers for recommendations if you don't. Research any potential Web designer you are considering just as you would any Web service from domain registration to Web hosting. Check out the design companies and do some comparisons, especially when it comes to experience with blogs and your blogging software. Don't forget to ask for quotes and compare them!

Part III
Fitting In and Feeling Good

The 5th Wave   By Rich Tennant

"He should be all right now. I made him spend two and a half hours reading prisoner blogs on the state penitentiary Web site."

In this part . . .

Blog in hand, you're ready to join the ranks of the top bloggers in the world. This part helps you get there in style. Get to know your readers in detail, focusing on their likes and dislikes, and find out how to cultivate a following you can be proud of in Chapter 8. Even great bloggers have off days or need the occasional inspiration, so Chapter 9 walks you through developing great content and breaking through writer's block. Also, discover how to keep your blog spam-free and friendly in Chapter 10. Comments you want, spam you don't!

Chapter 8

Finding Your Niche

In This Chapter

▶ Discovering blog genres

▶ Creating appealing blog posts

▶ Making connections with other bloggers

Chances are good that if you're blogging only for your friends and family, you have a captive audience that stays interested no matter what you choose to blog about on any given day. (Though, even your mom might get a little tired of hearing about what time you got up and what you had for lunch!)

For most bloggers, however, being successful is defined as attracting, keeping, and growing an audience of interested readers who can't wait for the next pearl of wisdom to leave your fingertips . . . preferably an audience that leaves comments and interacts with you and with other readers.

This is no small challenge: You're in competition with every other source of news, information, and entertainment in your audience members' lives (not to mention your own if you find it hard to find time for blogging).

The key here is to find a niche and exploit it fully. I have no way of knowing exactly what your niche is — that's something for you to figure out. I give you some ideas and suggestions to help you start turning your mental gears, but then you're on your own. After you've chosen a niche, though, the rest of this chapter helps you find out who your competitors are, what they're doing right, and how you can make the most of your subject.

Deciding What Belongs on Your Blog

Picking a niche and sticking with it can be tough to do. Fortunately, you get a lot of leeway in how you handle a subject, in evolving your own style, and in what you blog about. The medium allows for lots of experimentation, and your readers are likely to welcome new approaches and ideas as you go.

For your own peace of mind, however, it's often a good idea to pick a broad theme and then explore within it. Do you like books? Why not blog about what you're reading and make recommendations? It's then a natural leap to movies based on books, and to authors . . . even a simple idea can give you lots of room to grow.

Some subject areas have proven to be popular and successful blog subjects already. You can take on the competition and start a blog about

- ✔ **Your kids:** Baby books might have gone out of style, but that doesn't mean you can't document your child's growth in detail on a blog. *Mommyblogging,* as it has come to be called, is on the rise in a big way. Talk about a topic with an infinite variety of discussions, products, problems, and cute photos — this is it!

- ✔ **Your hobby or interest:** Blogs are beautifully suited to making connections, so feel free to use yours to become part of a community of folks that share your passion for knitting, sport fishing, geocaching, carpentry, or whatever your interest is.

- ✔ **Technology:** Many of the original bloggers chose technology as their focus, and what a great decision that was. There's a huge interest in technology and technology issues today. After all, more and more people have cell phones, personal computers, and MP3 players, and everyone has problems using them!

- ✔ **Politics:** Do I really need to explain that political commentary and criticism can make a good blog? A number of popular political bloggers have turned their online punditry into thriving careers in traditional media.

- ✔ **News of the weird:** Some very popular blogs make the most of the many strange Web sites by posting links and quick summaries of the site on their blogs. It's the lazy man's approach to surfing, and if you're interested in sharing the quirky oddities you find, you'll definitely find an audience for them.

- ✔ **Specialized news:** Offer a service for your busy readers by aggregating all the news on a particular topic, with quick tidbits and links to sources. This can work for both serious and comic topics — think cranial surgery techniques to coverage of the latest teen sensation.

- ✔ **A personal diary:** If you have enough going on in your life to keep *you* interested in it, you can stick with the tried and true blog. With a unique voice and great writing, you can attract readers who will to be friends.

Mommyblogging

Generally speaking, *mommyblogging* is memoir-style blogging, detailing the trials, tribulations, and general hysteria of raising children.

Quite a few mommyblogs start before much mommying is going on — before or during pregnancy — and then proceed through infancy and upward. Don't let the fact that you're not quite a mommy yet deter you from starting a mommyblog.

They are often hilarious, often heartbreaking, and so easy to identify with. If you don't have children, you certainly were one once. Frankly, kids are *funny*.

Many great examples of mommyblogs are out there; it's hard to pick just one to tell you about, but the blog Woulda Coulda Shoulda (`www.wouldashoulda.com`) is a good place to start exploring. Woulda Coulda Shoulda, shown in Figure 8-1, is written by Mir, a mother of two. Her blog has earned her coverage in *Parents Magazine* and a spot speaking about mommyblogging at the BlogHer Conference (`www.blogher.org`) in 2006.

Turning your offline hobby into a blog

Chances are good that you already have some offline hobbies that consume time and energy and are sources of great passion in your life. Chances are even better that you have plenty to say on the topic but too few people who are genuinely interested in hearing you expound about your hobby.

Figure 8-1: Mir's Woulda Coulda Shoulda is a memoir of a mother raising two children.

© Miriam Kamin

Find your compatriots online by starting a blog about your hobby and hook into a community of people who share both your passion for the activity and also your passion for news and discussion about whatever your hobby is.

Many terrific hobby blogs are out there; you can find great blogs about everything from scrapbooking to jewelry-making to collecting airline safety cards.

One of my hobbies is knitting, and let me tell you, the knitters have caught onto blogging in a huge way! Bloggers who knit share stories about frustrating patterns, exciting yarns, sales, and more. I read knitting blogs because I can identify with what the blogger is describing, but also because I often learn something new.

One fun knitting blog is Crazy Aunt Purl (`www.crazyauntpurl.com`), written by a knitter living in Los Angeles named Laurie Perry. Crazy Aunt Purl (shown in Figure 8-2) was started after Laurie found other knitting blogs and thought she could do the same. She describes the blog as "the true-life diary of a thirty-something, newly divorced, displaced Southern obsessive-compulsive knitter who has four cats." Her hilarious writing covers everything from knitting techniques to the traffic in Los Angeles, and it never fails to entertain.

Figure 8-2:
Crazy Aunt
Purl offers
knitting
techniques
and
engagingly
self-
deprecating
personal
stories.

Talking technology

Can anyone ever know enough about technology to make everything he or she owns function? At least for me, the answer is no. Just when I start to feel reasonably competent with computers, a hard drive fails. And how often have I brought home a new cell phone, ripped open the box with great excitement, and then failed utterly to figure out how to get my contacts imported? It's true — I need technology help.

And I'm betting you do, too. Technology bloggers have figured this out, as well as the fact that your appetite for new gadgets only increases the more frustrated you get. Don't you always think that a new and better device will solve the problems you have with the one you have now?

You can find a number of highly successful technology blogs around the Web, including some that have been in existence for years and years. Some of these are specialized to a particular kind of tool or software; some are just about conveying the latest and greatest across the field.

If you work in technology or just have a passion for it, you can start a blog around your enthusiasm. That's what Dennis Lloyd did when he founded iLounge (www.ilounge.com).

iLounge, shown in Figure 8-3, covers any and everything about Apple's iPod and iPhone devices. Started in 2001 shortly after Dennis Lloyd first laid eyes on an iPod, it has grown from being a blog into a true community site, with forums and photo galleries in addition to the news blogs.

Getting political with it

No matter which side of the Bible Belt you come down on, you live in interesting political times. You'll never be short of topics, from the latest senatorial scandal to the next presidential election.

Some of the most popular political bloggers have turned their online musings into full-fledged careers in the media, from talk shows to newspaper columns. And some traditional journalists have bowed out of newspapers and televisions to move to a blog.

This niche has room for many kinds of blogs, from those criticizing national policy to those covering local school board and city elections. If you have a craving to get involved in politics but don't want to run for office, a blog might be a great way to develop an effective voice. And if you're a politician, you can follow the example of politicians such as Huntsville (Alabama) Mayor Loretta Spencer (http://216.180.9.99/) or House Representative Ray Cox from Minnesota (www.raycox.net), both of whom have used blogs as a method of reaching constituents.

Figure 8-3:
iLounge
is the
essential
source for
all news and
issues for
the Apple
iPod and
iPhone.

For some, the urge to sound off on politics has produced entirely new publications. Take, for example, Truthdig (www.truthdig.com), which won a 2007 Webby Award in the Political Blog category. (The Webbys are the Web's equivalent of the Oscars.) Shown in Figure 8-4, Truthdig was started by journalist Robert Scheer and publisher Zuade Kaufman to be a source for political commentary and news that challenges the "wisdom of the day."

Pointing out the strange

If it's bizarre, chances are good there's a Web site about it. Many bloggers make a blogging career out of pointing blog readers to the strangest of the strange Web sites. These blogs are often called *link blogs*, consisting primarily of short descriptions and links off into the wild world of the Web. Today's blogger, in an attempt to cultivate the perverse, hilarious, and just weird, often adds more commentary, but the effect is the same: The reader gets a daily dose of random tidbits to enjoy.

A good example of a blog in this area is The Obscure Store & Reading Room (www.obscurestore.typepad.com), which focuses on news stories that are just too bizarre to be true — but are. Postings on the day this chapter was written ranged from stories about a boy who reported his own mother to 911 for bad driving from the car, and a social networking community called Enemybook (see Figure 8-5).

Figure 8-4:
Truthdig,
winner of
two Webby
awards
in 2007,
challenges
conventional
political
thinking.

Figure 8-5:
Get your
daily dose of
different at
Obscure
Store.

Reporting news

The offline world is full of general news sources — the 200-page newspaper that struggles to appeal to all its readers, the broadcast news show that does local car chases and the weather well, and the like — and not much else. Specialized news sources are hard to come by.

Online, things are a little different. Quite a few news outlets have opted to offer news personalization features, letting you customize the news you consume by topics. But many folks with specialized interests still have to look through a lot of news sources to find truly pertinent stories.

If you're doing that kind of research for yourself, you can start a blog that shares your findings with others interested in the same topic. Are you an economist collecting stories about garbage production in North America? Or a marketing expert who keeps track of the latest guerilla marketing tactics in order to keep on your toes, professionally? You can turn this research into a valuable blog for others who share your interest.

This format can be quite easy to produce, as well, because posts are frequently just pointers to a news story or article on another Web site — the value for readers in a blog like this is that the work of finding the news is already done, so sending them off site is actually an important part of the service you're providing.

Quite a few bloggers have opted to develop blogs in a specialized news area and parleyed that success into a new revenue stream or sponsorship, so this might even prove to be a wise business move, as well.

Even if you don't put advertising on your specialized news blog, keeping a blog of this kind demonstrates that you're on top of your field and promotes you to potential clients.

One journalist who has left traditional media behind in order to serve as a clearinghouse of news about the media in Los Angeles is Kevin Roderick. His blog, LA Observed (www.laobserved.com), shown in Figure 8-6, is a must-read for journalists in Southern California and across the country. His blog is becoming quite a little empire as he expands into city hall and business coverage.

Revealing it all

If nothing in this chapter has appealed to you so far, perhaps you're looking for the blog classic: a personal diary. Part memoir, part confessional, personal diaries on the Web cover every topic that life can serve up.

Figure 8-6:
LA
Observed
covers the
Los Angeles
media
space for
journalists
who don't
have time
to do it
themselves.

Personal diaries can be real snooze fests or tear-jerkers nonpareil. Much depends, of course, on the quality of the writing. But much also depends on what happens in the life being documented. *Life bloggers,* as they are sometimes called, must deal with whatever comes up next for them, from weddings to being fired or hired to being diagnosed with cancer.

These blogs are usually easy to relate to and easy to read; they're also often humorous or heart wrenching, and sometimes both. They take courage to write, whether read by millions or only five.

For a great example of a personal diary blog, visit Body of Work (www. elasticwaist.com/body_of_work), a San Francisco-based woman's experience with weight-loss surgery (see Figure 8-7). Anne Fitzgerald tells the story like it is — her writing is full of emotional and gritty detail, and also the mundane circumstances of changing jobs.

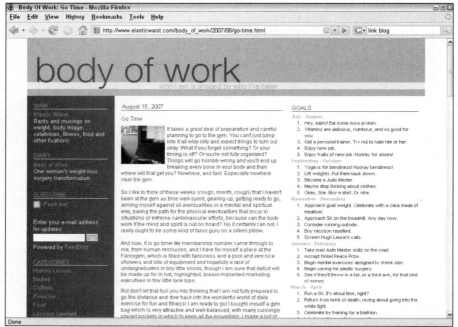

Figure 8-7:
Anne
Fitzgerald
bares it
all on Body
of Work,
a personal
blog
about her
experience
with weight
loss
surgery.

Learning from the Pros

With a topic chosen, you can work on producing a readable blog you can be proud of. In the following sections, you get ideas for setting up a blog successfully by cultivating your own talents, and observing what others are doing right.

When you blog, much depends on the quality of your writing and your ability to make a connection with your readers. Work on developing a dialogue with your readers. Life bloggers often do this by revealing common experiences that many people can identify with. Businesses can choose to start a blog that gives typically silent members of a company (like high-level executives or behind-the-scenes mechanics) a connection to customers.

Many blogs are maintained by more than one person; sometimes contributions by several different people can enliven and enrich the conversation, as well as decreasing the workload for any single blogger.

I cover creating great content in Chapter 9, and in this chapter you find out how to keep track of what is working for others.

Lurking on other blogs

The best possible way to figure out what will work on your blog is to see what's working on other blogs. If you aren't a regular blog reader, find some blogs and start reading!

The old, old Internet term *lurking* is used to describe Web users who look at blogs, mailing lists, online discussions, and forums, but don't choose to participate in them. There isn't anything wrong with lurking, though the word does sound kind of sinister.

The truth is that lurking is a great way to find out about what kinds communication and interaction are appropriate when you're new to a Web community or when you're planning on starting one yourself. The vast majority of Web users are actually lurkers; most people don't do more than read or look at blogs.

Start your lurking career by finding a few blogs you like, that you regard as competition, or that are interesting for some reason. If you want to see what a blog that has a very active, vocal audience looks like, find one with lots of comments and make sure you read them all. Many of the blogs mentioned in this chapter fall smack into this category, so why not start there?

If you want to see how a blog evolves, find one that has been around a while and look back through the site's archives to see how it got started. Most of all, pay attention to what you find interesting about the blog.

Here are some things you can learn about from lurking on a blog:

- **Posts:** Watch what the blogger (or bloggers) posts about, how often they post, what days and times attract readers, and see whether you can understand what prompts a blogger to post.
- **Interaction:** Pay attention to the posts that get lots of comments and response and try to understand what gets people talking.
- **Resource use:** Look for instances when the blogger chooses to include a link, a quote, or other resource, and what it adds to the conversation.
- **Design:** Keep an eye out for blog designs and styles you might like to imitate on your own blog.
- **Sidebar use:** Look at the blog sidebars for cool technologies and tools that the blogger is using, and that you might be able to benefit from.

Interaction is great, but some comments can be problematic because they are off topic or offensive, so you can use this opportunity to see how other bloggers handle bad comments, too. Pay attention to whether a blog comment policy is in place and how it's enforced. When does the blogger choose to remove or edit comments? Do you agree with his or her choices? How do you want to handle problem comments on your own blog? I talk more about handling spam and bad comments in Chapter 10.

While you lurk, keep a list of notes and ideas for reference later, especially for items that you think are good ideas but that you aren't ready to implement quite yet. It's easy to lose those first good ideas if you don't keep track of them somehow.

What works for someone else might not work for you, and it doesn't have to. It's still early in the life of the blogosphere, and you have plenty of room and time to try new ideas. Rules and standards that have been adopted by others are good starting points, but they aren't requirements you have to use if they don't work for you.

Participating by commenting

When you're comfortable, it's time to start participating in your favorite blogs! Leaving comments is the first way in which you can start interacting on a blog. They don't require a lot of time to write up, they help the blogger, and you might even further the conversation by leaving a comment.

Leaving comments lets you get some experience with participating in a blog audience, and when you have a blog of your own, it's an interesting way of letting others know about your own blog.

Many blog comment forms give you the chance to leave a URL when you post a comment, and your name is often linked to the URL. So, when you have a blog, leaving a comment with such a link is a bit like leaving a tiny, unobtrusive ad. When the blogger and other blog visitors read your comment, they might just choose to click the link and come visit your blog, especially if they like what you had to say.

You might also get visitors who *didn't* like what you say, too! You invite disagreement any time you put your opinion out into the world, but don't let that stop you from doing it.

Some bloggers have made the mistake of abusing this little privilege, and choose to leave comments that don't add to the topic or say much in order to get the link on the page. Don't make this mistake. Be a genuine member of the blogosphere and leave comments only when you truly have something to say. "Nice site" is neither interesting to read nor particularly helpful to anyone.

Leave comments that distinguish you as a thoughtful contributor to the topic. It's great if you can answer a question posed by the blog post or provide information that seems to be missing, but just leaving your own opinion is a perfectly valid contribution, even if you completely disagree with what the blogger is saying.

Reaching Out to Other Bloggers

Don't forget that other bloggers are your primary audience. These folks are online, already familiar with blogs, and you're likely to find other bloggers whom you have things in common with — maybe even the subject of your blog.

Meeting with bloggers in person and communicating with them online are terrific ways of networking and marketing your blog. Lots of bloggers list the blogs they read right beside their blog posts in the sidebar called a *blogroll,* so you might be able to generate some additional readership if you create relationships with bloggers.

Meeting in person

This is going to sound really old school, but you can turn online acquaintances into offline friends. In fact, it can be pretty fun.

For example, on a recent visit to Boston, I posted on the Rockin' Sock Club blog asking for yarn store recommendations, and I offered to meet with any knitters in town who wanted to get together. (The Rockin' Sock Club is a sock-knitting club put together by Blue Moon Fiber Arts. It's open only to members of the sock club.) The result was a great afternoon with people I never would have met otherwise.

You don't have to knit socks to get together with bloggers, though. Most cities have an active community of bloggers you can cultivate:

- ✔ Be sure to include your e-mail address or even a cell phone number on your blog and let people know that you'd like to make new friends. Look for similar information on the blogs you read if you're interested in getting in touch with a blogger.

- ✔ Look for bloggers who identify their location and get to know them on their blogs by posting comments.

- ✔ Visit Upcoming.org and Meetup.org and search for blogger get-togethers in your area. Many bloggers network with other nearby bloggers on a regular basis. You can even look up get-togethers when you're visiting a new place.

- ✔ Organize your own get-together and publicize it on your blog or on Upcoming.org or Meetup.org.

Using social networks

Social networking sites are designed to connect you with your current group of friends and then extend those connections out into their friends. Each of the sites I mention here has a different mechanism for making that happen, and different types of community interaction occur. LinkedIn (www.linked in.com), for example, is a professional networking site designed to showcase your work background and interests and make connections to others in your field.

You can make friends in these online communities like Friendster, LinkedIn, MySpace, and Facebook to find bloggers. After all, these folks are already online, so there's a strong likelihood that they can be found all over the Web, and not just on their blogs.

In fact, lots of bloggers regard their blogs as a form of networking and are already looking to make these kinds of connections via social networking Web sites.

Facebook (www.facebook.com) is more about cementing your social friendships, even for tracking down old friends from high school that you might have lost touch with. It has some great additional applications and games you can use to break the ice with a new friend.

Chapter 9

Creating Great Content

*L*ots of elements work together to make a blog work well, from a well-designed layout to fancy technical widgets, but none of those things can substitute for good content aimed at the right audience. In fact, if you write well (or podcast or take photos) and you're reaching readers who are engaged by your style and content, you can actually be successful without spending any time at all on how your blog looks. Good content can even make your readers forgive an awkward interface or missing bells and whistles like RSS feeds or categories.

So if you do nothing else to make your blog succeed, focus on producing great writing, photos, audio, or videos. Know what your audience wants and deliver it.

In this chapter, you get some pointers on writing well for the Web, and for understanding what your audience expects from your blog.

Knowing Your Audience

First things first: How well do you know your audience? Are you hitting the right notes to attract the readers you want in the quantity you want them?

Not all bloggers care about the number of readers they get, but they do care about getting the right eyes on their words. Regardless of whether you're number-obsessed or just focused on your niche, you need to understand your audience and what your readers are looking for.

You can get an idea about your audience by

- ✔ Looking at statistics software to track usage of your blog and what links get clicked

- ✔ Noting the content that gets the biggest and best response from your readers (or the response you want, even if it isn't the biggest)

- ✔ Looking at the blogs of your competitors to see what you can learn from their comment activity, search engine rankings, and other data

You might have to wait a while for statistics and comments, but looking at your competitors is easily done even if you're still developing your blog. I talk in detail about measuring site traffic and statistics in Chapter 15, so jump there if you want to find out more about the readers you already have.

Finding your competitors

To find your competitors, you must first define your own niche. Your niche consists of what you're blogging about, the topics you cover, and what words you use most frequently in your posts. These descriptive words are important because they're how you describe yourself and how visitors find you when they conduct a search on Google, Yahoo!, or another search engine.

Use these descriptive words to search yourself on Google or another search engine and add the word *blog* to your search. Investigate the results that come up and look for blogs with content (never mind the look and feel of the blog for now) that's similar to the content you're creating or want to create.

You can also use one of the blog search engines like Technorati (`www.technorati.com`), Google Blog Search (`http://blogsearch.google.com`), or IceRocket (`www.icerocket.com`). Figure 9-1 shows the results of a search on Technorati using the terms *blogs, blogging, audience, niche,* and *success.* These results show posts from blogs talking about these topics.

The idea is to find other blogs that inhabit your niche. After you find blogs that match this description, spend a week or two investigating these blogs. Your mission: Find the secret of their success. You want to know how those blogs get readers and how they keep those readers coming back for more.

Discovering the secrets of success

As you watch your competitors' blogs, you have a chance to learn from them about the topics they blog about, of course, but also about how they're reaching out to their audience.

Figure 9-1:
Use
Technorati
to find
the blogs
of your
competitors.

Remember that your competitors might not be doing things right. Part of your job as you look at these blogs is to decide whether your competitors are actually reaching their audience successfully or whether they're falling short. You can learn as much from a blog that doesn't appear to be succeeding as one that is.

As you visit these blogs, keep a journal of your impressions. Investigate how these bloggers are handling publishing and outreach by watching the following:

- **How frequently the blogger puts new posts on the blog:** Frequency of blog posts is a big deal. Any blogger will tell you to post "frequently," but almost none can tell you want that really means. I talk more about how often you should post later in this chapter, but one way you can explore this idea is by noting how often your competitors choose to post to their blogs. Are they creating new posts daily or even multiple times a day? Or are they posting a few times a week or even once a week? As you become a reader of that blog, do you find yourself wanting more content or less?

- **What time blog posts are being published:** Time of day can have a surprising impact on how a blog post is received. Think about it this way: You need to reach your audience members when they're likely to be sitting at their computer. If your audience is stock brokers, you want to time your posts so that new content becomes available just before business hours start on the East Coast, not during dinner time on the West

Coast. If you're targeting teens, try to publish before or during after-school hours and not while they're sitting in homeroom.

Sure, your readers can visit your blog anytime and pick up content that is posted in the middle of the night, but they'll be impressed with a blog that always seems to have fresh content just when they want it.

✔ **The length of posts on the blog:** You might be surprised to know that the ideal length of a blog post is a hotly debated topic among experienced bloggers. Some bloggers swear by the "short and sweet" recipe that guides most Web writing: Blog posts should get to the point quickly and allow readers to get back to their busy days with the information they need. Others find that longer posts — even essays — do the job, keeping readers on the site longer and providing more thoughtful commentary. The truth is that the topic of your blog, as well as your audience's appetite and available time, dictate the natural length of your blog posts. Looking at your competitor's blogs can tell you the number of words they find optimal in a blog post, which is a good starting point for your blog.

✔ **When the blogger links to outside Web sites:** Linking to other blogs and Web sites is a great way to serve the reader. By pointing out other sources of information or even other blogs, you help them become more knowledgeable about your topic and keep them engaged with it. So, when do your competitors choose to link to other sites, and what sites do they link to? Are the links designed to entertain, educate, or inform? Are links included in the text of the post or broken out at the end? What makes you click a link yourself?

I talk a lot more about linking other sites as a strategy for reaching your audience later in this chapter.

✔ **When the blogger addresses his or her audience directly:** Lots of bloggers use a very personal writing style that directly acknowledges the reader, kind of like this: You might enjoy being addressed directly by a blogger, so that the conversation feels more personal. Or, depending on the topic of your blog, perhaps a more formal, almost academic approach works better. Either way, check out how your competition is handling this issue. When do they ask the readers for input or feedback, and how do they phrase those requests? Do readers actually respond, and to what kinds of approaches?

✔ **Use of multimedia like photos, audio, and video:** Though the majority of blogs are made up of lots and lots of words, that doesn't mean you can't throw in the occasional (or even frequent) picture or video. In fact, bloggers do it all the time to dress things up visually and keep readers interested. Take a look at how your competitors handle these issues. Are they using photos to illustrate the ideas in the posts, or just to attract the eye? What about animation or video? Do posts with these extras get more comments or fewer? Do you like getting information in these other formats or is it just distracting?

- ✔ **Posts that get lots of comments and posts that get very few:** A blog that gets lots of comments is a sign that the blogger is resonating with his or her audience — even if just to make them mad. A blog with no or few comments is probably just leaving people flat and maybe just isn't being read. The truth is that not all bloggers get hundreds of comments every time they post. Some blog posts just get better response than others, and part of what makes a blogger successful is being able to know what makes those posts really work, so that the success can be repeated. Watch your competitor's blogs to see when a post gets a big response, and look at what that response is.

  Also watch for the posts that don't get any response — you want to figure out why those didn't work so that you don't make the same mistake!

- ✔ **The writing style of the blogger:** Having good content is key, and for most bloggers, that comes down to having an accessible and readable writing style. For those blogs in your niche that are doing well, what is that style? Personal? Professional? Humorous? What notes are hitting the right buttons for readers and making them come back to the blog again and again? What approach do you yourself find more readable and engaging?

You can use these same points of analysis on your own blog, too. After your blog has been up and running for a while, take a look at your own content with the same critical eye you just used on your competitors. What are you doing right and wrong?

This can be a hard exercise to do. I'm sure you think everything on your blog is great — after all, no one sets out to write a bad blog post! Still, it's likely that some of your posts were more popular with readers than others, and if you can figure out why they worked better, you can repeat that success again and again. In fact, I believe that developing a critical eye for your own content is a huge key to making your blog succeed: This medium doesn't hold still, and you need to be able to adapt your style and content as your audience grows and changes. Consider conducting this kind of survey of your content a couple of times year to make sure you stay on track and topical to the folks you want to attract, even if that really is just your immediate family!

Profiling your audience

With your competitive analysis done (yep, that's what you just did in the last section!) and after a review of your own content successes and failures, it's time to picture your audience in your mind's eye.

This is a fun visualization exercise. What you want to do is create a clear picture for yourself of just who is in your audience. If you don't have the audience you're targeting at this point, this might be an exercise in developing a picture of who you *want* in your audience.

You don't actually have to draw a picture, though. This profile can be created in words that describe the characteristics of your ideal audience member. You can include anything you want in this profile, from shoe size to personal hangups — any detail that helps you to know this person better, and to create better content for that person on your blog is helpful.

It's a total copout answer to say "My ideal audience is anybody who is interested in *[insert your blog topic here]*." You already know that, or this person wouldn't be on your blog. It's all the details that make this person different, unique, and interesting that you're trying to capture.

Take Gizmodo, as shown in Figure 9-2. Gizmodo (www.gizmodo.com) is a techie blog featuring information on gadgets and other nifty technical devices. The blog's tagline is "Gizmodo, the gadget guide. So much in love with shiny new toys, it's unnatural." Right away, you know that the audience for Gizmodo is more that just those "interested" in gadgets — Gizmodo readers adore gadgets, see them as playthings meant to entertain and amuse, and are perhaps unhealthily engaged by them, perhaps at the expense of other hobbies and pursuits. And they want their gadget news piping hot, fresh off the presses. Doesn't that tell you more about what kinds of posts are going to work best to attract and keep these kinds of readers?

Figure 9-2:
Gizmodo focuses on the fanatical gadget enthusiast.

Some of the concepts and facts you *might* want to explore for your profile are

- Age
- Gender
- The nature of their interest in your topic; for example, familial, personal, emotional, shared passion, and professional
- Geographic location and proximity to you or to the topic of your blog
- Lifestyle: workaholic, homebody, retired, world traveler, and so on
- Occupation
- Education level
- Marital status
- Interests and hobbies
- Income
- Political leanings

Heck, it might even be useful to think about what your ideal audience member reads, eats, or wears, his or her sleeping habits and style of personal hygiene, and so on. If a specific detail seems like it might inform your writing and content, throw it into the mix.

With a reader profile in hand, you can be more targeted about what you choose to write about, and how you address that audience.

Writing Well and Frequently

I've said it before and I'll say it again: The primary ingredients for a successful blog are

- Good content
- Frequently updated content

But what do I really mean by *good* and *frequently?*

Good content compels, satisfying the readers' immediate interests but leaving them hungry for more. Think of a blog post like an appetizer: It should whet the appetite, pique the palette, and sustain the diner until the next course arrives. You don't want to give your reader's Thanksgiving dinner here — you want them to come back and come back soon.

Respecting copyright

Anything and everything you see on the Internet is protected by copyright. Copyright is just what it sounds like: "the right to copy" an original creation. Copyright law protects authors by giving that right solely to him or her.

Unless the creator of an image or photo specifically licenses his or her copyright to you, you may not reuse it, even if you give the author credit or link back to the original story. (This is true of all photos and videos, too.) There are a few exceptions: you can quote a news story or a blog post on your blog if you only use part of it, and as long as you don't take credit for the work. Commentary and critique also earns you the ability to excerpt a piece of text or other work. But don't think that just because you are the subject of a story or blog post that gives you the ability repost the entire article on your blog or Web site. It doesn't. When in doubt, ask and get permission. That never hurts!

As a general rule, blogging has evolved into quite a personal, conversational medium, and textual blogs have a strong feel of the author and his or her personality. The first blogs were actually online diaries, and even today most bloggers choose to use words like "I" or "my" in their blog posts, creating an intimate and open feel. This is true even on corporate blogs. This is called *first person* writing, and differs dramatically from most corporate communication, which at best refers to the company as "our" and at worst only refers to the company by its full and official name.

Take, for example, the McDonald's blog, Open for Discussion (http://csr.blogs.mcdonalds.com), written by McDonald's Vice President Bob Langert. In an August 20, 2007 post, Bob writes

> "We all have one — a pet peeve that we just can't ditch. I was recently reminded of my #1 pet peeve while reading the latest account of McDonald's Moms' Quality Correspondents. They reported that McDonald's beef is 100% pure USDA-inspected beef. Frankly, I don't think this should be any kind of big 'Aha', and I am amazed that so many people question this established fact."

Figure 9-3 shows this post.

Writing in the first person isn't as easy as it looks (or reads); after all, most people spend years training to write more formally and commonly produce all kinds of documents in which first person writing is emphatically not suitable: memos, reports, new stories, invoices, and so on. It can be tough to find an authentic, genuine voice that really feels comfortable. My best advice is to just practice, practice, practice.

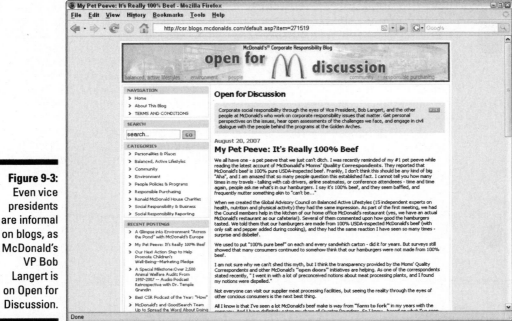

Figure 9-3:
Even vice presidents are informal on blogs, as McDonald's VP Bob Langert is on Open for Discussion.

Think of your blog posts like letters or e-mails. Speak directly and simply, as you would in a personal note or letter. Try not to overthink your words, but don't go right into stream of consciousness (fun to write, hard to read).

One of my favorite techniques for making my blog posts readable is to close the door of my office and read my post out loud. If it sounds close to something I might actually say in conversation, it hits the right tone for a blog post — at least on my blog.

When it seems appropriate, try using humor and jokes, especially if you can be self-deprecating. People just love self-deprecating bloggers. Here's an example from Stephanie Pearl-McPhee's Yarn Harlot blog (www.yarn harlot.com):

> "I think that I can't be the only one who finds LA a little hard on the ol' self esteem. There is an alarmingly high ratio of tall, beautiful people compared to us ordinary souls, and it usually doesn't take long for me, the shabby and usually bra-less to feel out of place."

Sometimes I find it difficult to write to some anonymous audience member and get a conversational tone, so I imagine that I'm writing to a good friend. If I can be interesting enough to hold her attention, it ought to do the trick for my readers, too!

Being informal and conversational doesn't necessarily mean you can completely ignore spelling, grammar, and sentence structure. Some bloggers do opt for a completely unedited approach, right down to not using capital letters, but keep in mind that writing that isn't well-formulated is actually harder for people to read, not easier. If yours is a business or professional blog, spelling and grammar are even more important because these little details will influence your credibility. Do your readers a favor and use the grammar and spellcheck functions of your word processor.

On the other hand, many blogs have made a reputation based on using incorrect spelling or grammar! An example is the funny blog `www.icanhascheez burger.com`, which has built its popularity largely off of bad spelling in hilariously captioned photos of cats.

Many bloggers like to quote news articles and blog posts, and then expand on them. That's fine, but be sure you understand the rules of copyright law when you choose to use someone else's words — it's always best to ask permission! For more, read the sidebar "Respecting copyright" in this chapter.

Good writing resources

The Web has some great resources to help you improve your writing, or just dress it up a little.

Google Definitions: (`www.google.com`) Get quick definitions by launching Google and typing **define:** followed by the word you need a definition for in the search box. In the following figure, I searched for **define: blog**. I use this resource constantly.

Copyright Law: (`www.copyright.gov`) Get the goods on what you can use on your blog without running afoul of the law protecting other authors' text. You might particularly want to read the areas around fair use, especially if you plan to write reviews.

Bartlett's Quotations: (`www.bartleby. com/100`) Visit this collection of 11,000 searchable quotations created by Bartleby.com. You can search by keyword or look up quotes by author or author's lifespan.

Ask Oxford's Frequently Asked Questions: (`www.askoxford.com/asktheexperts /faq`) Get the experts' answers to common spelling, grammar, word usage, and symbols from the Oxford University Press. Wordsmiths, prepare to spend a few hours reading mesmerized by this fascinating resource.

Roget's New Millennium Thesaurus: (`http:// thesaurus.reference.com`) Get immediate suggestions for synonyms and antonyms in this simple to use Web site, along with a dictionary and encylopedia.

Yale Web Style Guide: (`www.webstyle guide.com`) This guide covers everything from good Web design standards to graphics production, but the blog writer will benefit most from Chapter 6, which covers links, titles, and common online styles.

Getting Interaction Going with Comments

Comments are such an important part of a blog. It's such a sad thing when a blogger opts, through choice or necessity, to turn off commenting because the blogger loses some of what makes blogging such a dynamic, exciting medium: the interaction between blogging and readers. It isn't only the blogger who loses out when comments are removed either — most blog readers read and enjoy the comments left by others and often form a strong community feeling for fellow visitors.

Comments get turned off when a blogger simply doesn't have the time or desire to read and respond to comments or when the tenor of the comments becomes a problem. Popular blogger Heather Armstrong is selective about allowing comments on her blog Dooce (www.dooce.com) because her religious views and style of blogging generate a lot of negative interaction with readers in the comments. Political bloggers often have similar problems.

I talk more about handling spam and undesirable comments in Chapter 10.

For other bloggers, time is the main issue. A popular blogger can get hundreds of comments on a single blog post, and it takes time to read and respond to those, much less remove any inappropriate comments. Spam can also be an issue. Just as with e-mail, spammers have discovered that they can throw their unwanted commercial messages (anyone need a refinance?) into blogs, and even with the best blog software, some of those messages end up on the blog and must be removed. (If spam is a problem on your blog, check out the next chapter, which is entirely devote to filtering and preventing spam.)

Still, the vast majority of blogs allow comments, and they benefit hugely from the interaction and fun that comments can generate. On a blog like Grey Matter from the writers of the TV show Grey's Anatomy (www.greyswriters.com), for example, readers really get involved with the show's writers. In the comments, readers share their thoughts on the show, offering feedback and suggestions.

Comments are key if you want to have a dialogue with your readers, whether you're reaching out to your parents or to your customers.

Just because your blog posts have a comment form, though, doesn't mean that people will just jump in and start commenting. You need to tailor your posts to solicit dialogue and feedback, perhaps even by going so far as to ask specifically for responses.

Ask your visitors to tell you stories, answer questions, suggest directions for your blog, or discuss any other topic you want to hear about. For instance, if you're blogging about a frustrating travel experience, you might ask your readers for tips for the future. Or, if you're looking for a new laptop bag, get your readers to recommend bags they like.

Specific, rather than general, questions work better to start a conversation.

If the comment areas of your blog are looking a little bare, ask some friends to help you out by reading and commenting for a few weeks. Comments tend to generate more comments, if you can get the ball rolling.

Of course, the problem might also lie with your content or approach, so don't be afraid to experiment with your topic or style to try and get better results from your comment forms.

Blogs with active comment communities

As you experiment with comments, it can be useful to see how sites with vibrant, active communities handle the onslaught of opinion and discussion. Here are some popular blogs that have developed an involved and vocal audience that you can explore:

BoingBoing: (www.boingboing.net) This grandfather of blogs brings together the weird and wonderful from all over the Web for the entertainment and bemusement of its readers. Readers are healthily active in the comments, and the blog features a navigation item labeled Suggest a Link that encourages readers to send in their suggestions for future posts.

Gizmodo: (www.gizmodo.com) This gadget guide keeps you abreast of all the latest in shiny tech toys, from car stereos to mobile phones — and does so in multiple languages, to boot. Comments on this blog range from the rabid fan to the disgruntled critic and add as much value as the blog posts.

Nuts About Southwest: (www.blogsouthwest.com) Folks from all levels of the Southwest Airlines organization post to this blog, which covers things like new boarding procedures, dress codes, and food offerings. Judging from the hundreds of comments on some posts, Southwest is getting plenty of feedback from their customers on their experience with the airline.

Yarn Harlot: (www.yarnharlot.com) Stephanie Pearl-McPhee is an avid knitter turned knitting book author. You simply won't believe how popular her blog is or how many of her readers comment on her humorous posts about knitting projects and her family life.

The Pioneer Woman Cooks!: (www.thepioneerwomancooks.com) Warning! Reading this blog will make you very hungry. Ree, wife to a cattle rancher, posts mouthwatering recipes amply illustrated with photographs. If you're looking for ideas on what to cook for dinner, Ree has ideas. Judging by her comments, you can trust her cooking advice.

Truthdig: (www.truthdig.com) This news Web site won a 2007 Webby Award for Best Political Blog in both the juried and people's choice categories. The site combines commentary on current political issues with book reviews, podcasts, and interviews, and it gets loads of feedback from fans and critics.

Linking to Serve the Reader

Links — you need 'em. It's easy to worry that by providing a link to a news story or online article you're sending your readers away from your site into the black hole of the Internet, never to return. Partly, this is true. Your readers might in fact click the link and go read the article. But, they won't forget where they found the link.

On a blog, links are just as much a resource as any other information you provide. In fact, many blogs are actually collections of links around a topic or theme, pulled together to inform or entertain the blog's readers.

If you're providing good content and building it out with links, you're doing your readers a service they won't forget — one they'll come back to you for.

Joey deVilla doesn't shy away from adding links to his blog posts on The Adventures of Accordion Guy in the 21st Century (www.joeydevilla.com), as shown in Figure 9-4.

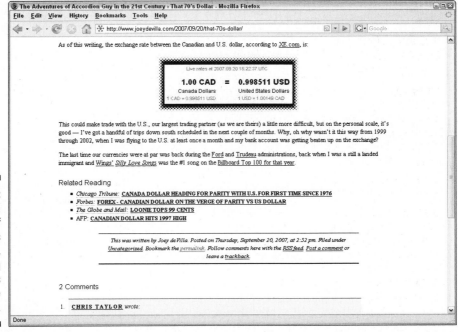

Figure 9-4:
Joey deVilla adds lots of links to his blog posts, helping his readers get more information.

In a September 20, 2007 post about the Canadian dollar's parity with the U.S. dollar, he included links to bios of the U.S. president and Canadian prime minister in office during the last time the currencies were equal, and he provided links to pop culture references current at that time. As well, he collected a list of news stories that cover the event.

Speaking of dollars, links are really the currency of the blogosphere. Lots of bloggers point their readers to blog posts they find especially interesting, even going so far as to quote the other blogger. Bloggers regularly build lists of links to blogs they read called *blogrolls* (see Chapter 12) that live in the sidebars of blogs.

In general, bloggers are generous about linking to other blogs and Web sites because the favor is frequently returned. As the saying goes, "You have to spend a little to make a little."

Adding links to your posts is a good thing . . . unless you're irresponsible about what you link to. Take your responsibility as a publisher seriously and don't send people to resources you think are suspect or throw them into an adult-oriented site without warning.

When you link to a blog post, be sure you link to the permalink URL and not just to the blog's home page. A *permalink* is the unique Web address for an individual blog post — the permanent link to that page. You should use the permalink and not the blog's home page as your link because the blog might be updated any time after you create the link, pushing the post you mention down or even off the blog's home page.

Breaking Through a Blank Screen

Even outstanding bloggers hit dry spells and can't think of a word to write at times. You can safely anticipate a day sometime in the lifespan of your blog when you literally have nothing to say to your readers, no matter how much enthusiasm you have for your topic.

It will pass, but sometimes you need a little help pushing back to a productive spot. Here are a few tips for making it through your dry spell:

- **Stockpile a few evergreen posts.** In newsrooms across the country, journalists regularly create *evergreen stories* (stories that can be printed or televised at any time and still be interesting). You can also put together a few evergreen blog posts that you can keep on hand against a day when your creative juices are taking a break. These kinds of posts are also nice to have ready for days when you're sick or on vacation but still want to have something for your blog. Lots of blog software allows you to schedule a publication date for a blog post in the future, so you can even set these posts to go up automatically and take a well-deserved break.

✔ **Ask a friend to guest blog for a few days.** Bring some new perspective to your blog when you have none left yourself by asking a friend, colleague, fellow blogger, or even a critic to write some blog posts for you. Your readers might enjoy the change of style and tone (and if they don't, they'll just be that much happier when you come back!). Be sure to return the favor when your guest blogger has a dry spell.

✔ **Recycle an oldie but goodie.** When you can't think of exciting new content, bring out a great post from your archives. New readers appreciate seeing something they missed, and old readers might find new information in a second read. Professional blogger Darren Rowse points his readers to a list of "Best of" posts on ProBlogger (www.problogger.net). In fact, Darren pulls out the best posts of all time, for the month, for new readers, and just some of his favorites (see Figure 9-5).

Figure 9-5: Darren Rowse points people to favorite posts from the past as well.

✔ **Hold a contest.** When the well has run dry, you can hold a contest. Ask your readers to submit funny photos or write a caption for one of your funny photos. Show them a bottle of jellybeans and ask for guesses about how many pieces of candy are in the bottle. You get the idea: Distract them with shiny, happy prizes! But make sure you are fair and impartial in how you award prizes. If you say you'll hold a raffle, be sure to actually do so!

✔ **Post a photo.** Instead of 1,000 words, put up a single photo. Take a picture of where you usually blog, show off your new laptop, or just take a walk in your neighborhood. You can dig out a photo of you as a kid, or show that embarrassing haircut you had in the '80s. Laurie Perry does just this on her blog, Crazy Aunt Purl (`www.crazyauntpurl.com`), with hilariously captioned photos from an '80s high school career. Check out the big hair in Figure 9-6.

✔ **Post about the books, movies, or television you're consuming.** Tell folks about the other media you're enjoying. You can even hook up an Amazon Associates account and earn a little money off your recommendations. (There's more on how to do this in Chapter 16.)

✔ **Give out your favorite recipe.** Dig out the cookbook and find your grandmother's fudge recipe or your mom's apple pie and share with your readers. Better yet, take a break from the computer and make the recipe yourself so you can put up a photo with your post.

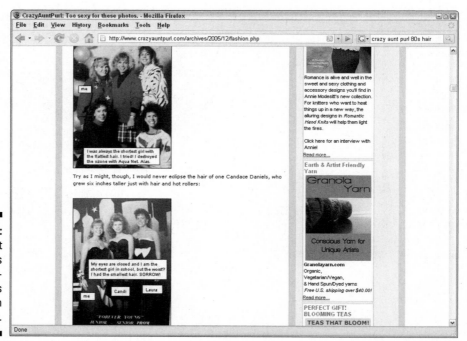

Figure 9-6: Crazy Aunt Purl shows embarrassing photos on a down day.

✔ **Blog from a new location.** Sometimes breaking the routine can shake loose those recalcitrant brain cells. Try blogging from another room in your house, or heading to the local Internet cafe or coffee shop.

✔ **Record an audio podcast.** If you can't write, talk! Give the gift of your voice to your readers — listeners — by trying something new and different. You might be pleasantly surprised and make podcasting a regular feature of your blog. Chapter 14 covers podcasting extensively.

✔ **Do an interview.** Ask a friend, colleague, neighbor, child, parent, boss, or public figure if you can interview him or her for your blog. Type up a few questions, e-mail them off, and when the answers arrive in your inbox, a little copying and pasting should do the trick.

✔ **Take a quiz.** Let your readers know what superhero you are or what color your personality is by playing with some of the fun quizzes and polls online. The superhero quiz is at `www.thesuperheroquiz.com` (I'm Spider Man), and loads of others are available on `www.blog things.com` and `www.quizmeme.com`.

✔ **Ask for suggestions from your readers.** Appeal to your readers for helping finding new topics to post about. Also, look through your old posts and see if you can expand on a post that worked well; check out comments and e-mails from readers, too!

Chapter 10

Handling Spam and Comments

In This Chapter

▶ Identifying spam on your blog

▶ Dealing with spammy comments on your blog

▶ Using technology to deal with spam

▶ Handling negative comments on other blogs

Spam! It's everywhere, lurking in your e-mail inbox waiting to pounce on an unsuspecting click. It also hangs on your blog hiding in the comments — you might never escape it! Fortunately, you can slow the stream of spam messages and even block most of them from appearing on your blog.

I don't recommend disabling comments just to keep out the spam. Blog comments are crucial for the life and health of your blog; if you want your blog to be more than just another Web site, to have real conversations with your readers, you simply can't forego comments. You just have to take the good with the bad. And I won't lie about the bad: Fighting spam can consume valuable time and energy. If you're serious about blogging, it must be done, no matter how unrewarding it feels. It's like taking out the trash: no fun, but if you don't do it, your house will fill up with garbage and become uninhabitable.

Unfortunately, comment spam isn't the only thing you need to worry about. Blog comments are like a playground where you need to play referee for your community. You might end up with some opinionated, cranky readers that leave nasty comments directed at you or other commenters. In situations like this, you must draw a line in the sand about removing inappropriate, offensive comments.

In this chapter, I show you how to fight the good fight against spam and how you can develop a community spirit on your blog through comments.

The amount of spam you're bound to get isn't a reason to avoid blogging. After all, junk messages aren't anything new. You see spam in your e-mail all the time; heck, you even see it in your snail mail box, and you probably aren't about to stop getting mail delivered, right?

Recognizing Unwanted Comments

Any unwanted message that's posted into the comment area of your blog is *spam,* especially those with links to fabulous drug cocktails, unbelievable mortgage opportunities, and solutions to certain . . . ahem . . . anatomical size problems you don't have.

The first time you see a spam comment on your blog, you might not recognize it. The first spam posts on blogs were obviously not real comments: incomprehensible text, inappropriate images, and links to pornographic Web sites made these comments stand out. But, as the blogs evolved, so did the spammers, and today's spam comments might look like anything from a sincere compliment to a request for more information. Figure 10-1 shows a spam comment that was left on one of my blogs.

Your brain and eyes are what protects your blog from the outside world. If something looks suspicious to you, check it out so that you can protect yourself, your readers, and your search engine ranking.

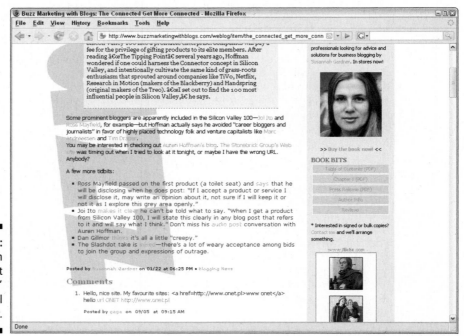

Figure 10-1:
A spam comment "disguised" as a real comment.

Because you're the first line of defense, you need to get a feel for the comments that are legitimately posted on your site. Take some time and see what your community is like. If your blog community takes some time to grow, venture out onto other blogs and see what people are saying:

- ✔ Look at real comments and see how are they are written.
- ✔ Get involved and add your own commentary to other blogs.

It might seem a little odd, but when you take the time to read real comments, you'll be better at spotting the spam.

Spam has certain styles. Spammers attempt to weasel into your site by looking like they have personal or generally harmless content. Sometimes you won't be able to tell a legitimate comment with poor grammar and spelling from a spam comment with similar attributes. Spammers are counting on this confusion. Sorting the wheat from the chaff can be a tricky bit of business, but with a few tips, you can get through the spam onslaught with as little frustration as possible:

- ✔ **Personalized and customized messages:** This type of spam is created by a real human being as opposed to an automated bit of programming. Usually a human being, paid by a spam company, visits your blog, reads a few posts and a few comments, and then customizes messages that fit in with the tenor and style of the site. Often these messages are even directed to you by name. You can easily miss these messages when you're watching for spam comments.

   If the link included with a comment isn't related to the subject of the comment or the topics on your blog, the comment is probably a fake, no matter how on topic it might seem to be.

- ✔ **Generic commentary or questions:** Another time-waster is the generic message spam. These messages either request you to do something or make a very nonspecific remark. Comments like "You've got the same name as I do,", "Have you seen the new video?", "Check out my blog?", "Need you to do something for me," or "Your blog is broken you need to see this" are quite common.

- ✔ **Flattery:** Finally, there's flattery. Comments like "Your blog is awesome" or "I like your blog, click to read mine" are very common. As a general rule, regard these kinds of brief praise with suspicion (well, unless your blog really is awesome, of course!). Real fans usually elaborate more about what they like about your writing.

In general, a spam comment invariably includes a link, usually to an advertising Web site or site designed to look like a blog. The spammers are hoping that you or your blog visitors will click the link, giving them a traffic boost and potentially allowing them to collect a fee based on the number of times the site is visited or a link is clicked. Look closely at comments that include links.

Many comment spammers are annoyingly ingenious about finding ways to disguise their messages. (Some aren't — you can easily recognize the comments about Viagra or that contain gibberish as spam.) But the generic nature of comments gives them away. Keep your wits about you so that you can identify new trends and formats in comment spam techniques as they appear. The techniques described in this chapter can help you prevent or remove spam, but the human brain is endlessly inventive, which keeps the spammers a step ahead of any software solution to the problem.

Don't just leave comment spam on your blog and let your readers sort through the mess. Spam attracts spam: If you don't remove these kinds of comments, you actually end up with more spam on your site. And, as your readers click the spam links, spammers realize that your blog is untended and flock to it. So delete your spam. Your readers will thank you.

Understanding why spam exists

Junk snail mail, e-mail spam, and blog spam all exist for the same reason: because someone, somewhere makes money on them. This can be hard to believe if you just look at a spam comment — lots of it doesn't really make much sense, much less look like something you might click.

The thing is that spam comments aren't necessarily designed to make you click them or to make your readers click them. What blog spam is usually intended to do is raise the profile of a site linked to from the comment in the search engines. Search engines use secret formulas to determine the result listings you see when you do a search. The formula works to determine and display the most relevant results — the ones that best match your search terms — at the top of the list. One of the ingredients in this secret formula is the number of Web sites that link to a site, and another ingredient is the words that are used for that link.

So, when you write a blog post about a company with a product you love and link to the company, you're really doing it two favors: You've praised them publicly, and you've given it a little boost in the search engine rankings that helps it come up a little higher the next time someone searches for the product you reviewed. Aren't you nice? Now imagine that ten more customers do the same thing on their blogs. The company gets lots of search engine love for all those different links.

Spammers are trying to scam this process by creating dozens, even hundreds, of links from many different Web pages to the Web site they're attempting to boost in the search engine rankings. When a site is high in the search engine rankings, you know what happens: It gets visited more often.

Ultimately, the goal of comment spam might in fact be to get people to visit a particular Web site, but it's a fairly indirect path to that result. Once on the Web site, the unfortunate visitor might be given a chance to buy a product, click a link, provide information he or she shouldn't about bank accounts, or view a page with ads on it. And that's where the profit is made.

Unfortunately, spam isn't the only unwanted comment material you might deal with. Some of your legitimate commenters may use language you don't want on your blog, or post personal, offensive *flames*, or attacks, aimed at your or other readers. You're just as entitled to remove this kind of comment as you are to remove spam. In most cases, the techniques described in the next section can be used to handle flames and spam comments alike.

Moderating Comments

The single best solution for keeping spam off your blog is to read each and every comment left on your blog individually, removing those that are spam or are inappropriate. This act is called *moderating*. Moderating your blog comments can add overhead to your blogging time, but if you're dedicated to making your blog successful and useful to your readers, it's time well spent.

There are ways to manage the time you spend looking through comment lists, but the method you choose as your primary line of defense depends on how your community grows.

Moderating can be done by you, your community, software, or a combination of all three. Table 10-1 covers the pros and cons of three approaches you can try. Some bloggers have strong preferences at the outset, but you can experiment with the best setup for your blog and readers.

Table 10-1	Comment Moderation Options	
Approach	*Pro*	*Con*
Review all comments *before* they're posted on your blog.	No spam ever appears on your blog unless you choose to allow it.	Comments are delayed before they're posted, making your blog less spontaneous and slower-paced.
Review all comments *after* they are posted on your blog.	Comments appear on your blog more quickly, making conversation quick-paced.	You must review and remove unwanted comments frequently, probably daily.
Asking your readers to notify you of inappropriate comments.	Cuts down on your comment moderation hours by pointing you to problem comments quickly.	Turns your readers into police, a role they might enjoy too much or not at all, changing the conversational tenor.

continued

Table 10-1 *(continued)*

Approach	Pro	Con
Letting software weed out the bad stuff.	Using a combination of blacklists and whitelists (see more on these technologies later in the chapter) means you don't have to read through lots of spam yourself.	Software needs to be kept up to date as spammers work out new ways to cheat the system, so budget time for behind-the-scenes technical work; ineffective against personal attacks or flames.

Using a combination of the methods in Table 10-1 to control spam is the easiest way to maintain your sanity. If your site becomes a popular location for online discussion, it's likely you will experiment with each of these methods to find one that suits you and your readers, while letting you keep enough time in your schedule for actually writing new blog posts!

Some blogs have communities that build quickly, whereas others take more time. You might need to change your spam prevention methods from time to time in order to take advantage of the community desire to help.

Establishing community guidelines

Before you get sucked into spending hours upon hours checking people's comments on your site, one method to stave off the hordes might be to write some community guidelines. Such guidelines should be straightforward and list clearly what's expected of users that leave comments on your site.

Your rules may exclude anything you want. Common blog rules outlaw comments with

- ✔ Racist or bigoted speech
- ✔ Sexually explicit content
- ✔ Discussions or descriptions of violent or criminal acts
- ✔ Unlicensed copyrighted material
- ✔ Threats, harassment, or personal privacy violations

It's up to you to enforce these rules, but simply having them in place can deter trouble makers from posting at all, particularly if you're scrupulous in applying your guidelines quickly. I talk more about types of guidelines you might want to consider in Chapter 3.

The blogging software solution you use might also have a set of standards in place that both you and your visitors must comply with. For examples, Microsoft Windows Live Spaces, a hosted blogging solution, has a community code of conduct that you must enforce on your blog (shown in Figure 10-2). Every hosted blogging service has their own set of rules and you should be aware of each of them. Don't get caught breaking the rules!

Any guidelines you create might need to be adapted over time, especially as your blog grows in popularity or changes its focus. Be sure to set a time every so often to review your own guidelines and make changes. You might include your visitors in the development of the community guidelines. There's no harm in checking with your readers about things you do to protect them. They'll love you for it.

Editing comments

Sometimes a comment is legitimate but needs to be altered in some way. For example, you might prefer to remove profanity from otherwise legit comments or to edit a long Web link that's breaking a page layout. Whatever the situation, editing a reader's comments is something that should be done delicately.

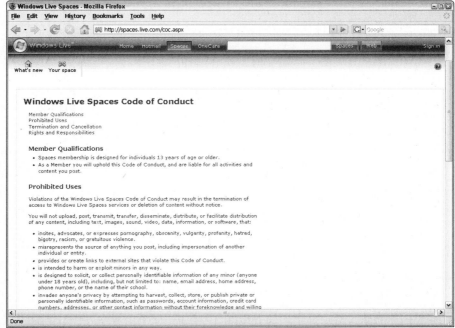

Figure 10-2: Microsoft Windows Live Spaces has a community code of conduct for their system.

Microsoft product screen shot(s) reprinted with permission from Microsoft Corporation

Some of your readers might react poorly to having their words edited, and of course the last thing you intend is to insult a reader by pointing out spelling or grammar issues. Use a sensitive hand, but remember that a comment on your blog is as much a part of the conversational give and take on your blog as your original blog posts. Not only that, you're responsible for the words on your blog, and may feel you have a duty to remove hateful or offensive language, especially if your blog is read by younger audiences.

Your blog is your domain, your kingdom, and your place in the world where your word is final. You can read all kinds of helpful tips that will guide you through some of the difficult phases, but ultimately you call the shots.

Of course, when you do choose to edit a comment, you might want to alert readers that you have done so and why, as I have done in comment #7 in Figure 10-3 on my own blog. It's also a good idea to lay out circumstances where you'll edit comments in your blog comment policy (see Chapter 3). Both these techniques can head off accusations of censorship.

An edited comment

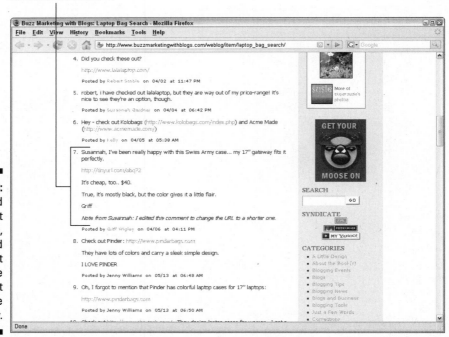

Figure 10-3:
If you need to edit comments, it's a good idea to let people know that you've done so and why.

Getting help from readers

If you have a vibrant community eager to help or if another interested party that you trust is willing to help you review comments, let them! For a blog that has existed for a long time and developed a real following, comment moderation can be a huge load. You can spread out some of that responsibility to trusted readers who have proven to be rational, responsible, and regular visitors. As the blog grows and evolves and your community builds, approach some of these folks about giving you a hand and check to see whether you can set up your blog software to give them access to the comment moderation area. If you trust these folks, they can help you delete spam, as well as edit and remove inappropriate and offensive comments. If you're lucky, you might receive requests by readers to help.

Moderators are a great solution for blogs that have a large number of comments posted every week. These trusted readers often feel invested in the community and welcome the chance to give back in a meaningful way. A few diligent helpers that can work with little to no direction and oversight can free up busy bloggers for the real business at hand: writing blog posts.

Another type of helper moderation is allowing the community members to develop their own sense of what is and isn't appropriate for your blog. Many different blog packages have additional plug-ins that allow you to give the community certain rights when it comes to spam moderation. Comment flagging and comment ratings are two of these:

- ✔ **Comment flagging** is when a reader can mark a comment as problematic. A site moderator (you) reviews the marked comment and then makes a judgment about whether the comment should be on the site. The Think Salmon Web site (`www.thinksalmon.com`) uses comment flagging to help cut down on spam; Figure 10-4 shows the "Flag as inappropriate" links readers can click to report an inappropriate comment. There are flagging plugins for ExpressionEngine, WordPress, and Movable Type. Be sure to check your own blogging software documentation to see if you have or can add this functionality.

- ✔ **Comment ratings** also help you (and your readers) make judgments about the usefulness of a comment. With a comment rating system, your visitors can vote on comments, generating tallies of popular and unpopular comments. Spam comments, logically, would be voted down, allowing you to automatically remove them after a certain vote count is reached or to review and delete them as you desire. You can see comment ratings in action on the Little Green Footballs blog (`www.littlegreenfootballs.com`). In Figure 10-5, the plus and minus boxes beside each comment can be clicked to vote a comment up or down. Check your blog package to see if you have a comment rating system is available for your blogging software. There are ratings plugins for WordPress, ExpressionEngine, and Movable Type, and others.

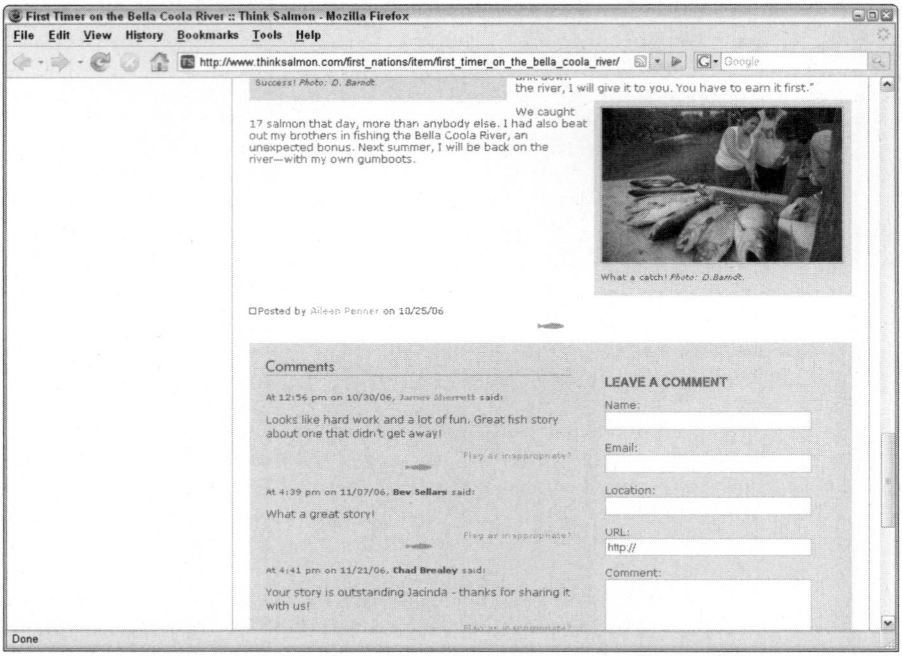

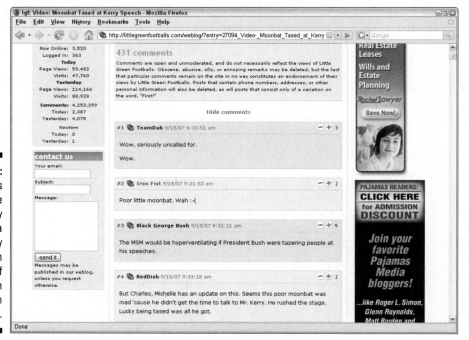

Figure 10-4: Readers can mark spam comments themselves on the Think Salmon Web site.

Courtesy of Pacific Salmon Foundation

Figure 10-5: Readers can indicate the quality of a comment by voting with the click of a button on Little Green Footballs.

Giving your community the ability to vote on whether or not a comment is appropriate is a great way to get your community involved. If your community is large enough, voting might be the quickest way to make them feel as if they have a say in the content of your blog.

There are a couple of draw backs to voting systems that you should consider before opting to have the users vote.

- *The number of votes:* You have to pick the right number of votes required before a comment is removed from the site. If you set the number too low, comments will disappear too easily, and some nonspam but nonetheless unpopular comments are likely to be removed. If you set the number too high, the spam simply sticks around for a long time with a low rating. The right number varies for every site, so you might need to experiment to find the right one for your blog and even change it as your audience grows.

- *Unjustified or biased votes:* Your audience might use the ratings to express their opinions about the quality of the comment or their disagreement or agreement with it, rather than simply using it to mark spam. Basically, your idea of what is being rated might differ from how your audience decides to actually use the functionality. Watch carefully when you implement a system like this to see how your readers use it, and ensure that users have access to your terms of service or community guidelines. Be sure to tell them what the ratings mean to you!

Fighting Spam with Software

Spam is a pain. But, think for a moment about how much you're really getting: Do you get three every few weeks, or are you getting 500 an hour? If you're receiving only a few every month, you might not need to install any software because moderating the few problem comments yourself isn't all that onerous. For blogs that get dozens of comments, however, spam fighting can be time-consuming. The following sections explore some of the many blog software solutions available to make this task a little faster and easier.

Protecting your comment form

The tools described in this section are designed to make it harder for spammers to fill out the comment form on your blog. The idea is to prevent the spam from ever reaching your blog so that you don't need to deal with reading and deleting it.

These tools do that job fairly well, but they also present something of a barrier to people who legitimately want to leave a comment; remember, the idea is to cut down on spam, not real comments! Keep your audience's needs and abilities in mind when implementing.

CAPTCHAs

A CAPTCHA (an acronym for something really long and boring) is a challenge-response test. That is, it's a question that your reader must answer correctly in order to post a comment. On a blog, CAPTCHAs are most commonly implemented in such a way that they can be completed by humans but not by computers. A CAPTCHA on the World Hum travel site (www.worldhum.com) requires the would-be commenter to duplicate the letters and numbers shown in an image in order to submit a comment, as shown in Figure 10-6.

CAPTCHAs were created to stop spammers from adding comments to blogs by using automated scripts sent out to try filling out any Web form they find, especially blog comment forms. But spammers are inventive: Some blog comment scripts are now proving capable of recognizing letters and numbers in an image, so many sites that use CAPTCHAs distort the text being displayed by stretching it.

Other sites use CAPTCHA questions that are simple for humans to answer, like trivia or mathematical questions. For example, "What color is a red balloon?" These kinds of CAPTCHAs are a bit newer and have yet to prove their effectiveness, but you might want to check into them and see for yourself how they work.

Your blog software may have CAPTCHA technology built in or you might be able to add one using a plugin. Check your blog software's documentation and support tools for suggestions on installing and configuring a CAPTCHA system.

User registration

A popular option with larger communities, especially online forums, is one that requests or even requires that users who want to leave comments sign up for a user account. These accounts are free, but to complete the registration process, you must provide a name and valid e-mail address, thereby cutting down on the number of spam scripts that can use them. Sites that require registration actually prevent anyone who isn't registered from leaving a comment; sites that simply request registration reward it by recognizing members or by marking that user's comments in some highlighted way.

One benefit to this setup is that you can keep a record of everything the poster adds to the system, easily identifying your most frequent contributors and visitors. Also, if a poster gets out of hand or if an automated spam system is able to acquire an account and post under that user name, you can simply close the account and stop the person from posting again using that account.

Registration is increasingly common in blog software, so be sure to check your documentation. If it isn't available, look for a plugin.

Screening for spam

Another defense against spammers is software that filters the incoming comments in various ways to identify and remove comments that look like spam.
These are great tools for the blogger: They run at all hours of the day and
time, and they don't require any effort on your part. But an automated
process is never as smart as a human, so you might occasionally lose a valid
comment when using a filtering system.

A third-party software solution called Automattic Akismet (see the sidebar on
Akismet in this chapter) is the clear leader when it comes to spam filtering,
though many blogging software applications have added their own internal
tools as well. Check to see if your blog software has any of these technologies
in place for you to use — chances are good that some of them are available. If
you don't find them, check `http://akismet.com/development/` to see
if you can add Akismet to your blog.

Keyword filtering

Keyword filters are a decent way of identifying incoming comment spam. This
kind of filtering is probably the oldest type of protection for blog comments
and might not work all the time because spammers have become much
smarter since this technology was first used. Spam filtering usually works by

comparing incoming comments against lists of words and/or phrases associated with spam. Matches indicate spam, and those comments are yanked.

Keyword filters are typically updated frequently to keep up with the ploys in use by spammers. Some of these lists contain Web addresses and other computer identification information as well as keywords. Users are also allowed to submit and maintain their own lists should custom spelling or other methods of tricking the antispam system come into use (for example, "V1agra" instead of "Viagra").

Several services over the years have allowed different blog tools and platforms to take advantage of a central keyword listing. These kinds of lists are usually updated and managed by a third party, an individual committed to helping the community or a private business, as in the case of today's most popular antispam system, Akismet (see the sidebar with the same name in this chapter).

One problem with this kind of filter system is that some spammers leave nice messages with bad links. These messages are allowed because they aren't offensive or violate any rule you have. Check to make sure that your spam system is up to date every week.

Blacklists and whitelists

A blog *blacklist* is a method of keeping spam off your Web site by preventing certain known spam systems from accessing your comment system or your Web site as a whole. By specifically identifying spammers from certain addresses, countries, computers, or using certain URLs, those individual spammers can be blocked, keeping your blog much safer.

Most blogging software comes with some kind of blacklist system built in or a system that can easily be added with a plug-in or third-party solution. Consult your blog software documentation to be sure you understand how to keep your blacklist up to date and how you can contribute to the blacklist.

Whitelists perform the opposite action of a blacklist by specifically permitting certain visitors or types of visitors. A whitelist is a preselected list of visitors that you know won't post spam on your blog. They're frequently used in conjunction with a blacklist. Whitelists are especially useful for accepting comments from visitors who have been misidentified as spammers in the past. Essentially, you're making your blog accessible to certain people or computer networks. If you want to guarantee that your mother, for instance, can always post to your blog or even set it up so that she doesn't have to comply with a CAPTCHA or other antispam technique, add her to the whitelist so that she can post with impunity. Whitelists are uncommon, so if your blogging software isn't one that offers this functionality, you probably won't find a good third-party solution.

Akismet

One antispam service is worth a special mention: Automattic Akismet (www.akismet.com). The Akismet service has been around since the latter half of 2005, and it's one of the best spam-filtering systems in the world. Plus, it's very easy to use. As you moderate your comments, a simple series of links and buttons helps you make quick choices about good and bad comments.

Akismet works by running your comments through a central data center. The Akismet system runs a number of tests each time a comment is submitted, and if the comment passes all of the tests, the comment is automatically posted to your site. Comments that fail the tests are held in a queue for your review so that you can identify any comments that are actually valid and post them. (Or, you can just delete them all and forget about them.)

The software updates itself and maintains the blacklist it uses, so after it's installed on your blog, you don't have to do anything to keep it up and running. Akismet is free for personal use but requires a monthly fee for commercial use. Also, some deals are available for nonprofit organizations.

IP banning

Similar to blacklists, IP banning prevents certain IP addresses or a range of IP networks from accessing your Web site. IP banning is probably the oldest method of protecting blogs.

An IP (Internet Protocol) address is a series of numbers that identify a network, a computer, or any networked electronic device within a computer network. Devices such as printers, fax machines, computer desktops and laptops, and some telephones can have their own IP addresses.

Many blog software solutions offer lists of banned IP addresses collected from other users of the same software who have identified spammers, and you can automatically update your own list to prevent those spammers from posting to your site.

A potential problem with banning networks or certain IP addresses is that the offending poster may connect via a different IP the next time he or she posts something. Banning by IP address can work for known spam companies but is highly fallible because so many computers regularly obtain new IP addresses through their Internet Service Provider. IP banning can also affect people who shouldn't be blocked. For instance, if you block a computer on a particular network, others using the same network but who are blameless might end up using the offending IP address at some point and be blocked. Many bloggers discount IP banning as having no real usefulness in today's mobile world.

Dealing with Coverage on Other Blogs

You can't do much about negative blog posts or comments about you on other blogs, though many a blogger has stayed awake all night worrying. (It doesn't seem to help.) It's easy to post a comment responding, but doing so when you're feeling angry and emotional might not be a good idea.

You're taking part in a public conversation and that free speech means that people can openly express their opinions about you, your blog, your opinions, your business — you name it. Negative criticism can be hard to take, especially when you feel it's unjustified. Before you send off an angry e-mail or post a comment, sit back and take a little time to consider your options. If you can be objective, try to understand how you're being criticized and whether the critic has a point.

Here are a few ways in which you can handle a case where another blogger posts a negative statement about you or your blog:

- ✔ Point to the negative coverage on your own blog and get some other opinions on the issue without taking a position yourself.

- ✔ Ignore the post and comment about it only when your opinion is specifically requested.

- ✔ Post respectful comments on the blog in question and add to the conversation there.

- ✔ Counter the criticism, in a respectful manner, on your own blog.

Whichever path you choose, make sure you deal with the comment in a respectful manner. It's very easy to escalate a conflict online because you don't have to deal with people face to face. The anonymous feeling people get when they're on the Internet can make them say and behave in ways they wouldn't say to anyone in person. Try to take the high road as much as possible.

In some cases, criticism of an individual or business on a blog has led to legal ramifications, from copyright violation to libel. If you feel you might be in a situation like this, consult with a lawyer about the best course of action.

You might not be the only target of criticism — some blogs have been used as a way to publish attacks on everyone from public figures to personal individuals. There are even those who might choose to attack your readers and ignore you. These kinds of situations need to be dealt with quickly and with as much care as you can provide. Think of yourself as the referee in a situation like that, and protect others from personal attacks to the extent you can do so.

Part IV
Adding Bells and Whistles

The 5th Wave   By Rich Tennant

"As a blog designer I never thought I'd say this, but I don't think your blog has enough bells and whistles."

In this part . . .

If you've mastered the basics, you can have some fun! In this part, you can try some of the truly cutting-edge tricks being used by successful bloggers. Undecipherable acronyms become your friend in Chapter 11 when you find out how to handle all the flavors of RSS feeds, syndicating your content across the Web and on other blogs. Chapter 12 shows you how to add more bells and whistles to your blog sidebars than you can shake a stick at. Also, try saying your peace with pictures by using the tools described in Chapter 13. Or, say it by simply speaking, as I describe in Chapter 14's tour of the world of podcasting and video blogging.

Chapter 11

Reaching Out with RSS

In This Chapter

▶ Figuring out what RSS really is

▶ Putting RSS to work for your blog

▶ Tracking blogs in newsreaders

*N*o fashionable blog would be caught dead without a Web feed. Web feeds, or *RSS feeds,* are hard to describe (bad for me), but easy to use (good for you!). RSS *(Really Simple Syndication)* is an easy way for you to distribute your content, such as blog posts and podcasts, to your Web audience. Having an RSS feed on your blog is essential for both accessibility and promotion.

But what is RSS, really? Read on, friend.

If you want to find out more about RSS than I can provide in this chapter, either to get your blog into the world or to pull in other blog content, consider reading *Syndicating Web Sites with RSS Feeds For Dummies,* by Ellen Finkelstein (Wiley Publishing).

Getting the Goods on Web Feeds

RSS is one of the hottest technologies on the Internet today. Since 2003 — which is when blogs truly reached mainstream awareness — there's been an exponential adoption rate of RSS. Companies like Mozilla, Microsoft, IBM, and many others are finding new and interesting ways to use RSS feeds to share information both with their Web sites and with internal communication processes.

Put simply, a *Web feed* is a list of your blog posts designed to be read by software, not by humans. It's formatted using the XML markup language (eXtensible Markup Language), an Internet standard that allows your prose to be marked in a way that software applications can understand and display properly.

Why is RSS a good thing? Well, it means your blog's feed can easily be understood and displayed on other Web sites, from blogs to search engines. This is useful for sites that pull in news from multiple sources and can earn you traffic from those sites back to your blog.

But more importantly, RSS feeds can be read by newsreader software that any visitor to your site might use, and visitors can then access your blog quickly and easily. RSS feeds mean that visitors don't have to bookmark hundreds of blogs and check them every 20 minutes to see whether they've been updated.

Several different terms are used to describe the same thing in this chapter: RSS, Web feed, and news feed are a few. All of these are used interchangeably, but in fact the most accurate one is Web feed. RSS is simply a type of Web feed, and of course, not all blogs are news. Even though Web feed is the most accurate, I usually refer to RSS feeds, because that's how most blogs and bloggers refer to them.

Breaking it down further

Essentially, what RSS does is give your blog the ability to take the content on your blog and break it down into a basic text file. This text file is formatted in a special XML-format that makes up the feed. This plain-text version of your blog content is then distributed to other Web sites, search engines, and blogosphere tracking services. Figure 11-1 shows the code behind an RSS feed.

A few acronyms for RSS are floating around out on the Internet. Here are the acronyms you're most likely to see, and if you want to talk about RSS with your blog readers, you can use any of them, but the first one tends to be the most popular:

- ✔ Really Simple Syndication
- ✔ RDF Site Summary
- ✔ Real Simple Syndication
- ✔ Rich Site Summary

RSS is used to syndicate content on blogs, but it's also used by most mainstream news agencies to make their news information more accessible. News services like Reuters, CBC, CNN, and the Washington Post use RSS technology to spread their articles beyond their own Web sites.

Many Web browsers are starting to handle displaying RSS feeds in a more attractive format for humans by using the XML markup language. If you click an RSS feed link and find that everything is looking rather user friendly, you're probably using a browser that understands and formats XML nicely.

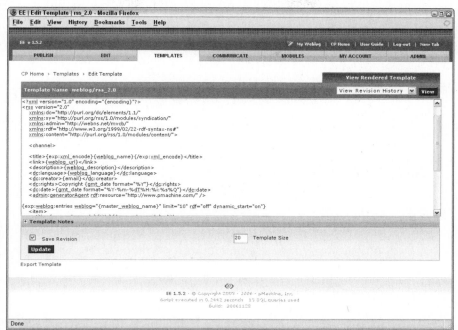

Figure 11-1:
Web feeds aren't very pretty for humans to look at.

For a really excellent short video that describes just what RSS is and how it works, visit the Common Craft blog at www.commoncraft.com/rss_plain_english. This video uses simple graphics and words to get across the concepts that make RSS so groundbreaking.

Confused yet? Well, don't worry, because nearly all blog software automatically builds your RSS feed and helps to advertise it to your blog visitors. So, you'll most likely be covered in any case, but knowing a little bit about it and why it's important to your blog is critical to your blog's survival.

Generating Web traffic

Some bloggers have a tendency to limit the distribution of their content and keep it off other sites. The reasoning goes that you worked hard to create that content, so why should other sites and software get to display it for free?

Actually, because of its ease of use, RSS can help you gain more users. Your Web site can travel farther than ever because RSS feeds can be distributed with little to no effort on your part. Because syndication of your content includes links back to your blog, chances are good that people who are exposed to it will click and come to your blog.

What that means is that because the RSS feed is only text, there's no reason for it to stay in one place. It can be picked up and displayed by any number of Web sites and blogs.

Creating a feed for your blog

Unless you really want to mess around in the code of your own RSS files, you shouldn't need to do anything special to get started with RSS. Most blog software already includes an RSS feed that pulls together and syndicates your blog. At most, you might have to turn on the option to have an RSS feed.

Then just blog normally and ignore the feed — your users will find it and subscribe, and your blog content will flow automatically into the feed.

If you don't have software that creates an RSS feed, you have a couple of options. If you're a programmer or coder, you can probably pick up enough XML to hand-code an RSS feed yourself. But an even better option is to use some of the third-party feed creation tools available today:

- ✔ **FeedYes (www.feedyes.com):** Use this simple tool to create an RSS feed from any Web site or blog. You can create multiple feeds and, with an account, edit and manage them. FeedYes is free.

- ✔ **Feedfire (www.feedfire.com):** This service lets you create RSS feeds for any Web site that doesn't already have one, and promises to let you do it without *any* programming. You can get started for free.

- ✔ **Feed43 (www.feed43.com):** Set up a feed for your blog quickly and for free. Increase the frequently with which your feed is updated by buying a higher level of feed, starting at $29 a year.

- ✔ **FeedForAll (www.feedforall.com):** You can use this tool to create and edit RSS feeds for your blog or podcast. You must be able to install software on your Web host to use this tool. Pricing starts at $39.95.

Chances are that your blog software already has RSS capability. Be sure to check your administrative settings and documentation. If it doesn't, you might also be able to add the functionality using a plugin.

Once a feed exists, you don't need to do anything else. Search engines and automated tools find it when they index your blog automatically, and your readers can subscribe to your feed when and if they choose to do so.

Subscribing to an RSS Feed

I'm sure you have some blogs you read regularly. Do you visit them every day or maybe even several times a day? Are you ever frustrated because the site hasn't been updated yet? Do you ever miss a post by a few minutes, and then read it hours or days later and miss out on the conversation? The solution to this problem is RSS.

Here's how the process works:

1. **Choose a newsreader to use.**

   There are tons, and I tell you about a few of my favorites later in this chapter.

2. **Subscribe to an RSS feed.**

   Don't worry — this is even easier (and cheaper) than subscribing to a newspaper or magazine, although the idea is similar.

3. **Check your newsreader.**

   When you subscribe to an RSS feed, new blog posts appear in your newsreader every time the blogger posts a new entry to his or her blog. When the blogger publishes a new post, the RSS feed is updated a few minutes later, and the newsreader checks the feed and alerts you to the new posts.

4. **Click, read, and** *voilà!*

   No more boring bookmarking and refreshing a blog over and over. You go to the blog only when it has new content, so you never miss anything.

You can subscribe to as many (or as few) feeds as you like, potentially keeping track of hundreds of sites all in one place.

Finding a Web-based newsreader

Web-based newsreaders are online services that allow you to aggregate your favorite feeds into a simple interface where you can read your subscriptions. These online services are usually free.

The big advantage to using a Web-based newsreader is that you can log in to the service from any computer, even if you're traveling, at the library, or using your son's laptop. In most cases, however, this means you need to have Internet access in order to read the blog posts because you have to be online.

Browser newsreaders

Some browsers have built-in newsreaders that you can use to subscribe to feeds and then read them. On the PC, users of Internet Explorer 7 can read, subscribe to, and manage feed subscriptions right inside the browser. Users of the Firefox Web browser can install a plugin called Sage (`https://addons.mozilla.org/en-US/firefox/addon/77`) to add newsreading capabilities to the browser.

On the Mac, you can use the built-in newsreader in the Safari browser to subscribe to and read feeds.

Google Reader

`www.google.com/reader`

Google Reader is a great Web-based feed aggregator. If you already registered with Gmail or other Google services, getting started with Reader is as simple as signing in at the home page. If you don't have a Google account already, click the Create an Account Now link.

Google Reader's interface is similar to the other Google Web products and features feed searching, RSS feed sharing, mobile access, and offline reading. Google Reader is shown in Figure 11-2.

Figure 11-2: Google Reader is an excellent online newsreader.

Bloglines

www.bloglines.com

The Web-based application Bloglines is super-simple to use, with quick tools for adding a subscription and sorting them into categories. One of the fun features of Bloglines is that you can produce a blogroll to put in your blog's sidebar, sharing the blogs you're subscribed to with your readers. It even carries over the categorization with it. You can mark some feeds as private if you prefer not to share them with the world.

NewsGator

www.newsgator.com

Like Bloglines and Google Reader, NewsGator is a handy online newsreader that you can use for free. In NewsGator, you can quickly subscribe to blog feeds, sort them into categories you choose, and tell at a glance which sites have new content you should check out. Newsgator also gives you some handy tools next to each post to let you e-mail the post to a friend, send the post via an instant messenger program, or save it in a Clippings file for later use.

When you sign up for NewsGator you can prepopulate your newsreader with popular blogs in categories like Sports, Technology, or Top Blogs. If you're new to blogging, this might be a terrific way to find some interesting blogs to read and learn from.

Choosing a desktop-based reader

Desktop readers are a little different than online newsreaders. You install these readers directly on your computer (so no Web-based tools are used), which gives you a bit more control over when your feeds are checked and updated. Best of all, a desktop reader actually downloads the feeds to your machine, so you can read blogs even when you don't have Internet access — perhaps on a commute or on an airplane.

Some people believe that a major drawback of desktop readers is that they cause your computer to run slower than it normally would, especially when it has to check a large number of feeds. Because there are so many differences between computers, I can't predict whether this will be a problem for you, but it's definitely something to watch out for.

FeedDemon

www.newsgator.com/Individuals/FeedDemon/Default.aspx

FeedDemon (shown in Figure 11-3) is a commercial RSS reader client that you can install locally on your computer. It downloads updates from your feeds on a regular basis that you can configure, and it features many great organizational tools that keep your feeds updated and easy to peruse.

FeedDemon, available from the folks at NewsGator, also downloads and stores any podcasts you subscribe to, and it transfers those to your portable audio player. As if that isn't enough, you can also set up custom "news watches" to keep track of topics or events you want to know more about.

FeedDemon is available only for Windows. You can try it out by downloading a free trial and then buy the full version for $29.95.

NetNewsWire

    www.newsgator.com/Individuals/NetNewsWire

NewsGator's Mac newsreader solution is NetNewsWire, a solid program that takes advantage of some of the preinstalled Apple software that come with today's Macs. As with FeedDemon, you can use NetNewsWire to read and organize feeds, as well as save them for later reference or send them via e-mail or instant messenger to a friend.

Podcasts are automatically downloaded and transferred to Apple's iTunes software, and you can even use NetNewsWire with iCal and Address Book.

The trial version is free, but the full version costs you $29.95.

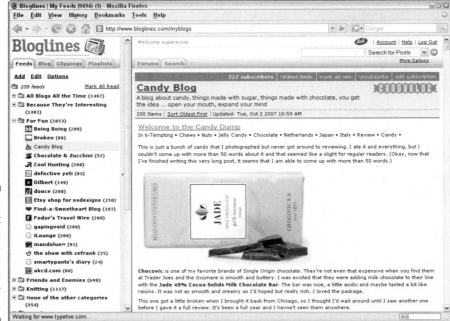

Figure 11-3:
Get FeedDemon working to read RSS feeds on your desktop.

AmphetaDesk

www.disobey.com/amphetadesk

AmphetaDesk is a free, open-source, cross-platform newsreader that should satisfy the truly geeky. Its code is highly customizable, so if you care to do so, you can customize the interface's look and feel and its functionality.

Signing up for a feed

When you've selected a newsreader, you can subscribe to a feed and start reading! This task has two steps: visiting a blog you enjoy reading and then subscribing.

Somewhere on the blog page, you might see a small orange icon, sometimes with the acronym RSS or XML in it. Or, you might just see a small text link to the feed.

Look closely — RSS feeds can be hard to find on the page. Because you really need to use the link only once, bloggers tend to downplay them in the design.

Alternet (www.alternet.org)offers several different RSS feeds, so you can choose between getting front page news stories, video stories, columns, and so on.

When you find the link or icon, click it. If you're using a Web-based news-reader, you might be subscribed automatically, or you might see an icon for subscribing using one of the most common newsreaders.

If you don't see a link or an icon to an RSS feed, copy the URL from the address bar of the browser. Return to your newsreader and click the button or link for subscribing to a new feed. Then paste the URL into the subscribe box, and the newsreader handles things from there.

Here's how subscribing works in Google Reader:

1. **Visit a blog or Web site and locate the feed link or icon.**
2. **Click the link and copy the URL from the address bar.**

   You can also simply right-click the feed link or icon and choose Copy Link Location or Copy Shortcut.
3. **In Google Reader, click the Add Subscription link in the left column.**

   A small box opens, as shown in Figure 11-4.

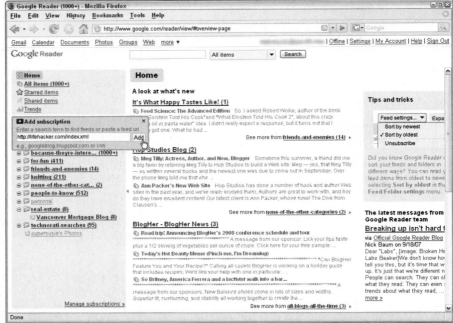

Figure 11-4:
Subscribing
to a feed is
quick and
easy in
Google
Reader.

4. **Paste the URL into the box and click Add.**

   If Google Reader finds the feed, it's displayed in the right column. If no feed is found, Google Reader notifies you.

5. **Repeat as desired!**

Making the Most of RSS

You can use RSS in all sorts of ways. Due to its high level of flexibility, RSS has been adopted into industries as diverse as financial sectors to breaking news stories. It's been widely adopted because of the Web site traffic it generates, attracting new readers from search engines and news aggregators. But that's not all RSS is good for. You can use RSS for these purposes:

- ✔ **Syndicating content:** In the blogosphere, syndication means that you publish your information on the Web so that newsreaders and other Web sites can display it.

- ✔ **Aggregating news:** Do you like other blogs which deal with similar topics as your own? You can use their RSS feeds to include their content on your Web site. You can link directly to it or, if your blog software has such functionality, draw those feeds in yourself.

✔ **Replacing e-mail newsletters:** Some RSS advocates make astounding claims that RSS will be the death of e-mail. Although this hasn't yet come to pass, RSS definitely has many advantages over e-mail newsletters. The most important is that you can avoid spam. How? You can simply choose to read an RSS feed rather than receive more e-mail; by not giving away your e-mail address, you don't put it at risk for being sold to a spammer.

✔ **Keeping communities updated:** RSS feeds are terrific for keeping people updated. Some feeds merely post information such as sports scores — as fast as a goal is scored, an RSS feed can be updated. What kinds of things can you share that people might want to know as soon as possible? Here are a few:

- Security bulletins

- Emergency weather changes

- Changes to bids on eBay or Amazon

- Product availability at retail stores

Because of the simplicity of the *use* of RSS technology (yes, the actual building of RSS feeds might still be too geeky for most bloggers), you can use it in many ways to augment the communication channels of your blog or within your community that you haven't quite figured out yet. Get creative!

Bringing It All Together

Offering a blog feed to your readers is a great way to advertise your Web site to the blogosphere, visitors, and search engines. And, the cost to implement this powerful technology is very low (nothing if you're using a blogging tool that is free). By using your feed, you can show your blog to the world!

If you haven't used RSS before, you might need some time to play with the technology before you figure out just what RSS can mean for your blog and your blog community. The bottom line is that being able to leverage the power of RSS feeds for your own blog definitely helps you get noticed. And you'll be seen long before any traditional Web sites that don't use blog software could dream of.

Get out there, blog about RSS, and show your users how very cool it can be! Share your new knowledge. Tell your visitors how they can use RSS feeds to read your blog.

Chapter 12

Building the Sidebars

*O*n a blog, lots of valuable information is contained in the *sidebar*. A sidebar is a column to the right or left of the main content of your blog.

Usually blog software comes with some content already in the sidebar, like links to your categories, archives, and RSS feed. But you can include a lot of other items in your sidebar. Many bloggers use sidebars on their blogs to have a little fun. They recommend books they like or let folks know what music they're listening to.

In this chapter, I talk about how to add some of these great items to your sidebar, starting with some terrific tools and walking your through a bit of code wrangling.

If you don't get enough sidebar fun here, don't miss Chapter 19, which has a bunch of other neat tools you might enjoy using.

Adding the Usual Suspects

Sidebars usually contain a mix of meat and potatoes features, and neat extras. Strike a balance on your blog that gets readers the basics and also plays up your personality. Figure 12-1 shows the sidebar for the Blissfully Aware blog written by Joshua Lane (www.blissfullyaware.com).

Archives   About text   Categories   RSS feed   Blogroll

Figure 12-1:
Blissfully
Aware has a
great design
that uses
two
sidebars on
the left of
the layout.

Usually blog software comes with some content already in the sidebar, like links to your categories, archives, and RSS feed. There are lots of items you can include in your sidebar. The following are some common types of sidebar content:

- ✔ **About Me:** You can provide quick bits of information describing you and what your blog is about (refer to Figure 12-1).

- ✔ **Archives and categories:** You might want to include links to category and archive pages so that your readers can quickly get to older content (refer to Figure 12-1).

- ✔ **Popular blog posts/recent comments:** Many blogs display a list of the most recent posts or a list of posts that have gotten a lot of comments. This is a good way to increase traffic on your blog.

- ✔ **Blogroll:** Some bloggers include a list of blogs or Web sites that they read and recommend to others. This is usually called a *blogroll*, though there may be Web sites included that aren't blogs (refer to Figure 12-1).

- ✔ **Search:** If you have a search tool on your blog, be sure to include the search box and submit button in your sidebar.

- ✔ **Syndication links to RSS feeds:** These links are important for letting readers subscribe to your blog in their newsreader (refer to Figure 12-1). See Chapter 11 for lots more information about RSS feeds.

- ✔ **Navigation:** If your blog is part of a larger Web site, you can include navigation to that site's content in your sidebar.

- ✔ **Contact information:** If you want people to be able to get in touch, give them quick access to your e-mail address or other contact information.

Many of these elements are built into the templates and layouts provided by your blog software. If you don't see them, check your blog software documentation to see if you can turn them on. It may also be possible to add these elements using plugins.

In the following sections, I discuss two of the more popular elements of sidebars: the About Me section and blogrolls.

Including About Me section

The sidebar of a blog usually contains what you might call a 10,000-foot view of the blog and blogger — that is, a high-level look at what the blog offers and is about. Often, these features focus on giving readers information about the blogger, from the blogger's name to what they read, eat, like, and are doing.

When I visit a new blog, I'm always looking for a little context to understand what the blog is about and whether I'm interested in reading it, and I check the sidebar for information to help me.

I know, I know. Putting a little bit of text about your and your blog (often called the *About Me* text) doesn't seem that exciting. But it's such a great way to let your readers know more about your blog and why you're blogging that I just couldn't leave it out. Frankly, I think this is the single best way to augment your sidebar.

The blog So Misguided (www.somisguided.com) has a great example of a nice bit of About Me text, which is shown in Figure 12-2. Without this text you wouldn't know, for example, that blogger Monique Trottier lives in Vancouver and is a *litblogger* (someone who blogs about literature), because she doesn't mention those facts in every post. The information here, however, is great information for new readers to have as they try to figure out whether So Misguided will appeal to them. Monique even includes a link to a longer biography for readers who just want to know more about her.

Figure 12-2:
The So
Misguided
blog tells
readers
about the
author and
the subject
in the
sidebar.

Lots of bloggers include contact information and even a photo in their About Me text, giving a quick snapshot to readers.

Many blog software applications have an option to add About Me text to your blog. Blogger and Typepad, for example, offer this feature, but in other blogs, you might need to get familiar with your templates in order to add this text. Unlike some of the other tools I discuss later in this chapter, you don't have to use any third-party tool to add About Me text to your blog. If you need a little hand creating the HTML for your About Me text, jump to Chapter 5. Here's a good example of how to code up your About Me text:

```
<h1>About Me</h1>
        <p>My name is Goldilocks, and my blog is about
        my quest for porridge and a great place to take
        a nap. You can read more about me <a
        href="http://www.myblog.com/my_life.html">here<
        /a>.</p>
```

Keep your About Me section short and sweet, giving readers the skinny in a few words. Save the lengthy prose for a blog post. One trick you can use is to write a long blog post with your bio and other blog details in it and then link to that post from your sidebar About Me section, as I've done in my Goldilocks code example.

Blogrolling

Blogrolls are a very common extra you might want to put in your sidebar. A *blogroll* is a list of blogs and Web sites that you regularly read, especially those you use for reference in writing your blog. Putting your blogroll in your sidebar is a good way to give your readers a sense that you aren't just making up stuff off the top of your head, especially if your blog is informational. It's also handy just to show your readers any writing you find inspiring or entertaining.

The blogroll (labeled Daily Reads) on Mandy Moore's Yarnageddon blog (`www.yarnageddon.com`) is shown in Figure 12-3.

Lots of blog software includes built-in methods for adding a blogroll or building a list of links, so check whether yours already has the tools you need to add a blogroll.

Figure 12-3:
Many bloggers include a blogroll of friends and resources in their sidebar.

If you can't add a blogroll easily in your blog software, you have two options:

- **BlogRolling (www.blogrolling.com):** This handy service lets you build lists of links, sort and organize them, and even keep multiple blogrolls. As with the other services in this chapter, you use BlogRolling to build your blogroll once, insert the code into your template, and then make changes on the BlogRolling site, which then automatically appear in your sidebar.

- **Newsreaders:** Look for a newsreader that allows you to build a blogroll based on the feeds you're subscribed to. Bloglines (www.bloglines.com) is one newsreader that lets you create a blogroll.

Creating Cameo Appearances

One of the really fun things about blogging is experimenting with all the great technical goodies you can put in your blog sidebar. With a little technical know-how, you can put tons of extra doo-dads and gee-gaws in the sidebar to let your readers know more about you and your life.

All things considered, these tools might be less useful for a business-related blog. These extras are just that — information that might dress up your blog but probably isn't crucial for your readers to have. Still, you can have some fun with these tools.

A few of my favorites include:

- **Photos:** Love to take photos? Of course, you should be illustrating your blog entries with your photos, but why not put a few in your sidebar as well?

- **Books and music:** Let your readers know what you're reading and listening to. Some tools even let you update a music feed instantly, so your readers know what you're hearing right this minute!

- **Instant updates:** Accessorize your blog with a quick update about what you're doing or where you are. A quick notice keeps your readers current even when you don't have time to write a full blog post.

- **Surveys:** Take the pulse of your readers with a quick multiple-choice survey.

- **Avatars:** There are some great tools for building avatars — visual illustrations of you — that you can then display right in your blog sidebar.

Very few blog software packages include the ability to add these kinds of elements, so in most cases you need to know how to edit your templates in order to add them. Check your blog software to find out whether you can add sidebar elements using a template editing tool in your software, or whether you need to get into the template code of your blog.

In general, most nonhosted blog software that you install on your own server gives you access to the templates that build your blog. With hosted blog software, there is more variation. Some offer template access, some offer it when you are using a premium or paid version, and others don't offer access at all.

Adding elements using your blogging software

If your blog software gives you a tool to add elements to the sidebar as part of the administrative interface, you're a lucky devil. This makes your life a little easier as you customize your blog.

Blogger (www.blogger.com) is a tool that gives you the ability to add elements to your sidebar without having to go into the template. Here's how you do it:

1. **Log in to blogger.com and click the Layout link for the blog you want to customize.**

    The Template tab of your blog administrative panel opens.

    If you're using one of the older Blogger templates, you might see a Template link instead of a Layout link on the Dashboard. Jump to Chapter 2 and read the section on upgrading your template.

2. **Select the Page Elements category.**

    The Add and Arrange Page Elements page opens.

3. **Click Add a Page Element.**

    A window opens with lots of page element options. Blogger offers quite a few custom sidebar tools as part of its interface, so be sure to experiment with these if you like adding to your sidebar. For example, Blogger has built-in tools for adding polls, photos, link lists, RSS feeds, videos and more.

4. **Click the Add to Blog button under the HTML/JavaScript header.**

5. **Give your element a title in the Title field.**

6. **Paste the HTML code for the tool you want to include into the Content field.**

    This HTML is usually provided on the Web site where you acquire the widget you are adding. I show you some specific examples of tools that work this way in the "Finding Goodies for Your Sidebars" section of this chapter.

7. **Click Save Changes, as shown in Figure 12-4.**

    The element is saved and displayed in the Layout view.

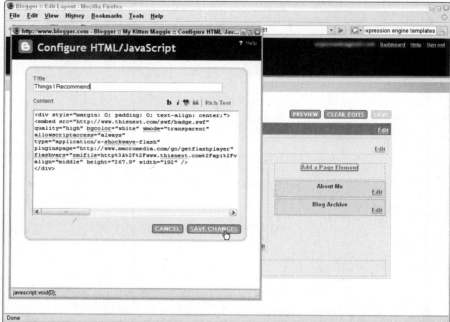

Figure 12-4:
Blogger
gives you an
easy way to
add
elements to
your
sidebar.

8. **If you want to change the order of the elements displayed in your sidebar, click and drag the new element to a new position.**

9. **Click Save.**

10. **Click the View Blog link and admire your new sidebar element!**

   Don't skip this step — you should always make sure that your blog hasn't been mangled by the new HTML code.

Blogger's tools might have changed by the time you read this book, so the steps I describe here might be different.

If you aren't using Blogger, but you see a tool in your blog software for adding sidebar elements, chances are the process is somewhat similar: After you choose an element, you can copy and paste some HTML code and choose an order for your sidebar elements. Refer to the documentation for your blog software for help.

Adding elements using your templates

In most cases, adding elements to your sidebar requires that you get your hands dirty in the HTML guts of your blog software. This is easy in some blogs, hard in others, and impossible in a few.

The process of adding third-party tool — sometimes called a *badge* or a *widget* — is similar no matter what blog software you use:

1. Visit the Web site of the tool you want to implement and set up your account, contributing content as required by that Web site.

2. Look for a link or option that allows you to add the tool to your blog.

3. Follow that site's directions to obtain the HTML code you need to put the tool on your blog.

4. Go to your blog's administrative interface and add the HTML code to your template, or use your blog's tools for adding sidebar elements.

Most blog software runs using a template of HTML code, so if you add your sidebar code to the template, it automatically appears on every page of your blog — assuming your software gives you access to the template and that you can figure out how to insert the code.

Don't be scared off by the gibberish of HTML, style tags, and blog software tags you see. As long as you don't delete any of that stuff, you won't do any damage! But just to be safe, copy everything in the template into a text file and save it in a safe place on your computer so that you can go back to the original code if necessary.

Movable Type (www.movabletype.com) is a blog software package that gives you the ability to edit and format templates.

Here's how you can add a sidebar element to your blog's templates:

1. **Log in to your Movable Type administration panel and click the Templates link for the blog you want to customize.**

2. **Click the Sidebar template.**

   The template opens with the HTML code, as shown in Figure 12-5.

3. **Paste the HTML code for the tool you want to include into the Template Body field.**

   This HTML is usually provided on the Web site where you acquire the widget you are adding. I show you some specific examples of tools that work this way in the "Finding Goodies for Your Sidebars" section of this chapter.

You might need to spend a few minutes looking at the code to figure out just where to put the new element. Look for words you recognize from your sidebar within the code, and use that to judge where in the order of the code to place your HTML. You might need to experiment to get your code placed properly by putting in your code, viewing the blog, and then moving your code to a new spot.

4. **Click the Save and Rebuild button.**

   Your new code is saved in the template and puts it onto your blog.

5. **Visit your blog and take a look at the page to make sure everything is appearing correctly.**

Movable Type's tools might have changed by the time you read this book, so the steps I describe here might be different in your version of the software.

The process for editing a template in other blog software is likely to be similar, but you might want to consult your software documentation to find out which template to edit.

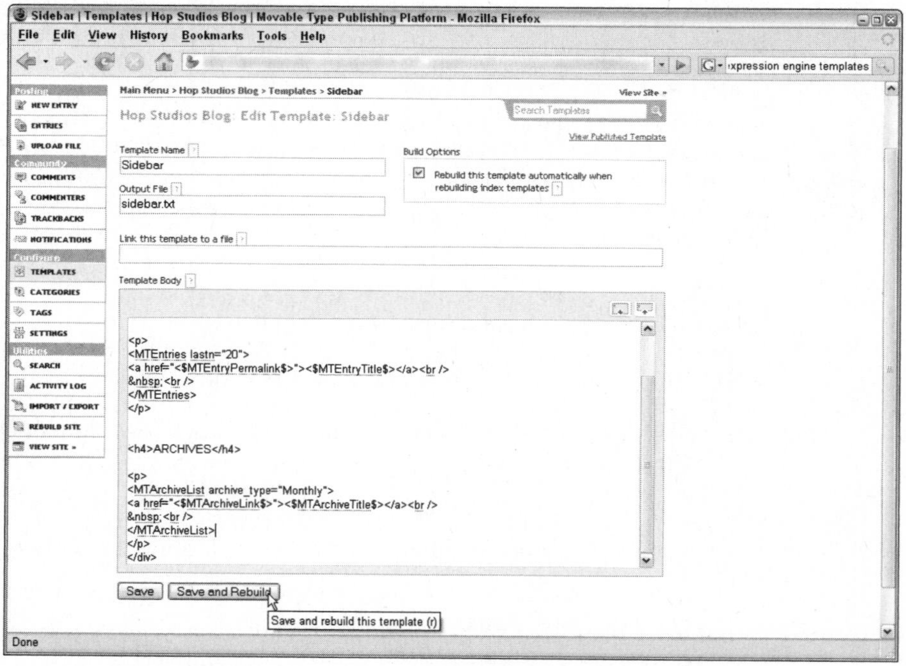

Figure 12-5:
You can add
HTML code
to your
Movable
Type
templates.

Finding Goodies for Your Sidebars

Now comes the fun part — putting third-party widgets and extras into your sidebar. I'm sure you can find a widget to fit your personality and blog, and in this section I show you a few of my favorites.

With each of the tools described, you generate HTML code that needs to be integrated into your blog. When you've obtained the code, refer to the "Creating Cameo Appearances" section of this chapter and follow the instructions for adding the code to your template or using a layout editing tool in your blog software.

Telling others about . . . your photos

These days, everyone's a photographer! This is thanks in large part to the relative inexpensiveness of digital cameras and the excellent photo-sharing and organizing services available for both personal computers and online.

Flickr is one of the best of the photo-sharing Web sites, and if you haven't already checked it out, you should do so. Pronto! I'll wait.

One of the neat tools that Flickr provides is the ability to create a badge to put in your blog sidebar. This badge shows your photos and is automatically updated when you add more photos to your Flickr account, so you always have the latest photos on your blog. If you like to put photos in your blog posts but take many more than you can use in your entries, you can still share those photos by using the Flickr badge.

Plus, the badge includes a link to your Flickr photos, so your blog readers can jump over to Flickr and look at all your great photos whether or not you decide to put them in your blog.

I've included a Flickr photo badge in the sidebar of my personal blog, Unfavorable Pink (`http://unfavorablepink.com`), which is shown in Figure 12-6.

When you have a Flickr account and have uploaded some photos, you're ready to create a Flickr badge:

1. **After logging in to Flickr, scroll to the bottom of any screen on Flickr and choose Tools from the Help navigation bar.**

2. **Click the Build a Badge link in the right column of the Tools page.**

3. **Choose whether to build an HTML or a Flash badge and click the Next: Choose Photos button.**

   The following instructions are for building an HTML badge.

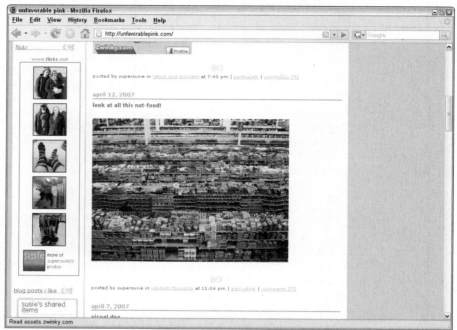

Figure 12-6:
Use Flickr to
put your
photos into
your blog's
sidebar.

   4. Click Yours to display your own photos on your blog.

   **5. Choose between displaying all your public photos, photos with a
   particular tag, or photos from one of your sets, and click the Next:
   Layout button.**

   **6. Select Yes or No to choose whether to display your Flickr icon and
   screen name in your badge.**

   **7. Choose how many photos you want to display in your badge from the
   drop-down list.**

   8. Choose between your recent photos or a random selection.

   **9. Pick the size of the images you want to display: Square, Thumbnail, or
   Mid-size.**

   10. Choose the orientation for your badge: Horizontal, Vertical, or None.

   For most blog sidebars, Vertical is the best orientation to use because it
   creates a thin badge.

   11. Click the Next: Colors button.

   **12. Choose the color you want to use for the background, border, links,
   and text of your badge by clicking the item you want to change and
   then choosing a color from the provided palette.**

   You can use this tool to choose colors that match your blog design.

13. **Click the Next: Preview & Get Code button.**

14. **Check out your badge to make sure it looks right. If you want to make changes, use the links across the top of the page to go back and make changes.**

15. **With the badge looking great, copy the code and go back to your own blog.**

    At this point, refer to the "Creating Cameo Appearances" section of this chapter and follow the instructions for adding the code to your template or using a layout editing tool in your blog software.

If you want to find out more about using Flickr to put photos into your blog posts, be sure to read Chapter 13.

Telling others about . . . your books

Are you an avid reader who always has a batch of books on the go? Do your friends constantly ask you for book recommendations or what you're reading right now? Why not share what's on your bedside table with your blog readers with a book badge?

A number of good Web sites right now let you create a catalogue of your book collection. LibraryThing (www.librarything.com) is a good Web site for cataloging your book collection. After adding books, you can tag them, write reviews, rate them, even record when you started and finished the book. As well, you can see what others thought of the book. Best of all, you can also use LibraryThing to put a badge of what you're reading on your blog.

After you've signed up for LibraryThing and added some books, here's how to create the badge, or widget, for your blog:

1. **Click the Tools navigation item at the top of any LibraryThing page.**

    The very first item listed is "Put LibraryThing on your blog."

2. **Click the Make a Standard Blog Widget link.**

    LibraryThing loads the configuration page for the widget.

3. **Choose a preset style by selecting the available layouts from in the pull-down menu.**

    LibraryThing previews each style on the right side of the page.

    Or, customize your widget by selecting options under the Customize It area:

    • *Show What:* Choose whether you want to display random books, recent books, tag cloud, author cloud, top authors, or top tags in your badge.

- *Tags:* Choose all tags, or select a single tag you want to filter the display by.

- *Show Entries:* Choose the number of books you want to display.

- *Book Covers:* Choose the book cover size you want to use (no covers, small, medium, or fixed width/height).

- *Book Text:* Choose to display the title, title and author, title and author without a link, or no text at all.

- *Show:* Choose to show a header, or only the books.

- *Style It:* Pick a style for your badge, or choose to create your own styles.

- *Associate ID:* If you are an Amazon Associate, you can enter your Associates ID to get credit for any purchases made from the link. I describe the Associates program in Chapter 16.

4. **Click the Make it! button.**

   LibraryThing loads the widget into the right side of the page, as shown in Figure 12-7.

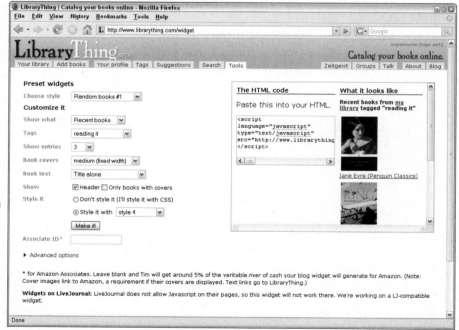

Figure 12-7:
Use
LibraryThing
to create a
book badge
for your
blog.

5. **Make any changes you need to the look of your badge, clicking the Make It button to see the updates.**

6. **Copy the HTML code for your badge. Head back to your own blog to add it to the sidebar.**

   If you need help placing the HTML in your blog, see the earlier section "Creating Cameo Appearances."

BookJetty (www.bookjetty.com) is another site you can use to catalogue your existing collection, tag books with keywords, rate and review them, and share your collection. Goodreads (www.goodreads.com) is another with similar services.

Telling others about . . . your music

If you like to listen to music, you can share your playlists and even the music you're listening to right now with your blog readers. Last.fm (www.last.fm) is a music-sharing Web site that lets you do just that.

Sign up for free and then install a little application on your computer that tracks what you're listening to in your normal music-playing software, sharing that information with the Last.fm Web site. When you install the software, it shows a list of available audio playing software — simply choose the one you use to listen to music. Last.fm calls this process *scrobbling*. As you build your music profile, Last.fm will start to make recommendations of music you might like, based on the likes of other Last.fm users who also listen to the same music.

You can also generate a personal radio station designed to play your favorite music with no advertising or DJs.

You can use Last.fm to create a badge for your blog:

1. **Click the Widgets navigation button at the top of any Last.fm page.**

   You see the Share Your Music Anywhere! page.

2. **Choose a color and chart for your badge.**
   - *Color*: Click to choose between red, blue, black, and grey badges.
   - *Chart*: From the drop-down menu, you can choose to display Recently Listened Tracks, Overall Top Tracks, Overall Top Artists, Weekly Top Tracks, or Weekly Top Artists.

   Last.fm displays the badge on the right of the page, and updates it as you make your choices, as you can see in Figure 12-8.

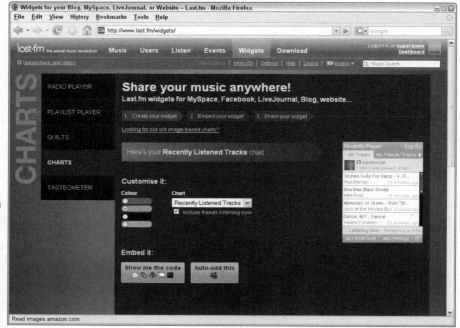

Figure 12-8:
Creating a
sidebar
widget with
Last.fm is
quick and
easy.

3. **Click the Show Me the Code button.**

4. **Copy the code and go to your blog so you can paste it into your sidebar.**

   See the earlier "Creating Cameo Appearances" section of this chapter to find out what to do with the code.

Telling others about . . . your interests

Most blog readers quickly become addicted to reading other blogs (don't even ask me about how hard it was to get any writing done for this book!), and use a newsreader like Google Reader (www.google.com/reader) to get through a lot of blogs quickly.

As you read blogs, you no doubt find posts that you think a friend or colleague should read. Maybe you'll find something so great that you want your own readers to check it out. Google Reader gives you a handy way to do just this. Every time you read a post you like, you can click the small Share icon at the bottom of the post.

You can start using Google Reader quickly by going to www.google.com/reader. If you already have a Google account, simply sign in to get started. If you don't have a Google Account, click the Create an Account Now link to register for free. I cover subscribing to blogs in Google Reader in Chapter 11.

Google saves these items, and you can quickly view them by choosing Shared items from the left navigation.

To put a badge that lists your shared posts on your blog sidebar:

1. **Sign in to Google Reader at `www.google.com/reader`.**

2. **Find a blog post you want to share, click the Share link at the bottom of the post.**

   Google adds the post to your Shared list. You can continue to add items to the Shared list at any time.

3. **Click Shared items in the left navigation.**

4. **Look for the "Put a clip on your site or blog" heading and click the link to get started.**

   Google Reader loads a configuration pop-up window, shown in Figure 12-9.

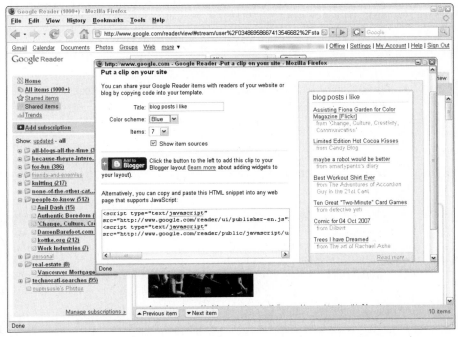

Figure 12-9: Share your favorite blog posts with Google Reader's blog badge.

5. **Give your shared posts a title, choose a color scheme, and select how many posts you want to share.**

   Google updates the badge preview on the right of the window as you make changes.

6. **Copy the HTML code from the code window and get yourself back to your blog's control panel to put it in your sidebar.**

   Read the "Creating Cameo Appearances" section of this chapter to find out how to integrate the code into your blog.

Surveying the Field

Everybody loves to answer polls, so why not add one to your sidebar or even a post? You might be able to find out useful information about your readers to use in getting advertising for your blog or to inform your choices in what you blog about.

You can create a quick multiple choice question to put in your sidebar using a number of different polling services. Some require you to create an account, some don't. If you use one that does require registration, you can keep track of your polls a little more easily, which is handy if you ever need to look at them later.

The term *poll* is used by scientists, media, and mathematicians to describe a sampling of a random number of people. By definition, a poll taken only by the readers of your blog can't actually be random. This type of questioning is better described as a survey. I'm just saying.

My favorite poll tool is PollDaddy (www.polldaddy.com). Using PollDaddy is free, and after you create an account, you can create multiple polls for your blog or Web site and even choose a variety of formats and styles to use with your poll.

After your create a poll, you can insert the HTML code PollDaddy provides in your blog sidebar or in a blog entry (see the "Creating Cameo Appearances" section of this chapter), sit back, and wait for the results to roll in. After your readers take the poll, they get instant results. After choosing an answer, the poll screen changes to show the reader the percentage of answers for each choice.

One especially nice feature of PollDaddy's polls is that you can create a *poll widget* specifically for your blog sidebar (see Figure 12-10). Insert the code into your template once and then use PollDaddy to control what poll is displayed in the widget, saving you from having to mess around in your template every time you want to change your poll question.

E-Mailing Your Posts

You've tricked out your sidebar with all kinds of tools, but there's one more you might want to consider: an option to subscribe to read your blog posts via e-mail.

Many of your readers will subscribe to your blog Web feed, and others will be content with visiting your blog periodically. But some readers might appreciate getting at least some of the content of your blog posts delivered via e-mail. The e-mail delivery option is a nice reminder to your readers that they should come and check out your blog — and it isn't spam because they need to sign up to receive e-mail delivery.

If your blog software offers e-mail delivery, great. If it doesn't, sign up for an account with FeedBurner (`www.feedburner.com`), a terrific service for all things related to RSS (which I cover in more detail in Chapter 11).

You can also use FeedBurner to create an e-mail subscription form that you can pop into your sidebar. Visitors to your blog simply provide an e-mail address, and from that point on, they'll receive a single daily e-mail with updates to your blog (assuming you've made any, and no matter how many updates you post).

You can see how easy this form is for readers to fill out on A View from the Isle (www.larixconsulting.com), a blog written by Tris Hussey. Figure 12-11 shows Tris' FeedBurner e-mail subscription form in the rightmost column of his blog.

TIP

To prevent people from adding addresses of any old person, the FeedBurner e-mail subscription requires readers to complete their registration by verifying via e-mail before delivery begins.

After you've signed up with FeedBurner and told it where to find your blog's RSS feed, use the Publicize tools to activate the e-mail subscription widget.

Figure 12-11:
FeedBurner lets readers subscribe to your blog via e-mail.

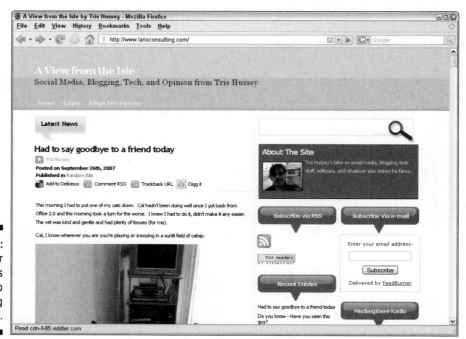

Chapter 13

Making the Most of Photos

In This Chapter

▶ Getting set up with a digital camera and editing software

▶ Using Picasa to edit your photos

▶ Putting Flickr photos into your blog posts

*I*t's a fact: People love photos! You can increase your readership and decrease your writing time by including photos in your blog posts or putting photo badges into your sidebar. Many bloggers have discovered that including a photo in a blog post, even if it's only tangentially related, ensures that the post is more likely to be read than entries without photos.

If you already have a digital camera and photo-editing software, you have the tools at hand to start putting photos into your blog quickly. But if you're new to photography, this chapter also includes some information about choosing a digital camera or software.

Putting graphics on the Web doesn't have to be incredibly hard to do, and today's wonderful photo-sharing Web sites make your life easy when it comes to getting photos online quickly. In fact, if you already have a Flickr account that you use to share your digital photos, you can jump right to the section in this chapter about integrating your Flickr photos into your blog posts — you'll be pleased as punch to find out how easy it is.

Getting Equipped

Today, digital cameras are quite inexpensive, and using one can expedite the process of putting your photos online. Most digital cameras can take photographs in file formats that can be used with no further processing on the Web, but as long as you're using a digital camera, you can pick up software that helps you convert your photos to the right format quite quickly.

The ingredients to getting photos onto your Web site are

- A camera, preferably a digital camera
- A way to get your photos from your camera onto your computer, like a USB cable or scanner
- Image-editing software to help you crop, resize, and touch up your photos
- A photo sharing service or blog software with file upload tools

Picking a digital camera

Digital cameras come in all kinds of price ranges and with tons of different features. When you take a photograph, the image is stored on a storage card or small hard drive, and many cameras have a nice preview screen that lets you see the results of your photography right away.

When you need your photos, you can remove the storage card from your camera and insert it into the card reader hooked to your computer, or even into a printer. Having a removable storage card is also helpful if you plan to take lots of pictures, because you can easily carry several with you, switching them out as you fill them. Some cameras can also connect directly to your computer.

Digital cameras usually come with several quality settings that determine the resolution of your image and the sizes that look good when you print your photograph. If you choose higher-quality settings, you can fit fewer images on your storage card, but the resulting files will look better, print more sharply, and can be resized more easily.

Today, even relatively inexpensive digital cameras are capable of taking high-quality images suitable for use in almost any medium, so the real challenge is to pick a camera that will suit your picture-taking style.

Be realistic about how you plan to use the camera and how comfortable you are with it when you look at the options:

- **Digital SLRs:** If you're a professional photographer or a dedicated amateur, the higher-end dSLR cameras are likely want you want. But they are also quite large cameras, which makes them awkward to carry and use unobtrusively on a day-to-day basis.

- **Low-end point-and-shoots:** If you're a photography amateur, super lightweight cameras are great gadgets that get lots of admiring glances. But they might lack important features, and their tiny size might also make them hard to use and hold steady.

- **Mid-range:** If you're not a professional photographer but you want more than just the basics that low-end cameras provide, look for a good mid-range camera in size, style, and price.

Start your search by visiting CNET.com (www.cnet.com) and looking at the product reviews written by CNET editors and readers. Reading through the reviews can really help educate you on the options and features, and it can give you a feel for the price ranges that include the feature package you want.

With some CNET recommendations in mind, head for a camera or good electronics store and test drive some cameras. You need to feel physically comfortable handling and using any camera you purchase, no matter how well it was reviewed online.

If you're more comfortable using a film camera, you aren't out of luck! You can still use film photos by scanning the photos to create a digital file. Or ask your film processing shop to provide you with a CD of your photographs along with prints.

Choosing photo-editing software

You also need to find a program to help you edit and organize your photos. You have loads of options, at all pricing levels. In fact, your computer might have come packaged with image-editing software, or the digital camera you purchase might include software.

When you're looking for image-editing software with the ultimate goal of getting your images online, consider these criteria:

- ✔ **File formats:** You need to be able to create images in the right format for display on the Web. These formats are JPG, GIF, and PNG.

- ✔ **Standard editing tools:** At a minimum, you need image-editing software that allows you to resize, crop, rotate, and adjust brightness and contrast in your photos. These tools should be quick and easy to use.

- ✔ **Organizing tools:** Software that helps you keep track of your images with thumbnail previews, naming schemes, and search are useful, especially if you take lots of photos.

- ✔ **Photo sharing:** A program that integrates with the blogging tool you use or with a photo-sharing service like Flickr isn't required, but it can really help you speed up the amount of time it takes you to get a photo online.

With these ideas in mind, don't forget to think about whether you want to be able to do more than just get photos into shape for online publication. If you plan to print photographs, be sure you look for photo-editing software with good tools for printing.

I cover two software programs (Picasa and iPhoto) in the next sections. Other image-editing programs also work well for touching up and formatting photographs:

✔ **Adobe Photoshop Elements:** $99.99, Windows only, www.adobe.com/
products/photoshopelwin. This program is suitable for users who
have the patience to learn how to use a full-featured program, but
don't have the most exacting standards; it's a great compromise between
basic software and high-end software.

✔ **Adobe Photoshop Lightroom:** $299, Mac and Windows, www.adobe.
com/products/photoshoplightroom. This software is intended to
be used specifically for photography, and serious amateur photographers and professionals find this program valuable for managing large
collections of photographs.

✔ **Adobe Photoshop:** $699, Mac and Windows, www.adobe.com/
products/photoshop. For anyone who isn't a designer or very serious
photographer, Adobe Photoshop can be overkill. But it's a great program.

✔ **Adobe Fireworks:** $299, Mac and Windows, www.adobe.com/products/
fireworks. Though you can use Fireworks to process photos, it's really
intended to be a Web graphics production tool. If you have it already,
go ahead and use it, but if you're looking over your options, I would
recommend some of the others on this list for photo editing.

Picasa

```
http://picasa.google.com
```

Picasa, from Google, is priced competitively (it's free) and works especially
well for photographers who want to get their photos online. Its organizational
tools are highly developed, allowing you to do everything from automatically
import and name photos from your camera when you hook it up to your
computer, quickly label and tag your photos, rate good photos, and create
photo "albums."

The editing tools are good, but they sacrifice some fine control in favor of
being easy to use. You can crop, straighten horizons, fix red-eye issues,
adjust color and contrast, and make other edits to your photos easily.

However, it's the photo sharing tools that really set Picasa apart. You can use
tools to e-mail photos, get them onto the Web, create online slideshows, and
put photo collections onto other devices. Printing photos is also quite easy
to do.

Picasa (shown in Figure 13-1) is available for Windows only.

Later in this chapter, I walk you through using some simple editing tools
in Picasa.

Figure 13-1:
Quickly
import, edit,
and share
photos
using
Picasa.

iPhoto

www.apple.com/ilife/iphoto

If you're a Mac user, you have a great image-editing program in Apple's iPhoto (see Figure 13-2). You have all the basic tools for cropping, straightening, adjusting color and brightness, and resizing. Plus, you can dabble with fun effects and increase or decrease highlights and shadows in your photos.

The organizing tools are also excellent: You can categorize, tag, caption, and title your photos quickly and easily, and the simple search interface helps you find old photos.

If you don't want to publish photos only to your own blog, use iPhoto to publish to the .Mac Web service, put up slideshows and albums, and share your photos with groups of friends and family.

You can also use iPhoto to print a real photo album, calendar, cards and individual prints. iPhoto frequently comes packaged on new Macintosh computers, but if you don't have it, head to the Apple Store (http://store.apple.com) and buy a copy of iLife, which includes iPhoto and other digital applications.

Figure 13-2:
iPhoto is
Apple's
solution to
image
editing and
organization
tools.

Choosing a photo-sharing tool

When you're ready to put your photos online, regardless of whether you ultimately want to include images on your blog, you have plenty of options. Photo-sharing Web sites have become full-fledged members of the Web 2.0 movement, offering friend lists, tagging, and other sophisticated tools.

The media darling in this space is definitely Flickr (www.flickr.com). For avid photographers, Flickr has nearly replaced the need to have a blog at all, because many of the best blogging tools are integrated into the Flickr service.

On Flickr, you can

- Create a list of friends whose photos you want to follow.
- Upload and organize photos by using tags (keywords), sets, and collections.
- Start groups around a visual theme and add your photos to other groups.
- Set privacy controls to dictate who can see your photos.
- Use your photos to create books, prints, calendars, business cards, DVDs, and stamps.
- Post photos in your account and receive comments (see Figure 13-3).

Figure 13-3:
When you post photos on Flickr, your friends and other Flickr members can leave comments for you.

✔ Create slideshows of your photos.

✔ Browse other members' photos and leave comments.

Basic Flickr accounts are free for 100MB worth of photos each month — you can display only your most recent 200 photos though. Pro accounts cost $24.95 a year, and receive unlimited uploading and image display.

Later in this chapter, I show you how to put Flickr to work for you in adding images to blog posts.

Flickr isn't alone in this space; it just happens to be my favorite. You can also upload your photos to Photobucket (www.photobucket.com), Shutterfly (www.shutterfly.com), SmugMug (www.smugmug.com), Snapfish (www.snapfish.com), and Webshots (www.webshots.com), among others.

Whatever service you choose, look for tools that will make your life easier when it comes to putting your photos on your blog. For example:

✔ Look for services that allow you to create a photo *badge* (a bit of code that displays your photos) to put in your blog's sidebar. I talk more about using Flickr for this purpose in Chapter 13.

✔ Look for services that let you post a photo to your blog or give you code to put the photo in your blog post.

Choosing Visuals for Your Blog

Far be it for me to tell you how to take photographs — I'm a rank amateur when it comes to photography. But I can give you some tips on taking photos that will be useful for a new blog post, and that's what the following sections are all about.

Taking photos

Posts with photos are more likely to be read than those that don't have them, and readers respond well to them. The real secret is that, most of the time, your photos and images don't have to have a strong relationship to what you're blogging about. In fact, they can go off on a tangential topic or idea.

This isn't always true. After all, if you're blogging about your new mobile phone, a picture of that phone really is the way to go. And if you're talking about your recent trip to Peru — well, you need some pictures from your trip. But if you're just pontificating or talking about a favorite book, think about adding a photograph as more of an accessory.

Bloggers often add pictures of their cats to posts that just need a little zing, as Claudia does in her blog (www.claudiasblog.net) in the post shown in Figure 13-4. I don't really know why this is. Are bloggers more likely to be cat owners than the general public? Do they just like their cats more? At any rate, it's hard to object to looking at a cute picture of a cat.

If you want to take photographs to put on your blog, the trick is to keep your eyes open all the time for visuals you are inspired by or interested in. Finding such things isn't rocket science, but it does require you to be thinking about your blog and your camera more often than you might normally. In fact, some bloggers find that carrying a camera with them actually helps them find things to blog about and helps them illustrate regular blog posts.

Here are a few tips for taking photos for your blog:

✔ Carry your camera with you when you leave the house, even if you're just running down to the grocery store.

✔ Keep fresh batteries in your camera so that when you need to use it, it isn't dead. If possible, keep a second set of batteries in your camera pouch. (By the way, digital cameras quickly suck up battery juice, so you really should buy rechargeable batteries.)

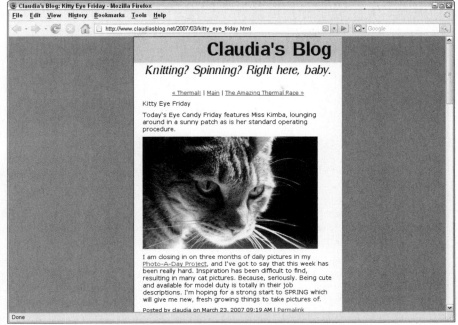

✔ Don't worry too much about taking the perfect picture. Just take the picture!

✔ Take photos of the people you meet and talk to and your friends. Be sure to ask them whether you can use their photo on your blog. Then, when you blog about going to a movie with Sam, you'll have a photo of Sam to include.

A word on copyright

If you see a photo on the Internet, you can bet you bottom dollar it is protected by copyright, even if the photographer hasn't explicitly said so. Copyright is literally "the right to copy" an original creation and protects the author by giving that right solely to him or her. Unless the creator of an image or photo specifically licenses his or her copyright to you, you may not reuse it, even if you give the author credit or link back to the original image. (This is true of all text, too, including books, news stories, and so on.)

So, when you see a photo or image that you think would look great on your blog, look to see whether the author has given permission for it to be used with a Creative Commons license (`www.creativecommons.org`) or ask for permission to republish the work. Don't just steal it.

Using art from other sources

One nice thing about the Web: There are tons and tons of photos, images, graphics, and visuals out there to inspire you. Some bloggers have taken advantage of this by including some of those great visuals in their blog posts. This is popular with readers and a great idea, as long as you have the rights to republish those images. (See the sidebar "A word on copyright" in this chapter.)

Here are some tips when you need images other than your own:

- ✔ **Checking the public domain:** Some materials are designated *public domain* works, which means they can be used for any purpose, by anyone, though you must still give the author credit. If you're interested in featuring public domain and licensed images on your blog, do a search for "public domain photos" in your Web browser. There are a number of good resources that you can investigate.

  In the United States, anything published before 1923 is considered to be public domain, but this isn't true in other countries.

- ✔ **Searching through Creative Commons:** You can also look for works that have been specifically licensed for republication using the Creative Commons licensing tools. To find things you can use, visit `http://search.creativecommons.org` and do a search using keywords that describe the material you're looking for.

- ✔ **Asking for permission:** If you see something you like and want to use that is protected by full copyright, consider just asking whether you can use it. Many photographers, especially those who don't make a living selling their work, are willing to let you use their work, especially if you give them credit!

Many of the photos on the Flickr (`www.flickr.com`) photo-sharing site have actually been licensed for use on other Web sites and blogs. When you're looking at a photo on Flickr, check the copyright information on the right side of the page.

Editing Photos

Now it's time to edit a photo! As long as you have the rights to do so, you can edit any photo. In general, you can do what you like to photos you acquire from a public domain Web site or a picture you take yourself. Photos that you obtain permission to use, or use under a special license, may have restrictions when it comes to making edits, so be sure you understand what you're allowed to do. In the following sections, I show you how to do some of the most common photo-editing tasks by using Picasa.

Most of the edits you want to make most frequently are resizing, cropping, adjusting lighting and contrast, and adjusting the color of a photo. For each of the following tasks, you should have Picasa running and have a photo available to edit.

When you edit a photo in Picasa, no changes are saved until you choose Save from the File menu. When you do this, Picasa saves the changes. At the same time, it creates a copy of the original image, so that if you ever need to start fresh you can.

Getting photos into Picasa

Before you can edit a photo, you need to get it into Picasa. Here's how:

1. **With Picasa installed on your computer, connect your camera to your computer.**

   You can also put your card into a card reader or printer, if that's how you usually move photos from your camera to your computer.

   Windows displays a pop-up window asking what program you would like to use.

2. **Choose Picasa from the available programs and click OK.**

   Photos begin to load in Picasa's Import Tray.

3. **Click Import All to bring the photos into Picasa.**

   The Finish Importing pop-up window opens.

4. **Create a folder name for the photos.**

   You can use the Browse button to set a location for the photos to be saved. The default location is the My Pictures folder.

   You can also add information about where the photos were taken, the date, and given them a description, but this information is option.

5. **Click Finish.**

   Picasa finishes importing the photos, and returns you to the photo Library.

Cropping a photo

Cropping a photo allows you to remove unneeded or unattractive parts of an image. For example, if you take a picture of a group of friends and then want to include a photo of just one of the individuals in your blog post, you can crop out the other people in the image.

To crop a photo you've imported into Picasa, follow these steps:

1. **Open Picasa and double-click the photo you want to edit in the Library.**

   The Editing screen opens.

2. **Click the Crop button at the top of the Basic Fixes tab.**

3. **Choose to crop to a preset size, or to crop manually.**

   If you're cropping to a preset size, simply click the size you want to use.

4. **Use your mouse to click and drag over the area you want to retain in your photo, as shown in Figure 13-5.**

   As you click and drag, the area that will be cropped out of your photo is slightly grayed out, leaving the portion that will be retained at the original brightness.

   If you want to start over, click Reset, and the cropping box you created is removed. If you don't want to crop after all, click the Cancel button to exit the Crop tool.

5. **Click the Preview button to see how the cropped photo will look.**

   Picasa displays the cropped photo.

6. **Click the Apply button to crop your photo.**

   Picasa displays the cropped photo.

Figure 13-5:
Cropping manually lets you choose a specific area you want to keep in your photo.

Adjusting brightness and contrast

Sometimes, despite your best efforts, photos end up being too dark, or too light. With photo editing software like Picasa, you get a second chance, because you can make adjustments to brightness and contrast.

To adjust the brightness and contrast, follow these steps:

1. **Open Picasa and double-click the photo you want to edit in the Library.**

   The Editing screen opens.

2. **Click the Tuning tab on the left side of the application.**

3. **On the Tuning tab, click and drag the slider bar under Highlights to adjust the brightness of the image.**

   Picasa adjusts the image being displayed as you move the bar.

   If you are lightening the photo, watch the brightest parts of your photo to make sure they don't get too bright, losing information you want in the photo. If you are bringing down lightness, watch the darker areas of your photo so that you don't end up with too much black in your photo. Let your eyes be the judge of a well-adjusted image.

You can have Picasa make an educated guess about the brightness settings you need by clicking the Auto Contrast button in the Basic Fixes tab. Click the Undo Auto Contrast button if you don't like the results.

Adjusting color

Color is another area that frequently needs a little adjusting. I've taken too many greenish photos in fluorescent lights! With a little help from photo editing software like Picasa, I can turn my friends back to their normal skin colors.

To adjust the color of a photo, follow these steps:

1. **Open Picasa and double-click the photo you want to edit in the Library.**

   The Editing screen opens.

2. **Click the Tuning tab on the left side of the application.**

3. **On the Tuning tab, click and drag the slider bar under Color Temperature to adjust the color tone of the picture.**

   Color can be tricky to adjust. As a good rule, look for an element in the photograph that you know should be a particular color, and adjust the overall color to make that element look right. Then look at the overall picture and adjust if necessary. Elements you can use for the purpose include eye color, skin color, sky, and other consistent elements.

You can have Picasa make an educated guess about the color settings you need by clicking the Auto Color button in the Basic Fixes tab. Click the Undo Auto Color button if you don't like the results.

Resizing a photo

Resizing a photo actually occurs when you export the image out of Picasa, so you don't need to resize until you've done all your other edits. When you export, you're creating a file you can upload to your blog, so don't skip this step!

You resize images in order to make them larger or smaller. Digital cameras common take larger images than you need for display on a blog or Web site, and it's not a great idea to make your blog visitors download a great big image when they don't need to. Usually, you resize your image to be smaller when you plan to put it on your blog.

To resize and export, select the photo in Picasa you want to export:

1. **Click the Export button at the bottom right of the Picasa window.**

   The Export to Folder dialog box opens, as shown in Figure 13-6.

2. **Click the Browse button to choose the location where you want to save the file you're exporting.**

3. **To resize your image, click the Resize To button under Image Size Options.**

4. **Enter a pixel width you want to use for your new image.**

   You may need to experiment to find the right pixel width for your particular blog design, but a good rule is to choose a pixel width of 400 pixels.

   You can also use the slider bar next to the pixel field to change the width.

5. **Choose an Image Quality setting from the Image Quality drop-down list.**

   For Web graphics, Normal is a good setting to choose.

6. **Click OK.**

   Picasa exports your image to the folder you chose.

If you plan to upload your image to Flickr, don't worry about resizing the image when you export. Flickr can handle large files and will resize the photo for you.

Figure 13-6:
Export and
resize an
image in
one step by
using
Picasa.

Inserting Photos into Blog Posts with Flickr

With a photo prepared for use on your blog, you're ready to upload it to the Web. You can take two approaches here:

- ✔ **Uploading directly to your blog:** If your blog software supports it, you might be able to upload your image directly into your blog post. In Blogger, for instance, you can use the Image Upload button in the New Post interface to upload an image. You can read more about how to do this in Blogger in Chapter 2.

- ✔ **Other online sharing sites:** If your blog software doesn't include an image-uploading tool, you can upload your photos to online sharing sites such as Flickr. You can then add your photo to your post.

Here's how you add photos to Flickr:

1. **Log in to your Flickr account and choose Upload Photos from the home page, or click the arrow next to the You navigation button and choose Upload Photos from the menu that appears.**

   The Upload Photos to Flickr page appears.

2. **Click the Choose Photos link.**

   A Select File dialog box opens, showing files on your computer.

3. **Navigate to the location of the photo you want to upload, select the photo, and click Open.**

   Your photo goes into an upload queue on the Flickr page.

   If you want to upload more photos, click the Add More link and add those photos to the queue as well.

4. **Make sure that your Privacy setting is set to Public so that your photo can be viewed when you put it on your blog.**

5. **Click the Upload Photos button.**

   Flickr displays a progress bar and notifies you when your photo has been fully uploaded.

6. **Click the Describe your photos link.**

7. **Give your photo a title, description, and tags that describe it.**

8. **Click the Save This Batch button.**

   Flickr adds your new photo(s) to your photo page.

9. **Click the photo you just uploaded from your photo page.**

10. **Click the All Sizes icon above the photo, as shown in Figure 13-7.**

    To post your photos directly from Flickr onto your blog and skip the rest of the steps, click the Blog This icon next to the All Sizes icon. Flickr shows you the starting point for configuring the connection between Flickr and your blog. Have the Web address for your blog's publishing interface, your username, and password ready.

11. **Scroll down the page to find the HTML code for your photo, click in the code box, and copy that code into your Clipboard by pressing Ctrl+V (⌘+V on a Mac) or choosing Edit⇨Copy.**

12. **Go to your blogging software and start a new post.**

13. **Paste the code from Flickr into your post entry field.**

    Type your post as you normally would after the Flickr code.

14. **Publish your post and be sure to check to see how it looks on the blog.**

In Figure 13-8, you can see a photo from Flickr posted in Gillian Gunson's blog Gillianic Tendencies (`www.gunson.ca/blog`).

Figure 13-7:
Clicking the
All Sizes
icon gives
you access
to the HTML
code for
your photo.

Figure 13-8:
Use Flickr to
add photos
to your blog
posts.

Flickr uploading tools

You have five ways to upload your photos to Flickr. You can use the method described in this chapter, you can download the Flickr Uploadr tool and install it on your computer, use a plug-in for iPhoto, or upload via e-mail. If you upload via e-mail, don't forget that you can use your mobile phone to e-mail pictures directly onto your Flickr photostream.

To find out more about the Flickr uploading tools, go to www.flickr.com/tools.

Chapter 14

Saying It Better with Podcasts

*A*t this point, you've set up a blog and sampled what life is like for the average blogger. Maybe you've chosen what it is you'd like to talk about, written a few posts, and have hit that publish button more than once. Seems almost easy, doesn't it? Of course, you need to do quite a number of technical things, but after everything is set up and working properly, writing your thoughts and publishing them on the Internet is simple! How could it get any more challenging?

Enter the podcast. Basically, a *podcast* is either a video or an audio file that's published on the Internet for people to download and listen to or view. This is normally done using blog software but publishing a podcast can be done in various ways — it's just easier when you already have a blog to use! The audio podcasts are a lot like radio programs, and the video podcasts are comparable to short films.

The production process for a podcast is (in theory) simple: You go out into the world, record a video or some audio, edit it on your computer, and then upload the files to your blog for release onto the Internet. The files are then downloaded by your blog's readers, who can still leave comments and interact with your blog in the usual way.

Intrigued? There's no denying that podcasts are attracting a whole new audience to the blogosphere. With software being improved and portable hardware units being created to consume these kinds of media, podcasting might be something you should seriously consider adding to your blog.

If you want to become the coolest podcaster in your neck of the woods, check out *Podcasting For Dummies,* by Tee Morris and Evo Terra.

Podcasting in ancient times

In 2003, a number of bloggers thought it would be interesting to record their thoughts out loud and then publish the audio, usually as MP3 files, through their blogs. Some started releasing audio blog entries on a regular basis. What happened next was a bit of a surprise. Because of the rising popularity of MP3 players such as Apple's iPod, the audience for these podcasts grew extremely quickly. And, thanks to RSS feeds, it was easy to retrieve and download the latest recordings. People from all over the world started listening, recording, and publishing their own audio blogs. Several audio blogs became popular enough to gain some notice within the mainstream media. A hidden audience had been discovered.

In fact, most people believe the word *podcast* comes from the Apple iPod device, a popular MP3 player that can store and play podcasts and music. This is close, but not the whole truth. Podcasts arose at the same time that Apple's device came on the scene, and the name *podcast* was conceived by bloggers to echo the idea that these audio files could be listened to on the go in a handheld device. But the files could always be played by many devices, and in fact, most podcasts are listened to on a computer, not an MP3 player. Some say the word comes from a combination of the acronym *pod* (*pod* standing for portable-on-demand) and the word *broadcast,* but this meaning evolved after the word itself, probably in response to Apple's attempts in 2005 to try to restrict the commercial use of the word *pod.*

Although some bloggers were also experimenting with video, it took until 2005 for videocasting to really start to gain traction. Two technological shifts helped make this happen: iTunes, the program most people used to subscribe to podcasts, started supporting video, and YouTube, the video-sharing site, made uploading and sharing video a much more common online activity.

Portable video cameras were fairly cheap, and a number of online services like file storage and video hosting started catering to new video producers. Video blogging was born and, with the advent of YouTube and Google Video, became one of the most powerful mediums on the Internet. And, the most amazing thing is that demand for such podcasts continues to grow.

Deciding to Podcast

Podcasts come in all flavors. You can find personal podcasts, technical podcasts, sports reports, music samples, recorded social gatherings, previously recorded radio broadcasts, book reviews, and audio books. If you can think of a topic, there's probably a podcast for it.

Knit Picks (www.knitpicks.com) is a knitting yarn and supplies company that offers a regular podcast about knitting activities, techniques, books, and guest interviews in an informative and entertaining mix. The Knit Picks podcast subscription page is shown in Figure 14-1.

Blogs and podcasts can look very similar; the main difference being that a podcast entry contains a media file that can be downloaded by the consumer either by directly accessing the Web site or by subscribing to your syndicated blog feed, also known as the RSS feed. A "blog feed" is another name for RSS feed.

Figure 14-1:
Get knitting
tips and
tricks from
the Knit
Picks
podcast.

If you've already subscribed to a number of blogs, you know that a syndicated blog feed contains information such as the title of the post, the main content, and maybe some author information. (Find out more about RSS feeds in Chapter 11.) A podcast feed, in addition to the typical entry information, contains a link to a media file. If a consumer subscribes to a podcast feed with an RSS reader, most modern readers automatically download the files so the users can listen or watch at their convenience.

Reaching a wider audience

Many people like to read and enjoy taking in a well-written blog post. However, some blog readers enjoy listening to what you have to say as an audio recording. As well, some blog followers like to watch rather than read your blog post. This is especially true if you have a compelling voice or are more photogenic than average. (I've been told I have a face for radio.) Podcasting can help you reach a different audience.

Also, some of the things you want to talk about might work better as an audio recording rather than a text post, like interviews, soundscapes, or special events. And video is even more powerful: You can show off much more of your personality than you can with just a text blog and demonstrate things that might be difficult or impossible to convey with just words.

Using a podcast, you also can reach your audience in different locations: People might listen to you as they drive or commute, or they might watch your videos on their television or their hand-held iPod.

Think about when and where your podcast might be played and use that to help focus and inform your entries.

Choosing between audio and video

If you're ready to take the plunge into the production of a new podcast, you need to decide what format you want to use. Both audio and video require some specialized skills to produce.

Your level of technical competence and comfort can determine what medium you choose. You'll also need to consider what type of podcast fits with your blog's purpose — videocasting, for example, would be a poor choice for a blog targeted to those using low-bandwidth connections.

Here are a few tips that can help you decide on what type of podcast you should use:

- Audio is

  - Easier to produce than video due to a larger availability of open source software; most software for professional video editing is expensive.

  - Easier and generally quicker to edit than video.

  - More portable than video. Fewer portable devices are designed to deal with video than with audio.

  - Smaller than video files, making them less expensive to store on a Web host.

- Video

  - Is more compelling. The visual and auditory components combined are more likely to keep a viewer from being distracted.

  - Can be shorter. Audiences will likely be satisfied with a 2-4 minute video podcast, whereas they might want a much longer audio podcast.

  - Gives you more visual elements to work with — both when you're designing your blog and in individual entries.

  - Has more related sites online where you can upload and share files.

  - Requires the viewer's attention, whereas audio podcasts can be listened to while completing other tasks. You can listen to an audio podcast while driving to work, for example.

Video and audio files can be very large. When you upload them to your Web server, you will fill up your available disk space more quickly than you will with text and photos. As well, distributing audio and video requires more bandwidth. Be sure to keep an eye on your disk space and bandwidth usage so that you aren't hit with unexpected overage charges. Ask your Web host how to keep tabs on those elements, any fees you may accrue, and if you need more space and bandwidth.

Planning Your Podcast

The first thing you need to create a podcast is the desire to make it the best experience for the listeners that you can. If you aren't having fun, it shows in the final result. Remember, even if your very first podcast is a little frustrating, it'll get easier.

Here are a few key ingredients needed for a good podcast experience:

- **Planning:** You don't need to write a script every single time that you decide to record a podcast — although some podcasters do this — but it helps when you jot down a few notes or create an outline to follow.

- **Timing:** Technically speaking, you can use as much or as little time as you want in your podcast, but you may find that your end product is better when you give yourself some limits. Give some thought to how much time you can reasonably expect your audience to give you, and target that length for your podcasts. In general, podcasts range from a few minutes to an hour.

- **Recording conditions:** When you want to record anything, you need to take into account environmental considerations before hitting the record button. Is the environment you are in quiet enough? Are there fans or computers running in the background that will annoy the listeners' ears? For video, is your situation sufficiently lighted to produce watchable video? Try to eliminate distractions, like phones ringing or people walking by. And if you can, do some test recording that you can listen to or watch so that you know what the quality of the final product will be before you record your entire podcast.

Blogging with text is relatively easy in comparison to recording a podcast, and it's also easier to hide your inexperience because you can rewrite and edit before posting. Audio and video can also be edited, but it is harder to remove stuttered speech or inappropriate facial expressions. Practice can help eliminate awkward moments.

Here are several reasons that creating a podcast is a major decision:

- **The learning curve:** Many bloggers who might otherwise want to podcast don't because of the learning curve to build and maintain a podcast. As wonderful as podcasts can be, writing, recording, uploading, hosting, and promoting one require a high level of technical proficiency.

- **Planning ahead:** A single podcast, like a blog entry, can be about anything, so it helps to have a clearly defined topic before you start. Unlike text editing, where you can just rewrite and rewrite, producing an audio or video podcast can be a one-shot situation. If a phone rings in the middle of an interview, or someone walks in front of the camera at just the wrong moment, you're in trouble. Re-creating the situation may not be possible. Try to organize your recording session to minimize this kind of disruption. As well, make sure you have enough time to record the entire podcast in the same location so that you don't have awkward changes in the background noise that distract your listener or viewer.

- **Finding your voice:** You need to establish the tone of the piece before you go forward. How is the format of your overall podcast going to determine how you shoot or record it? Will you have some kind of traditional show format, or will you decide to improvise the entire program each time? Taking these kinds of questions into account when you're planning out your first podcast can help you make your program a success.

If you get stuck thinking about what type of podcast to add, ask your readers for suggestions. Even if only five or ten readers respond, you can get some good ideas and direction.

Here's a short list of podcast ideas that have been successful for other podcasters. Use this list to spark your creativity to find other topics that interest you:

- **One-on-one interviews:** Fascinating people in your neighborhood are just waiting to get on your podcast — especially people involved in a cause, an organization, or a business. Discover more about your family's background or the adventures of your friends. See who in your acquaintance might fit the theme and direction of your podcast.

- **Show your expertise:** Show off what you know and share your knowledge with others — maybe even teach your audience how to do something.

- **Soundscapes:** All around you are fascinating sounds you can document. Record yourself walking through a forest or park. Make some observations about your surroundings and describe what each of the sounds is and how they're important to you. Remember, what's ordinary for you (waves at the beach, a passing train, construction noise, or a barn owl) might be fascinating for someone living on the other side of the country.

- **Events:** A performance at your local coffee house, a city hall meeting, or a surprise party all might make for an interesting podcast. Make sure to get permission before recording or publishing your podcast.

✔ **Discussions:** General discussions in social settings can reveal some great conversations. Take your recorder along to your next BBQ or evening social and direct the conversation along a theme or idea.

If you take the time to plan out what things you want to share with your subscribers, you can make it happen by taking the time to plan. With a recording device, a plan, and someone else to talk to, you can have a complete podcast episode in no time.

Assessing the Tools

Making your podcast requires a bit more than your ten fingers and a computer keyboard. Podcasts require recording equipment for audio and video. Here's what you're looking at:

✔ **Computer:** You need a computer of some kind. This can be a desktop or a laptop, although laptops might be more flexible and allow you to edit on the go. The computer must be able to handle the editing of audio files and, more importantly, video files. Video is a computer intensive process and requires an updated computer with a lot of disk space in order to process the large files you may be recording. Audio files can also be fairly large.

✔ **Microphone:** Microphones these days are built into almost every laptop, and external microphones are easy to buy. Purchasing a good microphone from a professional audio store is the best way to go because the microphones that you would get from the average computer store or on the typical laptop are poor quality. Ask a podcaster or the staff of a good audio store for advice about the best microphone for the kind of recording situation you expect to be in. Expect to spend at least $40 for your microphone — it's not the item to economize on.

✔ **Sound-recording and -editing software:** To record or edit recorded audio files, you need some kind of editing software. Solutions range from free to the price of a small automobile. Let your budget be your guide. A good strategy is to start small and upgrade when you know more about podcasting and your own needs. I talk more about software options in this chapter, but a good starting point for audio software is the free program Audacity (`http://audacity.sourceforge.net`). A high-end solution is Sony's Sound Forge (`www.sonycreativesoftware.com/products/soundforgefamily.asp`).

✔ **Video camera:** If you can afford one, get one. You can also rent cameras or borrow them from family or friends. Many digital photo cameras and some cell phones also have video options and can be used for a video podcast if you aren't too worried about the quality of the video, though audio is usually quite poor from those devices. Almost all Apple computers now come with a built-in video camera, but you can't really pan around with a desktop machine, so your video might look a little boring.

✔ **Video-editing software:** Of course, you need a tool to edit your video masterpieces once you get them off your camera and onto your computer. This can be home grown software that comes with your operating system, or you can search out some commercial alternatives. Apple users can get started quickly with iMovie (`www.apple.com/ilife/imovie`); for Windows users, an entry-level option is Microsoft Movie Maker (`www.microsoft.com/windowsxp/downloads/updates/moviemaker2.mspx`). For high-end video editing, check out Apple's Final Cut Pro (`www.apple.com/finalcutpro`), Avid Liquid (`www.pinnaclesys.com/PublicSite/us/Products/Consumer+Products/Advanced+Video/Liquid+Edition/Avid+Liquid+7`).

Recording and editing audio

Unless you're the sort of person who never deviates from a script or says "um," you need some kind of software to edit your audio or video. You can spend thousands of dollars on dedicated, high-quality equipment, or you can spend very little and use whatever you have at hand.

I suggest you give the sound editor Audacity (`http://audacity.sourceforge.net`) a try. It's available for Windows, Mac OS X, and Linux/Unix. Audacity (as shown in Figure 14-2) is the program of choice for many podcasters, largely because it's free and open source. Audacity is a *multitrack recording* program — which means you can have two pieces of audio, like a voice and a piece of music, and you can mix the two at different volumes or even fade from one to the other.

Recording and editing video

Getting video onto your computer requires more specialized equipment than audio recording. Fewer options are available in the freeware market, and editing video usually requires a more powerful computer than audio does.

Jahshaka

`www.jahshaka.org`

Jahshaka is an open source, cross platform, free piece of video-editing software that wants to power the new Hollywood. It's available for Windows, Mac OS X, and Linux/Unix.

The software is a *nonlinear video* editor — which means you can access any part of your video clips, delete bits of them, and splice them together in any order, without having to actually modify or destroy the original video clips. You also get additional functions such as effects rendering, animation, and audio track editing. Jahshaka supports many different video file formats.

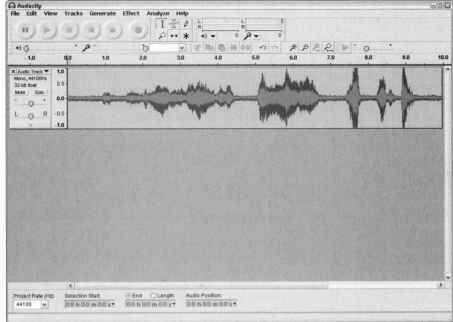

Figure 14-2:
Audacity is a popular audio-editing software program.

iMovie

www.apple.com/ilife/imovie

For Mac users, iMovie is a great option. Free with the computer, iMovie is a video tool designed to make recording, editing, and publishing video as simple as possible. This tool is quick and easy to learn, but it's fairly limited in its range of effects but it does get the job done. If you want more functionality, you'll want to research some commercial video solutions.

Dressing Up Your Podcast

Nothing spices up a podcast like a little intro or background music. But podcasts, even if they're produced and released at no cost to the listener, aren't exempt from copyright restrictions. The trick is to find music and/or images that are in the public domain or that are licensed for republication.

Let me be clear: Even if you use only a little bit of a copyrighted song or give the performer credit, you're still violating copyright if you don't have a license or other permission to use the music. The same goes for using copyrighted images and video clips in videocasts.

A quick word about video and codecs

When you get into editing audio and video, you eventually run into something called a codec. *Codec* is a technical word for compression and decompression. You see, video files and audio files are normally compressed to create file sizes that are small and don't fill up your hard drive or create files too large for your users to download.

Codecs are the mathematical rules that compress movie files for storage and decompress them to play on your computer. Codecs are part of every media player you use for music and videos. Some video files, without any compression, would be more than ten times in size than they are with a codec to compress them.

Fortunately for podcasters, some common formats are accepted by blog software and blog audiences. If you stick with MP3 for audio podcasts and MPEG for videos, you should be fine.

The good news is that plenty of this material is available for you to use. The term *podsafe* has appeared to describe music, sounds, and other clips that are made available for free unlimited use in podcasting, but there's no one specific license that means podsafe, so be sure to read the terms and conditions before you integrate sound or audio into your productions.

Creative Commons Search

http://search.creativecommons.org

Creative Commons is an organization that has evolved a set of licenses you can use on your own content to permit or disallow use by others. If a publisher applies a Creative Commons license that allows republication, you can search for and find that content in the Creative Commons Search area, specifically requesting content that you can use for commercial purposes or modify (see Figure 14-3).

Some of the types of licenses are:

- ✔ **Commercial use:** Permits use of the content for business and revenue-generating purposes.

- ✔ **Non-commercial use:** You may only use this media for non-commercial podcasts.

- ✔ **Attribution:** The work can be used only when credit is given to the creator.

- ✔ **Derivatives allowed:** This media can be cut, chopped, and excerpted to create new works.

- ✔ **No-derivatives allowed:** Media must be left intact and unchanged.

Figure 14-3:
Search for licensed content to use in your podcast on Creative Commons.

Magnatune

www.magnatune.com

Magnatune is a record label that helps artists to promote their music, share their music, and make some money doing it. The label and the artists sell their albums on CD and via download and split the money evenly. The music on Magnatune (shown in Figure 14-4) is available for download and purchase but also is available to podcasters. To help promote their artists, podcasters are granted a waiver to use their music without paying a royalty fee.

Podsafe Music Network

http://music.podshow.com

The Podsafe Music Network is a place where artists provide tracks from their albums for sharing and use in podcasts. Everything is released using a Creative Commons license, and registered users can create play lists and download tracks to share on the podcasts.

Figure 14-4:
Magnatune is the only record label that specifically allows non-commercial podcasters to use music for free.

The Freesound Project

http://freesound.iua.upf.edu

Music is great, but what about sound effects? What podcast wouldn't be improved by a few barking dogs and fart noises? I'm kidding, of course. Sound effects can really add a lot of value to your production, from realistic sounds of dialing a phone to a spring breeze. The Freesound Project can help you dress up your podcast.

Use their simple search box to find Creative Commons licensed sound, and contribute your own sound effects.

Publishing Your Podcast

Putting your podcast into the blogosphere is fairly simple; you write a blog post about your podcast, upload your podcast media file, and then publish it using your blog software.

But before you do that, you have a couple of tasks: You need to give your podcast some metadata, and you must choose a file format to deliver your podcast in.

Assigning metadata

Metadata, simply put, is data about data. In the case of podcasts, metadata is data that describes your video or audio podcast. Why is this important to you? When you publish a podcast — whether audio or video — you need to provide descriptive metadata that can be read by podcast systems like Apple's iTunes and in the RSS feed. After all, the computer can't listen to or watch your podcast and figure out what it contains!

Common metadata types include

- ✔ Title
- ✔ Author name
- ✔ Publication information
- ✔ Topics covered
- ✔ Type of file
- ✔ Descriptions
- ✔ Keywords

Your editing software (both video and audio software packages) ask you to enter metadata when you create your audio or video files, and software like iTunes that is designed to support podcasts also offers you a chance to provide metadata.

Choosing a format

Creating video and audio for general release means that you need to choose a file format your audience can consume.

Audio podcasts

Most audio bloggers release audio files in the MP3 format. It's easy to create and, with the popularity of MP3 players like the Apple iPod, easily played on a variety of devices. Most computer users are familiar with the format, and there's good built-in support in browsers and preinstalled audio players as well.

Other options are available, such as OOG, an open format, and AAC, a format popular on Apple computers. The Apple iPod won't play OOG files, which is a significant issue for most audiences. AAC has some nice features like audio bookmarks.

Video podcasts

Apple QuickTime files (MOV) are the standard format for videocast delivery, but you can also use Flash Video (FLV) or Microsoft Windows video files (WMV).

In recent years, the rise of services like YouTube, Google Video, and other online streaming sites mean you have an alternative to creating video podcasts in a particular format. YouTube and Google video take most formats and convert them into a common streamed format that displays using those sites' custom players. This allows podcasters to not worry about their audiences' ability to view their video — though it's important to note that these video players stream the video, they don't allow it to be downloaded for viewing offline or on a portable device. They also usually have a length limit of about ten minutes but not every service has the same restrictions. Before you choose the video service you want, check what their limitations are.

Regardless of how you plan to distribute your video, it's to your advantage to produce your files in the same format you'll deliver them — this makes for cleaner delivery and better quality control.

Storing your podcasts

With a podcast ready for primetime, you're ready for the next major hurdle: where to put it online. Posting your podcast poses two problems:

- **Storage:** You have to have somewhere to put the actual file. Audio and video files are larger than text files, so disk space is the issue in storing them.

- **Bandwidth:** You have to account for the additional bandwidth required for your audience to download those files. Again, it takes more bandwidth to deliver audio or video to your audience than it does text or images.

You have two options: your Web-hosting server (the one that hosts your blog) or a free storage Web site.

Putting your files on your own Web-hosting server

Check with your Web host to find out how much disk space is available and what it costs to increase your allotment. Be aware that if you keep podcasting, you'll eventually run out of disk space even if you start off with quite a bit of space. If you are a video podcaster, you will want a hosting package with several gigabytes of storage space. If you stick with only audio, you will need a few gigabytes to start. As your podcasts grow, you will require more and more space, so, keep that in mind. I talk about choosing a Web host in Chapter 6.

Bandwidth is the second issue to look at. Most Web hosting packages comes with a standard amount of bandwidth included, and you're charged if you use more than that. Fees are pretty reasonable, unless your podcast because the hottest thing on the Web and your traffic becomes astronomical.

Most hosting packages come with a finite amount of disk space and bandwidth. You most likely can post only a certain number of podcasts before your hosting package runs out of space. Unless you have the dollars to spend, you'll probably need to find an alternative for storing your files.

Using a free storage and sharing Web site

Luckily for podcasters, there's a great service called Archive.org (`www.archive.org`), and all podcasters should be aware of its existence. Archive.org is the home of the Internet Archive, a nonprofit organization founded in 1996 to build an Internet library where researchers, historians, and the general public can store and access text, audio, moving images, software, and a vast collection of archived Web pages.

You can upload your podcasts to the Internet Archive for free, as long as you comply with its guidelines and describe your content. The system also provides and converts your video or audio format into other formats for increased accessibility.

Here are a couple of other places you can upload your podcast to:

- ✔ **YouTube:** (`www.youtube.com`) If you haven't seen a YouTube video on a blog or Web site lately, you must be living under a rock. This site has soared in popularity. When you upload a video to YouTube, your video is listed on the YouTube site and can be viewed and commented on there, but you can also grab the code for the file and embed it directly into your Web site or blog posts. Files you upload to YouTube are reformatted into Flash Video. They must be shorter than 10 minutes and under 100MB in size.

- ✔ **Google Video:** (`http://video.google.com`) This service of the popular search engine allows you to upload a video for free and then share it via e-mail or by posting it to your blog. You can upload AVI, MPEG, Quicktime, Real, or Windows Media files. You can also choose whether to have your files display in the Google Video search results.

Delivering your podcasts

With your audio and video online and your blog post created, the final step is to make sure your blog has an RSS Web feed. Podcasts are typically delivered to playback software (like Apple iTunes) through a subscription to your blog's RSS feed. I talk extensively about setting up and using RSS in Chapter 11.

Suffice to say that you need an RSS feed so that your viewers and listeners can subscribe to it themselves, but also so that you can promote your podcast using some of the handy podcast promotional directories and software out there.

Promoting Your Podcast

Publishing your podcast on your Web site is a good start to publicizing your podcast, but you can get the word out in more effective ways. If you already have a good promotional system built into your site and a decent-sized audience, you can get users to subscribe to your podcast without too much additional marketing, but if you need a little more promotion, you can use a number of strategies.

Adding your podcast to FeedBurner

FeedBurner (www.feedburner.com) provides custom tracking and customization of podcast feeds. If you submit your podcast to Feedburner's service, you can implement some good promotion tools to help your podcast get more play.

FeedBurner has a lot to offer bloggers and podcasters. FeedBurner gives you the ability to track the number of subscribers to your feed and also provides you with tools to make your feeds compatible with every RSS reader available. You can also use FeedBurner to add metadata to your files, and keep track of which podcasts are actually being downloaded.

When you use FeedBurner, your podcast is also added to the major podcast directories, making sure that people can find your podcast.

To use FeedBurner, you must already have an RSS feed. If you're using blog software, it's likely you already have a feed. Check your documentation for more information, and jump to Chapter 11 for more about RSS feeds. Follow these steps to create a feed with Feedburner:

1. **Go to http://feedburner.com.**

   The home page appears, as shown in Figure 14-5.

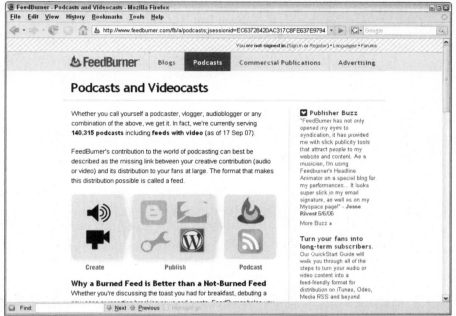

Figure 14-5: Start delivering your podcast by using FeedBurner.

2. **Create an account on FeedBurner if you don't already have one.**

3. **On the FeedBurner home page, paste the Web address (URL) of your RSS feed into the Start FeedBurning Now field.**

4. **Check the I Am a Podcaster! box.**

5. **Click the Next button.**

   FeedBurner verifies that the feed is working and loads the Welcome screen.

6. **Give your feed a title, if it doesn't already have one.**

   You can also customize the feed address, if desired.

7. **Click the Activate Feed button.**

   FeedBurner creates your new feed and loads a screen that displays the Web address of your feed.

8. **Click the Next button.**

   FeedBurner loads the podcast configuration screen.

9. **Fill out the configuration screen:**

   • *Create podcast enclosures from links to*: Choose the kinds of files that should be included in your podcast — any, audio, video, or images.

- *Include iTunes podcasting elements*: Deselect this box if you don't want your podcast listed in Apple's iTunes Music Store.

- *Category*: Choose a category from the drop-down menu. You can also choose a subcategory.

- *Podcast image location*: If you have created a graphic for your podcast, paste the Web address of the graphic into this field.

- *Podcast subtitle*: Expand on your title in this field.

- *Podcast summary*: Provide a short description of your podcast.

- *Podcast search keywords*: Provide descriptive keywords for your podcast.

- *Podcast author e-mail address*: Fill in your email address.

- *Include "Media RSS" information and add podcast to Yahoo! Search*: Deselect this box if you don't wish to be included in Yahoo! Search.

- *Contains explicit content*: Select yes, no, or yes (cleaned). Use the information icon if you want help understanding how FeedBurner defines explicit content.

- *Copyright message*: Provide a short copyright message.

- *Podcast author*: Fill in your name.

10. Click the Next button.

FeedBurner loads the traffic statistics screen.

11. Fill out the Feed Traffic Statistics screen:

- *Clickthroughs*: Select this box if you want to know when subscribers use your feed to come to your Web site.

- *Item enclosure downloads*: Select this box if you want to which podcast entries are actually downloaded by your subscribers.

12. Click the Next button.

FeedBurner finished burning your feed. You can begin monitoring subscriptions and activity on your feed using FeedBurner.

After you create a feed with FeedBurner, head to your site and put the link to your new feed on your blog and urge your blog visitors to subscribe.

After your feed is listed with FeedBurner, you can actually keep track of how many subscribers you have and how they're using your podcast, which is useful information if you plan to pursue funding or sponsorship.

Adding your podcast to iTunes

Due to the overwhelming popularity of Apple's iTunes software as the main podcast viewer, you absolutely must submit your podcast to its service — unless you, for some reason, don't want people to find your podcast.

If you have a FeedBurner feed set up, you've already taken care of some of the optimization to make your feed work well in iTunes. Be sure to use the FeedBurner feed address when you sign up in iTunes.

If you have the iTunes software installed on your computer, you can submit your podcast using the iTunes interface. You have to sign up for an Apple ID prior to submission of your podcast because each submission is associated with a user account. It's also a good idea to have a few entries in your feed and to make sure the feed is working well. Podcast submissions are reviewed by Apple iTunes staff prior to being added to the store. They can refuse podcasts for even very small reasons, and it is difficult to get added if you've been turned down once.

To submit your podcast, you must already have an RSS feed. If you're using blog software, it's likely you already have a feed. Check your documentation for more information, and jump to Chapter 11 for more about RSS feeds.

In order to get your podcast into the iTunes store, here are the brief steps that you need to follow.

1. **Start your iTunes software.**

2. **Click the iTunes Store navigation item in the left column.**

3. **Select the Podcasts link from the iTunes Store menu on the left side of the screen.**

   The Podcasts page appears.

4. **Click the Submit a Podcast graphic located in the middle of the page.**

   This link is also available under the Learn More menu on the bottom left.

   iTunes loads the Submit Podcasts page.

5. **Enter the RSS feed of your podcast in the Podcast Feed URL field and click the Continue button.**

   If you are not logged in to the iTunes Store, you're prompted to login at this point.

   iTunes submits your feed for review by Apple staff.

After you've submitted your podcast, it might take several days or even weeks until your feed shows up in the iTunes library of podcasts.

Getting listed in podcast directories

Podcast directories direct would-be listeners and viewers to known podcasts. Getting listed in these directories is an easy step in letting people know about your podcast. Most directories are organized by topic, and many of them offer subscription features to allow people to quickly sign up for your podcast. Listing your podcast in these directories is never a bad idea and will most certainly provide you with new traffic.

Here's where you should get your podcast listed:

- **Podcast Alley:** (www.podcastalley.com) This site contains a podcast directory as well as news and information about podcasting.

- **Podcast.com:** (www.podcast.com) Podcasts are organized by category (for example, entertainment or sports), and the home page displays a list of recently updated podcasts.

- **Odeo:** (www.odeo.com) Plans are underway to turn this excellent directory site into a resource for tools and functionality.

- **Podcast Pickle:** (www.podcastpickle.com) This is one of the older podcast directories and offers visitors organization tools for the podcasts they subscribe to.

- **Podnova:** (www.podnova.com) This is more than just a directory. You can subscribe, listen, view, read, and maintain your feeds online.

And if that doesn't do it for you, check out Robin Good's extensive list of podcast directories at www.masternewmedia.org/podcast_directory.

Part V
Marketing and Promoting Your Blog

The 5th Wave   By Rich Tennant

"I'm sorry. I'm answering e-mail right now. And since when does the Taco Bell Chihuahua have a blog anyway?"

In this part . . .

Blogs aren't just for the hobbyist, as you discover in this business-oriented part of the book. If you have a business idea up your sleeve or want to put ads on your blog, you'll love Chapter 15 for its tips on installing and understanding Web statistics tools for tracking your traffic. Get the lowdown on using blog advertising programs and tools in Chapter 16 and make a little money with your new blog. Businesses and nonprofit organizations aren't left out, either. Chapter 17 describes how today's companies are making use of blogs to reach customers and critics alike.

Chapter 15

Measuring Blog Presence

. . . .

. . . .

For a moment, picture your new blog running just the way you like it. The graphics are pretty, you're blogging every day, and comments are rolling in. Everything looks perfect, and you seem to be well on your way to a successful blogging career. But wait! Now imagine that, for no real reason, over a few weeks the number of comments left on your blog each day starts to decrease. Your visitor numbers are down. There doesn't seem to an obvious explanation, and you can't imagine why your readership is disappearing so quickly!

If you ever find yourself in this type of situation and you don't have any idea why your traffic is changing, you'll start asking yourself questions like "How many visitors do I have every day, anyway?" or "How many of my visitors have been here before?"

For you, it's time to understand your Web traffic statistics. Web stats can be especially important for you as a blogger because your audience numbers are affected each time you post.

Paying attention to what your blog is doing on the Internet is an important task, but it can be confusing and boring. Spending an afternoon peering at Web stats, especially if you don't know what you're looking for, can be a tedious experience. It's like . . . well, it's like watching paint dry. But, it doesn't have to be as painful as it sounds. Web statistics are very geeky, but these days, services that are available to bloggers (and Webmasters, in general) allow you to track your blog's success in some very interesting and informative ways by using a friendly interface.

For more help with Web analytics, check out *Web Analytics For Dummies* by Pedro Sostre and Jennifer LeClaire (2007) from Wiley Publishing.

Finding Out About Statistics

Even if you like the way your blog is performing, you should take a look at your blog stats once in a while. Some bloggers look at them daily to see what kinds of visitors appeared on their blogging radar overnight; some bloggers check their stats once a week or once a month. Whichever pattern you choose, keeping a good handle on your statistics is never a bad thing. Knowing how many visitors you have can help you improve your blog in the future — making it even more popular!

Your Web logs can tell you all kinds of things, and a whole lot more than just how many people read your site. For an example of what a typical Web stats tool looks like, check out StatCounter's measurement of the Find-A-Sweetheart Web site (www.find-a-sweetheart.com) in Figure 15-1. (You have to be logged in to view stats on StatCounter.)

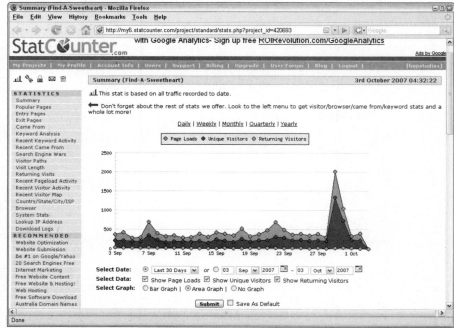

Figure 15-1:
Blogger Kathryn Lord uses StatCounter to track Web stats.

Using Web statistics, you can track:

- ✔ What countries your Web visitors are surfing from
- ✔ How long visitors stay
- ✔ How many visitors are there for the first time

- ✔ How many visitors have been to your blog before
- ✔ What pages your visitors start their visit on
- ✔ What pages visitors end their visit on
- ✔ What sites are sending visitors to you
- ✔ What search words are being used to find your site
- ✔ What browsers your visitors use
- ✔ What kind of computer your visitors use to surf the Web
- ✔ What screen resolutions your visitors set their monitors to

With some of the more advanced Web analytics software, you can see what pages are the least popular, find out how search engines handle your blog, and even see what errors or missing pages your visitors are getting. Lots of bloggers are especially interested in knowing what Web sites are sending visitors to their blogs, so they know where to invest time and energy in comments and discussion forums.

Knowing even a little bit about your traffic can help you make all kinds of strategic decisions about your blog, from what kind of design to use to the subject of a post.

Analyzing your stats

Web analytics are the trends that your statistical or log software shows you. Some traffic software helps break out these trends for you, but the most basic software simply displays the raw data of how your site is being used and lets you draw the conclusions. When people talk about Web analytics, they're referring to the process you undertake when you're looking through those stats and logs to figure out what visitors are doing on your Web site. Commonly, you look for trends about what content the visitors are viewing, how often they visit, and what other sites are directing traffic your way.

Pay close attention to your Web site logs and you can chart what your users are doing over time. You can see what your site visitors are reading and what keeps them coming back for more. You can then use this information for a variety of purposes (like, say, deciding what to blog about).

For instance, if you notice that a large bunch of readers are coming from a particular country (see Figure 15-2) and you don't live in that country, you should see what pages those visitors are viewing — and determine why they're coming to your site. You can then write more to attract additional visitors with similar tastes. In fact, noticing a trend like this one might help you really focus on a core audience you weren't aware of or even redefine what you do with your blog in the future.

Figure 15-2:
Track where
your visitors
live using
a stat
program like
StatCounter.

You can also break this information into dollars and cents. If you take the time, you can see what kinds of visitors are clicking advertisements on your site (if you have any). If more people are clicking a certain type of advertisement, you can use this information to sell ads to certain advertisers.

To understand what it is you're looking at when you're scanning your Web statistics or server logs, you need to know a series of terms. Most Web analytics software uses these terms, but you should always check to see how measurements are defined by the software's creators — these terms are commonly used the same way, but not always. I cover the most vital terms in the following sections.

You'll run into more terms than the ones I cover here, but the most important ones for bloggers are *page views, unique visitors,* and *repeat visitors.* Together, these three statistics give you the most accurate picture of how many visitors your blog receives and what they do while they visit.

Hits

A *hit* is an official request for a file from the Web server. The file can be an HTML file or a movie file. Essentially, any file available on a Web server to the surfing public counts as a hit.

Any given Web page causes multiple hits on the server when it's loaded, even though it's only one page. This is because multiple files are actually being called to display the page: the HTML file, any associated style documents, and all the image files. If an HTML file has five images, it counts as six hits — one for the HTML file and five for each individual image.

Hits are commonly misunderstood to indicate the number of Web site visitors or even the number of pages viewed, but they don't even come close to measuring those kinds of figures. Hits are pretty meaningless if you're trying to understand how many visitors you have, but they can be important if you need to get a feel for the load your site puts on the Web server.

Page views

A *page view* is normally defined as a "page" within a Web server log; if an HTML file is requested, the log says that this is a single request even if several files are needed to display the page. Each time a page of your site is loaded, it counts as a page view, and page views are a valuable measurement because you can get a better understanding for what kind of usage people are making of your site.

In Figure 15-3, you can see the page loads for October 6, 2007.

Advertisers are often very interested in the number of page views on a Web site (more is better), and most bloggers consider having lots of page views a number to brag about.

Unique visitors

Unique visitors are just what they sound like — individual visitors who visit your Web site. They're counted only once, no matter how many pages they view or how many times they visit. When you're looking at the number of unique visitors your blog gets, take a look at what time period is being referred to. Fifty unique visitors in one day, for example, is a much bigger deal than 50 unique visitors in a month.

Repeat visitors

Repeat visitors are blog readers that visit your site on more than one occasion and, usually, visit multiple pages. Pay attention, again, to the time period being discussed when repeat visitors are measured.

In Figure 15-4, you can see a graph breaking down the percentages of first-time visitors to repeat visitors on the Web statistics tool StatCounter.

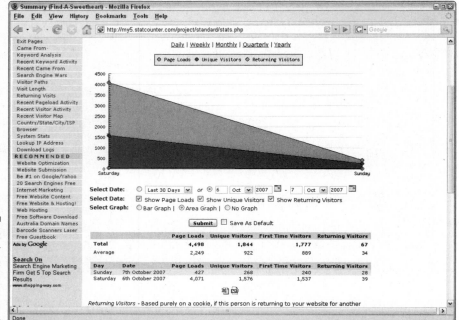

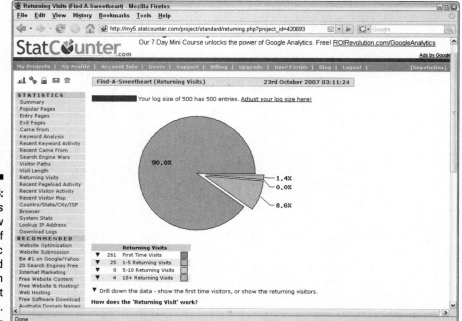

A lack of standards

Currently, no official standards are governing the world of server logs and Web statistics. No large corporations tell anyone how things should be done, what terminology should be used, or how statistics should be analyzed. The world of Web stats has, more or less, grown organically, and a set of rules has built from the community around the analysis of server logs.

There can be a lot of inconsistency in what's measured in different software tools and how it's measured. For instance, I commonly use two different programs to measure unique visitors on my own blog, and the two software programs rarely agree about what that number is. It's a frustrating fact of life. (Don't tell anyone, but I tend to use the bigger number.)

Knowing this, you might want to consider using at least a couple of Web statistics tools (I talk about some options later in this chapter) and comparing the results you are getting. Different Web analytics software treats server logs differently, and some software is certainly better than others. Most often, users find packages that create charts and graphs that represent their data are a better solution. Because no hard and fast rules exist, you're free to do research into what packages will work better for you.

Errors

Most stat software tracks *errors,* instances when your visitors get an actual error message when they try to do something on your site or when they try to view a page that doesn't exist anymore (or never did).

Track your error logs to find out where visitors are having problems and be sure to fix the errors.

Getting Web Stats

Many statistics software applications for tracking Web traffic are available for installation on your blog. But before you get too carried away, check to see whether your blog host offers Web traffic — tracking software or gives you access to your server logs.

If stat software is part of what your Web host offers you, be sure to review the offerings carefully. You might not need any additional tools, or you might want to supplement the preinstalled tool with one of those discussed in this section, if only to check the accuracy of the numbers you're seeing as much as is possible. Keep in mind that different applications can measure things differently, so the numbers may not be exactly the same.

Some bloggers like to look at the *server logs* for their sites. Server logs are simple text files that Web servers generate in order to keep track of information about who, when, and how a Web server is visited.

Most Web hosts provide access to stat software and server logs through an administrative control panel.

In the following sections, I cover the different services and software available. You should be able to find a service that fits you.

Web stats can be a difficult thing, and you might want to check them daily. But don't forget you have a blog to run, and that requires a concentration on the quality of the content you produce for your community. Try to avoid an obsession over your Web statistics because no amount of tinkering with Web analytics can make your blog popular. Your content is the only thing that will accomplish that.

Choosing hosted statistics software

Like hosted blog software, hosted Web statistics software is managed by the company that has created the software package. Typically, you install the software by adding a chunk of HTML code to your pages that communicates with the hosted software.

Google Analytics

```
www.google.com/analytics
```

In 2005, Google purchased a software package known as Urchin, created by a Web statistics company. Urchin has since been released as the online stats system Google Analytics

Google Analytics has a great interface with many options that you can customize and use to analyze stats to your heart's content. You can do calculations on visitors by using different criteria such as page views and number of visits. The Google Analytics system is free, but it requires a registered Google Account (which is free as well). To use Google Analytics (shown in Figure 15-5), you must be able to place some HTML code into your blog software templates so that it appears on every page you want to track. If you can't access the templates, this won't be an option for you.

StatCounter

```
www.statcounter.com
```

StatCounter is a free hosted statistics tracker and is easy for new users, thanks to good organization and explanation in the control panel.

Figure 15-5:
Use Google
Analytics to
check out
where your
traffic
comes from.

After setting up your site in StatCounter (see Figure 15-6), you must insert StatCounter HTML code into your blog templates so that it can track everything from what terms your readers used in search engines to a Google Maps interface of where your traffic originates.

Site Meter

```
www.sitemeter.com
```

Site Meter has been around since the beginning of stats tracking on the Web. This tool provides you with basic details about each visitor that comes to your blog and shows you what the visitor does while there, even down to what page they are on when they leave.

Site Meter (see Figure 15-7) has two levels of service: the free basic edition and the professional edition. The professional edition provides more information than the basic setup and grants to access to a longer history of your statistics, but the free edition is a good starting point for new bloggers. The professional edition starts at $6.95 a month.

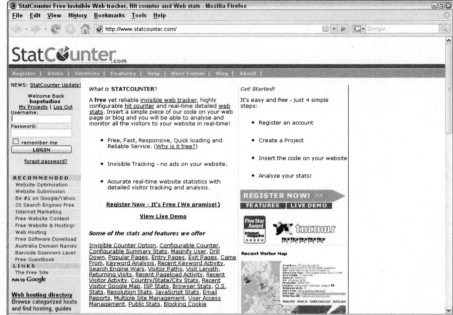

Figure 15-6:
StatCounter
is a free
online tool
for tracking
page views
and visitors.

Figure 15-7:
Site Meter
offers two
levels of
statistics
tracking.

Choosing installable statistics software

Web analytics software that you can install on your Web server and manage on your own is called *installable* software. If you want to use a specific analytics package your host doesn't normally provide, look into whether you can install software on your server. Some hosts can give you suggestions and may even assist you installing analytics software.

Installed software is usually used to measure the same kinds of things as hosted statistics software, but does so by analyzing log files stored on your Web site, rather than gathering information as a visitor hits your site. Some Web developers feel that these numbers are therefore more accurate, but that's a hotly debated opinion.

When you sign up for a Web-hosting package, the Web host probably has some kind of Web statistics available to you. These packages can range from open source software to custom, home-grown solutions.

Be sure to check the technical requirements for the package that you want to install to be sure that your server works with it.

Webalizer

```
www.mrunix.net/webalizer
```

Webalizer is an open source application that you install on your server. Because it's free to use, many Web hosts offer it as part of their standard Web hosting packages. Originally created in 1997, Webalizer lets you track hits, page views, geographical origin of your traffic, and other data.

Webalizer generates easy-to-read pages showing traffic broken down by month (see Figure 15-8), but you can also see traffic figures by day and even by hour. All the usual suspects are here, from page views to unique visitors to the top referring sites.

AWStats

```
http://awstats.sourceforge.net
```

AWStats is another popular Web statistics analyzer that you can install on your Web server. It has features that allow you to track visitors but also streaming media, e-mail, and FTP transactions on your server. AWStats requires the Perl programming language to be installed on your Web server to operate. (Most Web servers support this requirement.)

AWStats (see Figure 15-9) generates graphs and other visual indicators about the activity of your visitors month by month, letting you see the region and cities where traffic originates, the operating systems, and browsers used by your visitors, among many other measurements.

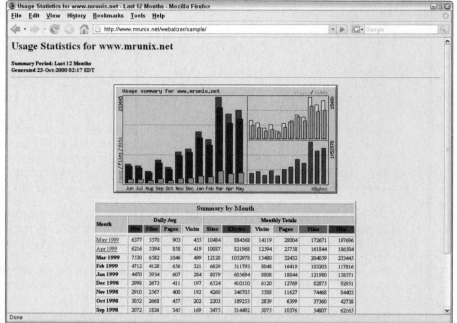

Figure 15-8:
This sample report from Webalizer is color-coded to show usage by month.

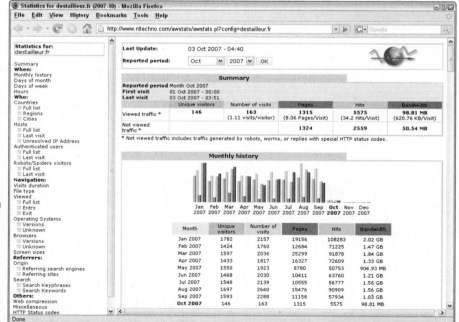

Figure 15-9:
AWStats offers an easy-to-read presentation of Web statistics.

Mint

`www.haveamint.com`

Mint is a recent entrant into the installable software field, and offers the usual suspects: new and returning visitors, the sites they get to your site from, search terms they use to find you, and so on. Mint also looks really cool, and you'll enjoy using the graphs and charts it produces.

A Mint license costs $30.

Finding Out What Others Are Saying

Watching the behavior of your site's visitors is important, but you can also find out a lot by monitoring mentions of you, your blog, and your topic on the Web (especially on your competitor's blogs!). Watching what's going on within the blogosphere is a huge task. You could spend hundreds of dollars to have others do it for you, or you could check out some of the simple tools available on the Web.

Blogosphere tools available to you include the following:

- ✔ **E-mail notifications:** Receive updates via e-mail about content or topics you want to keep up with.
- ✔ **RSS watch lists:** Keep current on topics using your favorite newsreader software. (Read more about RSS in Chapter 11.)

You can use these tools in a variety of ways by doing random manual searches and installing software designed to display Web information on your desktop.

The power of RSS and the syndication of news and blog feeds become apparent when you start trying to monitor certain phrases and keywords. RSS is one of the best ways to track what people are saying about your blog and about topics that you're interested in.

Google Alerts

`www.google.com/alerts`

Google Alerts (see Figure 15-10) are e-mail notifications that are sent to you based on keyword searches of Google's search system. Sign up for an account and then create an alert by entering keywords you want to be notified about.

In order to receive any e-mail from the Google Alerts system, you need to enter some keywords.

1. **Go to `http://www.google.com/alerts`.**

2. **Enter the keywords you want to be notified about in the Search terms box.**

3. **Select the type of Web content you want included in your search. Your options are news, blogs, web, comprehensive, video, and groups.**

4. **Select how often you want to be notified: once a day, as-it-happens, or once a week.**

5. **Type your e-mail address into the e-mail field.**

6. **Click Create Alert.**

    Google begins to track your search and send you e-mails as you requested.

When a keyword gets a hit, an e-mail is sent to you with the link. Automatic keyword searches can be done for all Web sites, blogs, video, and Google Groups, or a combination of all four.

These alerts work best when you create a specific and detailed search. Think about how you can refine your search to keep your results to a manageable number. For instance, if you want to track a particular news topic, use several keywords instead of just one.

Figure 15-10:
Google Alerts sends you e-mail if it hits your keywords in searches.

Do use:

```
knitting sock yarn hand-dyed
```

Don't use:

```
socks
```

TIP

Set Google Alerts to search for your name, your blog name, and any keywords you want to be aware of. Use these alerts to find out when people are talking about you, your blog, or the topics you're covering.

Technorati

```
www.technorati.com
```

Technorati is a search engine that focuses its energy on blogs and does it very well. Technorati publishes information periodically that gives people who use its service a "status" of the blogosphere. In its analysis, Technorati updates people on the number of blogs that are officially tracked, what trends in conversations have been ongoing throughout a given time period, and what the growth rate of blog technology adoptions has been.

To create watch lists of certain blogs, keywords, and names, you must sign up for a Technorati account (this is free). Once you are a member, you may create your watch lists.

1. **Log in to your Technorati account.**
2. **Click on Watchlists link in the navigation bar.**
3. **Under Add to Your Watchlist, type the search terms or URL you want to track.**
4. **Click Add.**

   A watchlist with results appears.
5. **Click the blog post you want to read.**

You can manage your watch list using the handy menu items on each watch list. Use these to view all the results for the watch list, open the list in a pop-up window, subscribe to the watch list via RSS, or remove the watch list. You can add more watch lists by repeating these steps.

My Watchlist for my name (susannah gardner) is shown in Figure 15-11.

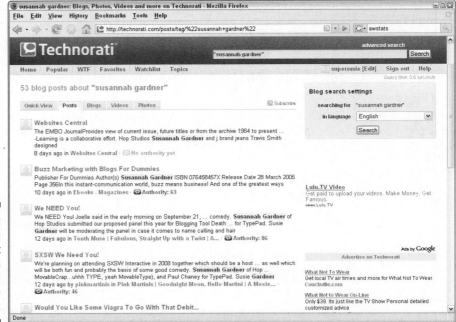

Figure 15-11:
Technorati
lets you set
Watchlists
of terms you
want to
track.

One of the really nice services offered by Technorati is the ability to subscribe to an RSS feed of your Watchlist terms. Anytime you see the small RSS
icon next to the word Subscribe at the top of your Watchlist, you can add the
feed to whatever newsreader you normally use to track your Watchlist as you
read other blogs!

Chapter 16

Making Mad Mad Money

- -

In This Chapter

▶ Checking out the advertising options

▶ Blogging for money

▶ Putting products on your blog with affiliate programs

- -

Advertising on your blog has never been easier. Many different advertising systems offer bloggers a free way to place ads on their blogs, and businesses have picked up on the fact that blog advertising can really work. Putting an ad or two on your blog is an easy way to earn a little money doing something you enjoy. You can turn a pretty penny and even earn a living from advertising.

Ever since Web sites came into existence, there have been online advertisements. From the first Web banners of the early Internet to today's contextual advertising systems, ads have run the gamut from wildly successful to being a waste of precious bandwidth.

In some cases, this has more to do with the readers than anything else — on some topics, blog readers are willing to look at ads and even click them, but audiences on other blogs just don't have the patience to wade through advertisements that clutter their reading pleasure. So rule one is to know what your audience can tolerate before you accept a big sponsorship!

Turning your blog into a retirement savings plan won't happen overnight, and the addition of advertisements to the average blog shouldn't be taken lightly. It all requires planning, patience, and a faith and trust in your readership. Depending on your readership, you might need to request input from them about the advertisements you choose to employ on your blog.

Finding Out How Advertising Works

Banner ads (rectangular ads usually placed along the top of a site) once dominated ad slots on the Web, but they have become less important as people have learned to tune them out. Then animated and blinking advertisements generated a few clicks, but ultimately managed to generate a massive backlash. Many of these moving, beeping, and blinking ads just proved to be an irritant rather than a successful advertising method.

Today's contextual advertising tools are actually intelligent; ads are matched by subject to the words and phrases you use on your blog. Generally, the result is ads that better suit your readers' interests, making them more likely to click the ads.

The first thing to do is decide whether your blog is meant for an advertising campaign. Many blogs can benefit greatly from advertisements. However, you should think about a few things before diving in:

- ✔ Does your blog have a design that's ready for ads?
- ✔ Does your blog software support the advertising system you've chosen?
- ✔ Will advertising earn you any money?
- ✔ Will your audience put up with ads?

Answering these questions isn't easy; in fact, it might be impossible to do unless you jump in and try using some advertising and observe the results.

Planning for advertising

You can use several kinds of advertising methods to turn a blog into a place where you can make a tidy profit. The last few years have seen an explosion of companies that want a piece of the action in the blogosphere, and these companies have come up with some creative ways to make ads easy to use, simple to implement, and easy on your readers' eyes.

If you're a new blogger or just new to advertising programs, it's easy to latch on to the first advertising system you find and commit to using it. Although this isn't necessarily a bad thing to do, you might want to take a look at some of the different ad systems out there and find out about how advertising tends to work in the blogosphere before you start using ads.

As you do your research, keep in mind that, if you decide to make that leap into monetizing your blog, you should choose software that allows you to control your advertising so that it doesn't overwhelm the blog audience you worked so hard to build.

A multitude of advertising companies offer bloggers simple solutions to monetize Web sites. Most of these programs work in similar ways but have unique delivery methods. Advertising programs range from text-only ads to flashy animations and even full-page advertisements that really get your readers' attention! As a blogger, choosing an advertising program that works for your audience can make the difference between an increase in readers and turning off your existing traffic.

Looking at the formats

You can deliver ads to a blog audience in four different ways. Additional methods are available, but most don't work as well in a blog. The most popular advertisement formats are

- **Text-based ads:** These ads are text-only and feature a link or links to the advertiser's Web site or service. Each ad is very plain, and most advertising systems limit your ability to customize their look and feel.

- **Graphical banner and button ads:** Banner and button ads can be static or animated images. These ads usually have pre-set sizes but can be customized to fit your blog design.

- **RSS ads:** Ads are a new addition to RSS feeds; as the format has taken off with the public, advertisers have jumped on the bandwagon. Such ads can be text or images and are linked to the advertiser's Web site straight from your RSS feed. See how this looks when the RSS feed is viewed in a newsreader in Figure 16-1. If you want to find out more about RSS, see Chapter 11.

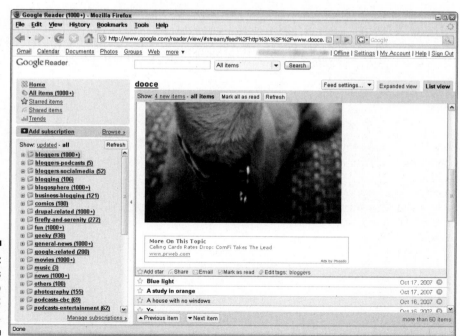

Figure 16-1: Place ads directly into your RSS feed.

✔ **Pop-up ads:** Pop-ups tend to be everyone's least favorite type of ad, but oddly enough, pop-up ads that open in a new window are still quite successful at getting people to click an advertiser's Web site. The readers might be fairly irritated by the time they get to the site, but they do click.

The Interactive Advertising Bureau makes recommendations each year about ad sizes and standards. You might find the recommendations useful in planning for ads. Visit www.iab.net/standards/adunits.asp to see what the options are.

Most ad programs today — with the exception of sponsorships — use contextual advertising that coordinates ad display with related editorial content. So, a blog post about skiing might be accompanied by ads for ski shops and resorts. A blogger who posts about say, blogging, ends up with ads for blog software and tools.

Contextual ad systems search your blog for keywords that match products that the advertisers have in their inventory. These ads are then displayed beside the topic keywords and, in theory, apply in the context of the Web page they appear on.

Contextual ads about blog polling tools appear on the Smiley Cat Web Design blog, as shown in Figure 16-2.

Figure 16-2: Contextual advertising puts blogging tool ads next to a post on the same subject.

Assessing business models

Money can flow from the advertiser to the blogger in different ways. Always read the terms of service for an ad program, because each advertising company has a different idea of how bloggers should be compensated. The usual business models for online ads are

- **Cost Per Impression:** In this model, advertisers pay for the number of times a page displaying the ad is loaded. The advertiser might prefer that a reader click its ad, but it recognizes that simply being visible on a blog also has value.

- **Cost Per Click or Pay Per Click:** The blogger makes money only when a reader clicks an ad and goes to the advertiser's Web site. This type of ad is very common in contextual ad programs, as well as on search engines in the sponsored results section.

- **Cost Per Action:** In this case, the advertiser pays only when the reader actually takes action after having viewed and clicked the ad on the blog. This can be anything from signing up to receive more information to actually purchasing a product.

- **Sponsorships:** When an advertiser wants to be actively associated with the content of your blog, it might offer to sponsor the blog or some part of the blog. A sponsorship is usually played up with premium advertisements and exclusive ad placement, and it's sometimes even thanked in the editorial content of the site.

Lots of bloggers have had the same great idea about the ads on their blogs: "I'll just click on these myself and send my Cost Per Click rates through the roof! I'll make millions!" Unfortunately, the advertising companies have figured out this little scheme, and they refer to it as *click fraud*. Advertisers spend good money to have their ads displayed, and companies that run advertisement programs go out of their way to make sure that clicks on those ads are good clicks. Make sure you understand what happens if you click ads on your own blog before you do it — some programs penalize or even ban bloggers that engage in click fraud.

Getting Advertising Going

Most bloggers choose to incorporate advertising programs by signing up with a company that serves as a middle man between the blogger and the advertiser. This company typically negotiates rates with the advertiser, tracks ad performance, and pays the blogger for advertising placement.

Although you can cut out the middle man and sell your own ad space, many bloggers find that the negotiation, tracking, and technical overhead isn't how they really want to be spending their time.

But even the most time-pressed blogger is likely to find the strength to listen when an advertiser contacts a blogger directly and offers to sponsor the blog. These arrangements are typically more lucrative for the blogger (and the advertiser, presumably) and are negotiated on a case-by-case basis depending on the audience, product, blog traffic, and other factors.

With your planning done, it's time to put ads on your blog. The good — and bad — news is that you have dozens of options to choose from. In this section, I show you a few well-regarded advertising programs to consider.

Google AdSense

www.google.com/adsense

AdSense is Google's contextual advertising program. This program is really the biggest player in the contextual advertising space. When you sign up for Google AdSense, you choose what kinds of ads you want on your blog, from text to images to videos. You can see examples of the Google AdSense formats in Figure 16-3.

Figure 16-3:
Google AdSense puts advertisers on your blog and money in your pocket.

Advertisers pay Google money when your blog visitors click the advertisements displayed beside your content, and those payments are distributed back to you. Successful bloggers with lots of traffic are able to earn a living from Google AdSense, but income varies greatly depending on the size of your audience and the how well your blog topics match the advertisers who contract with Google.

Yahoo! Publisher Network

`http://publisher.yahoo.com`

Yahoo! Publisher Network (shown in Figure 16-4) is another advertising system that displays ads in a contextual manner. You can customize the look of the ads that appear on your blog to blend in better by selecting color, size, and layout options. The Yahoo! Publisher Network also allows you to filter out ads from potential competitors so they don't appear on your site.

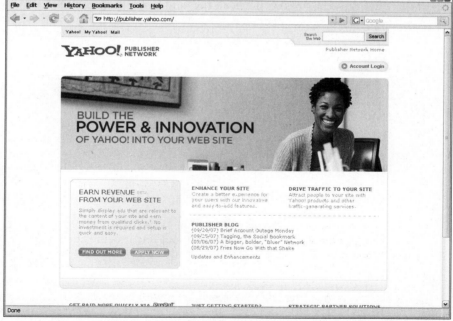

Figure 16-4:
You can filter out your competitor's ads if you use Yahoo! Publisher Network.

Text Link Ads

www.text-link-ads.com

Based in New York, Text Link Ads is one of the most popular and recognizable advertising systems that bloggers use. Designed with blogs in mind, these ads are a slightly different option than contextual advertising programs that try to relate ads specifically to your content. Instead, you get only simple links that you preapprove, which are related but much lower-key in look and feel.

You can display Text Link Ads on the same page with Google AdSense, Yahoo! Publisher Network, and other contextually served ads.

AdBrite

www.adbrite.com

AdBrite is an advertising marketplace similar to the others mentioned. Bloggers can choose between text and banner ads or full-page *interstitials* (splash pages containing a full-page advertisement). Interstitials are high-paying ads shown only once per visitor per day; they aren't as intrusive as they seem.

Putting Ads on Your Blog

How do these ads get onto your Web site? Most often, the programs you sign up for provide you with a bit of code that you insert into your Web site templates. Some programs have step-by-step instructions for popular blog software packages, but be aware that you might need to consult your blog's documentation for help with putting your ads where you want them.

Step one is to decide just where you want the ads on your page. The best thing to do when you're thinking about introducing ads into your blog design is to make sure the ads aren't overpowering.

Don't damage your reputation or credibility by overloading the site with ads or by associating ads too closely with your blog posts and content. Aside from pop-up ads, nothing is more annoying than having a blog design that's created around ads rather than a blog that has been designed to include ads.

At the same time, you need to place ads in spots where they will be seen. Bloggers have discovered a few truths about ads, although your results might differ:

✔ **Ads at the top and bottom of each page do poorly.** Advertisements along the top or the bottom of a blog are often ignored and rarely viewed because the site content is usually in the middle of the screen. As users scroll their windows to view site content, these top and bottom advertisements might never be seen at all.

✔ **Ads in the sidebars perform well but might interfere with navigation.** The left side of the Web site is a traditional place for ads. However, it's also a prime place for navigation tools and your Web site might require that such tools be located higher than the ads you wish people to view. As for the right side, not only are navigation tools sometimes placed here, but the content tends to flow on the left side of the screen, which means that some users might move windows about and miss these right-side advertisements entirely.

✔ **Ads within the content itself get clicked.** Some blogs have their ads placed within the content, and this works really well because visitors don't miss the ads. But, you need to be careful when you use advertising within your content. Remember that the content should be king, not the ad.

Try out ads in different places on your blog and see how your audience reacts, as well as how your earnings do. You might need to try several different locations before you hit on one that balances your readers' needs with your advertisers'.

Putting Ads in Your RSS Feeds

There's a debate around whether RSS feeds should contain ads. RSS has been used as a way to share information and only recently has it become a place to put advertisements. You might want to consider using them because many of your blog readers might be using RSS readers to consume the content of your blog.

RSS ads are simply banner or text advertisements that appear below or above the content displayed in your RSS reading program. The ads are usually smaller than typical banner ads you would find on the average Web site because they are meant to fit within the RSS feed.

Pheedo

www.pheedo.com

Pheedo (see Figure 16-5) is the pioneering company that began the feed advertising industry. In 2003, two people thought up an idea to place advertisements

Figure 16-5:
Pheedo was
the first
company to
create the
technology
to place ads
in feeds.

in RSS feeds and started Pheedo. Their business has grown into one of the largest advertising networks for RSS.

Feedvertising

www.text-link-ads.com/feedvertising

Feedvertising (see Figure 16-6) is a department of Text Link Ads that places ads within the RSS feed of your Web site. Feedvertising uses a similar system to its site-based ads for its RSS feed ads.

FeedBurner ads for blogs and feeds

www.feedburner.com/fb/a/advertising

FeedBurner, a Google-owned company, is full of feed experts. They have a program called FeedBurner for Blogs and Feeds that allows you to control the ads that go onto your blog and blog feeds. They have a significant ad network established.

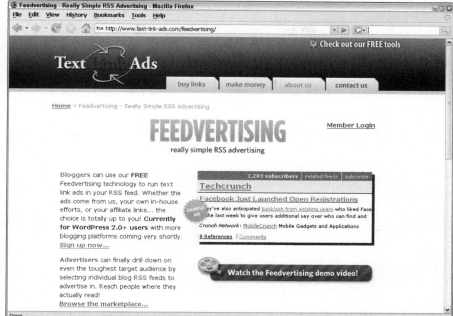

Figure 16-6:
Feedvertising
is an easy
way to put
ads in your
Web feed.

Getting Paid to Post

Being paid to post can mean a couple of different things. For many bloggers, it means getting paid in money or products to post a review or mention a company on a personal blog. But blogging for money can also lead you down the path of the professional blogger, where you write posts for other blogs.

Placing products on your blog

Some bloggers believe that getting paid to post about products or companies is a bad thing. However, blogging is hard work. Why would it be bad to get paid to talk about a product every once in a while?

Some bloggers fear that the influence of advertisers might take over the traditionally independent voice of the blogosphere. When advertisers offer money to bloggers to praise their products and services in a blog, it might not result in an honest review of the business. So, if you're paid to post information about someone else, make sure that you retain your ability to post your own honest opinion. You might even want to consider starting an additional blog to showcase content that you're being paid to produce as opposed to the content contained in your original blog.

Above all, let your readers know about products you've been paid to post about. You can head off accusations of deception.

You can either set up your own system or find a service that allows you to connect with companies that want to have their products or services advertised on blogs.

Sponsored Reviews

www.sponsoredreviews.com

Sponsored Reviews (shown in Figure 16-7) is a company that connects advertisers with bloggers who are willing to write reviews about the advertisers' products and services. This company is forthright with the expectation that you as a blogger will offer an honest opinion and even give constructive criticism about the products its advertisers create.

Figure 16-7:
Sponsored Reviews pays you to review products and services.

Pay Per Post

www.payperpost.com

Pay Per Post is a company that helps bloggers get paid for creating and publishing advertiser-sponsored content. The theory behind the company is that if you're a blogger, you'll inevitably write about some products you've used in the past or are currently using. Pay Per Post believes you should be paid for those kinds of posts.

Pay Per Post, shown in Figure 16-8, works somewhat like a job board where you accept bids to write about a certain product or service. The amount of money you get paid is determined by the advertiser and the amount of traffic you report.

Figure 16-8:
Pay Per Post pairs up bloggers with products they want to endorse.

Blogging professionally

Another way to offer your blogging services to those who might want them is to make a small business for yourself as a professional blogger. Believe me; companies are often looking for competent writers they can hire to contribute content to their blogs. This decision might take time away from your personal blog, but hopefully additional practice can help you to become a better blogger!

To offer up your service, check the blogger-wanted ads on job boards and see whether you're interested in writing about any topic. Also, be sure to post about your availability on your own blog's sidebar and in your blog. (You can read more about sidebars in Chapter 12.)

Two job sites where you can start your search for blogging jobs are

- **Jobs.Problogger** (`http://jobs.problogger.net`) is a popular Web site that provides help to bloggers so they can monetize their Web sites. The job board is highly active, and it's a popular place for blogger jobs to appear.

- **Performancing** (`www.performancing.com`) is a Web resource that was established as "a home for professional bloggers." If you want to find out job postings for new bloggers, you can check out their job posting forums.

When you begin blogging professionally, you're expected to keep track of any progress you make. Typically, this includes tracking either the number of posts that you create or the number of site visitors over a period of time. You can organize this information in various ways, but the tracking needs to prove that some interaction occurred between you and your readers.

Tying in Affiliate Marketing

If you ever blogged about a product you really like and just knew that you were helping the company who makes the product make a sale, you can now make some money from that sale with affiliate marketing.

Popular retailers have set up affiliate marketing programs, most notably Amazon. You sign up with an affiliate program, and when you blog about one of its products, you include a piece of identifying information that the company gives you. You earn cash when readers of your blog click the product and buy it.

If you find yourself blogging about items others might buy as a result of your recommendation, check to see whether the company that makes the product has an affiliate program and get yourself signed up.

In short order, your blog can contain links to books, DVDs, or other products that provide you with a commission on each product bought with your identification number.

Amazon Associates Program

`www.amazon.com/associates`

Amazon is the most recognized affiliate program available, and it's arguably one you're likely to benefit from using because many bloggers mention books and DVDs they've enjoyed.

Amazon Associates works by letting you create specially formatted links you can use on your blog to drive traffic to the Amazon Web site. Anything that gets purchased by a visitor who clicks your link earns you a percentage of the sale as a referral fee.

LinkShare

`www.linkshare.com/affiliates/affiliates.shtml`

LinkShare is another affiliate program that calls its program a *pay-per-action* marketing network. You can place ads, both text and graphical ads, on your blog and make money from any sales that come from the reader sales.

Seeking Sponsorships

Sponsorships are advertisements by companies that have either requested to be an advertiser or you have sought out to advertise on your site. Such sponsorship can mean one of two things:

✔ Sponsors might pay you to put their ads on your Web site.

✔ Sponsors might simply provide you with free goods or services in return for advertising on your Web site.

You need to think carefully about whether to take on a sponsor because not all sponsorships are equal:

✔ **Prominent placement or exclusivity:** A sponsor is different from the usual ad on your Web site because sponsors like a prominent placement on your blog — possibly including the exclusive right to advertise on your blog.

✔ **Acknowledgment:** You might be asked to use the phrase "This blog sponsored by . . ." or some variation of it to let your readers know that your blog writing is being funded by a specific company. Thanking your sponsor occasionally isn't a bad idea either.

✔ **Time commitment:** Sponsorships often run for a set length of time, usually much longer than a standard ad would run. Sponsorships of several months to a year aren't unheard of.

Getting sponsors interested in your blog is probably the hardest advertising strategy, though it's also the most lucrative. To find a sponsor, you need to "sell" your blog from the design to the content. You need to make the sponsor want to post its advertisements on your site — not someone else's. Keeping your blog dynamic, on topic, and written well is critical when you're seeking sponsors.

As hard as it is, however, one of the best things sponsors do for your blog is legitimize your work. Many bloggers might be viewed by the public as just "another blogger" within the static of the Internet. But, with sponsors that believe in what you're doing, you can attract other professional relationships, like speaking engagements or press interviews. Being regarded as an authority is always helpful.

Urbanmoms.ca Kitchen Party (`http://urbanmoms.typepad.com/kitchen_party`) is an example of a sponsored blog. This site for Canadian women who like to cook (and who have kids) is "hosted" by Cuisinart. Cuisinart gets some billing in the blog's header and in one of the sidebars.

Negotiating a sponsorship experience

Sponsors can be demanding advertisers. Unlike developing your own monetization plan, sponsorships can change the way you advertise on your site. Some sponsors demand exclusivity — that means they're the only business of that type on your site, and you might have to turn away other potential sponsors. Others might demand that you always write about their product or services in a positive way. It can be a true balancing act. But the rewards can be worth the work.

Here's my recipe for a successful sponsor/blogger relationship:

✔ **Be clear on your topic.** Know who you are and what it is you're writing about. Nothing is worse than having a blog that isn't clear about its subject when you're seeking sponsorship. Sponsors want a very clear idea about the content you're creating and about what you can do for them.

Keeping your blog on topic is more important when sponsors are actively using their brand identities on your site. Make sure that they're aware of everything you might write about and so that there are no surprises or objections to editorial content.

✔ **Be clear on what you're promising.** Be sure both you and your sponsor understand exactly what influence and control — if any — the partnership offers the advertiser. You should be very clear about how you'll handle both content and advertising placement of the sponsor; the advertiser should be up front about its expectations of you.

✔ **Know your audience.** Educating yourself on your audience is critical if you're seeking paying sponsors for your blog. With increased sponsorship, it becomes imperative that you address the question of who your audience is. You need to document the activity in your community, track your comments, and analyze the information from your Web statistics. (Check Chapter 15 for information on Web statistics and traffic software.)

Create a report of your statistics to prove to any sponsors that you have the numbers that you claim you do. Don't use any guesswork when creating this report — your sponsors want to see solid numbers with data to back up your claims. Creating statistics reports is often required for sponsorship arrangements; the simple fact is that if you want to make money, you have to do some data gathering.

Another way to collect data from your audience is in the form of contests, polls, and other interactive experiences. There's no harm in asking your audience members who they are — and if you approach it in a professional manner, they might be happy to reveal a little bit about themselves.

✔ **Banner placement and visual cues.** If you've been accepting advertising for a while, you already have a good idea where ads appear to good effect on your site, and you probably also know what types of ads work best. One good thing about this is you can demonstrate the benefits of placement and ad types to any potential sponsors.

However, if you've never had ads on your site when you first seek a sponsor, be prepared to offer some ideas and suggestions for adequately highlighting the sponsor's ads and branding. Providing a design mock-up or some kind of visual representation is a good idea. Or you might even consider creating a demo Web site that actually shows the ads in the positions and formats you think will work.

✔ **Limit other monetization methods.** Some bloggers find that if they use other advertising systems at the same time as a sponsor, it dilutes the effectiveness of the sponsorships. Many sponsors ask to be the exclusive advertiser on your site or that you limit what other kinds of advertising and advertisers are used while they sponsor you. This isn't unreasonable, especially if you have a lucrative sponsorship agreement that compensates you for the loss of those ad spots.

Setting boundaries

Jumping to the professional level in the blogging world poses a few potential pitfalls and requires ongoing reinvention on your part. Set up and keep to some simple rules about what your professional limits and intentions are, and don't be afraid to write those down in a document you share with sponsors and your readers.

You also need to be ready to say no. Some sponsors might want more than you're willing to give. It can be a great thing to earn some money from your blog, but don't forget the reason you're blogging in the first place. Your blog is your territory and not your sponsor's. You are renting the sponsor space on your site, access to your audience. You aren't signing up for someone to tell you what to do. You already have parents for that!

Don't jump at every offer that comes in the door. It might be hard to do this when you're seeking your first sponsor, but you need to maintain a high level of professionalism — not just for yourself, but also for your audience. Just as you protect your audience from nasty comments and spam, you need to be sure that you give them an appropriate experience with your sponsors and advertisers. Protect the integrity of your blog and avoid sponsors that demand more time, editorial control, or space on your blog than you're willing to give.

Accepting Gifts, Not Obligations

Many companies offer news media access to products and services in order to generate press attention, and increasingly, bloggers are being offered the same goodies. After all, some blog topics are so specific that companies absolutely know that the blog's readers will be interested in their products. For example, a blogger who writes about cell phones might be targeted by a mobile phone company and be offered a free product or money in exchange for some kind of online review or feedback.

This kind of exchange can be a tricky situation because some bloggers regard the gift as some kind of bribe, or obligation to write something positive about the product in question.

In fact, that isn't the case. I know bloggers who accept products for review on the condition that they will say what they really think about it, and most companies are perfectly satisfied with this kind of arrangement. In addition, most bloggers who do these kinds of reviews are very up front with their readers about how they obtained the product in question and what agreement there is with the company that provided it.

If you're getting these offers, you would probably benefit from establishing such a policy. Most bloggers would agree that they don't want to be seen as taking bribes or favors from companies that just want the bloggers to say nice things about them. Your policy needs to lay out how you plan to deal with such situations.

Here are a few things to consider when you start to get product review offers:

- ✔ **Be clear about what you will do with the product.** Be clear with the product maker that you won't write a positive review if it isn't warranted. Make sure you're very specific about what you'll provide in return for the gift (if anything).

- ✔ **Be prepared to return gifts.** A lot of bloggers, especially those who are incredibly geeky, would love to receive a gift from a company with the latest and hottest product. However, if the demands are unreasonable or don't match with the blogger's vision, perhaps the right choice is to return the gift.

- ✔ **Donate what you receive.** One way to avoid an ugly scene with your audience or any sponsors of your blog is to take the gifts you receive, write your review, and then give the item away. You can send them to your favorite charity or hold a contest for your audience. This generates all kinds of goodwill from your community while avoiding any accusations of bias.

Keep to the core of what it is that makes your blog great. If you get an offer of a free product, think about it first and don't accept it right away. You can even go to your community members and see what they think if you require some advice. It really depends on you.

A Final Word of Warning

Advertising is a hard game, and the rules are always changing. If you make a dollar or two in the first few months of posting advertisements on your site, you're ahead of the game. But be careful, and be mindful of your audience. It isn't uncommon for blogs to lose readers and influence thanks to being overwhelmed with advertisements.

Don't make your blog a destination for ads; maintain it as a destination for blogging and the best content that you can create.

Chapter 17

Blogging for Companies

As a business owner or entrepreneur, you're probably wondering whether blogging can help you be more financially successful or allow you to promote your company in some way. Many of today's technically savvy businesses have started blogs and found them to be terrific tools for reaching out to customers, generating buzz about a service or product, building goodwill, or just informing customers about what they're up to.

If you're thinking about adding a blog to your outreach efforts but aren't entirely confident that it will be worth the time and effort, you're not alone. For many companies, it can be difficult to see the value in blogging. Some professionals worry about diverting time away from more crucial workplace tasks, whereas others worry about opening themselves up for public criticism.

And the truth is that even though blogging can be a really incredible tool for a business, it isn't right for *every* business. Nonetheless, in this chapter, I do my best to persuade you that blogging can work for you and your company, whether you're a lone-wolf entrepreneur just starting out or a Fortune 500 executive with more marketing staff than you know what do with.

If this chapter piques your interest, check out my book *Buzz Marketing with Blogs For Dummies* (Wiley). The book covers in depth what I can cover only briefly in this chapter.

Putting Blogs to Work for Your Business

A stigma still lingers around blogs. Many people still think of a blogger as a pimple-faced teenager who sits in his pajamas all day writing excruciatingly boring diary posts about what he had for breakfast. Blogs, for lots of folks, are equated with the worst kind of narcissistic navel-gazing. Those blogs do exist, of course, but the reality is so much more than that. Hundreds of non-profit organizations, small business owners, consultants, newspapers, and schools have moved into the blogosphere.

Why? Blogs are simple to set up, easy to publish, and have a proven track record for increasing search engine traffic to a Web site. For a company where time is of the essence and accessibility is a necessity — show me a company where these things aren't a priority, and I'll eat my hat — blogs are a low investment way to accomplish a lot. Don't believe me? Then perhaps you'll believe General Motors, McDonald's, Microsoft, Amazon, *The New York Times,* and Southwest Airlines; for all these companies, blogs are now an important addition to their business practices.

For a business or organization, you can use blog software to release company public-relations documents to the public, or you can go further and introduce blogs as part of your external communications to your customers and poten-tial customers. Some companies use blogs internally to coordinate work group teams or communicate across distances. Here are a few of the ways businesses are using blogs:

- ✔ Generating conversation and buzz about the company, its products, or services in the online space
- ✔ Reaching out with information and support to current customers, even resolving issues traditionally handled by phone customer service lines
- ✔ Creating new pathways to interact with the public about an industry or issue, including gathering feedback and input to guide future product development
- ✔ Defusing negative criticism or press by publicly addressing problems
- ✔ Demonstrating expertise and experience to potential customers
- ✔ Directly driving sales or action
- ✔ Collaborating across teams, branches, regions, or staggered shifts

When it comes to business, the main thing that a business blogger should consider is that blog software, implemented properly, can allow companies to improve their communications and organization with very little overhead. In some cases, blogs have even saved businesses money by delivering docu-ments and data online that was previously delivered via snail mail.

Businesses haven't been the only beneficiaries, either. Customers have bene-fited from increased access to news, information, support, and dialogue with companies with blogs.

Making blogs work for you can be simple if you have a communication strategy that's flexible and can evolve as your blog takes off. Blogs can generate sales, establish strong communication directly with customers, and are perceived as a friendly method of making customers happy.

You know blogging is important. You already know that it's a very good way to generate talk about your company. Do you need a little more convincing? Well, check out how some other companies are blogging.

McDonald's

```
http://csr.blogs.mcdonalds.com
```

McDonald's Vice President Bob Langert blogs on Open for Discussion, as shown in Figure 17-1. The blog focuses on the corporation's social responsibility and how McDonald's practices affect others. Langert's goal is to show a "personal perspective" on the issues of health, well being, and how McDonald's can be a part of that.

Figure 17-1: McDonald's VP Bob Langert tackles corporate social responsibility in Open for Discussion.

McDonald's Corporate Responsibility Blog "Open for Discussion" (c) 2007. McDonald's, The Golden Arches Logo and Ronald McDonald House Charities are the registered trademarks of McDonald's Corporation and its affiliates. Used with permission.

Hewlett-Packard

```
www.hp.com/hpinfo/blogs
```

Chances are good that you've owned a Hewlett-Packard product at some point in your computing life. Hewlett-Packard has built computers, printers, cameras, and high-end computer servers for years, building up incredible expertise across a range of consumer products. That knowledge is displayed in the HP blogs, which claim to convey the "unvarnished thoughts of HP employees." Topics range from computers to the Cannes Film Festival to gaming, and the bloggers come from all walks of the company's structure.

Wells Fargo

```
http://blog.wellsfargo.com
```

What could a bank possibly blog about, you ask? Apparently, banks can discuss a whole lot with their customers. Student loans, small business, and stock markets are all topics discussed on the Wells Fargo Blogs site. Wells Fargo Blogs gives multiple contributors a public voice in a variety of blogs from "The Student LoanDown" to "Guided by History."

Microsoft Community Blogs

```
www.microsoft.com/communities/blogs/
```

The Microsoft Community Blogs (shown in Figure 7-2) are one aspect of how Microsoft is reaching out to customers and potential customers. These blogs, written by software and hardware developers give interested readers a behind-the-scenes peek at their favorite products, and a way to interact with the developers.

Sun Microsystems

```
http://blogs.sun.com
```

Sun Microsystems also reaches out to customers using developer blogs. On the blogs, customers can seek out and talk directly to the people involved in the making of a product, giving customers a feeling of involvement and direct access not available from traditional marketing efforts.

It's pretty ingenious when you think about it — put your engineers and programmers to work helping you promote your products and services instead of just creating them!

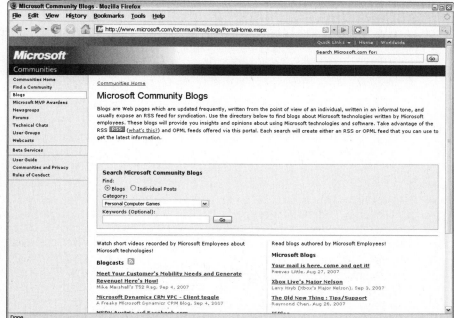

Figure 17-2:
Microsoft's
software
coders talk
about their
work to
customers
and other
employees.

Planning for Business Blog Success

Blogging for a business comes down to planning. Don't let the easiness of getting started with the technical side of blogging seduce you into jumping in without preparing. You need to decide what your goals are, decide who will blog, map out the topics you'll be discussing, and plan how you might integrate direct action or sales.

Setting goals

Before you jump in, you need to set goals that define how you'll know your blog is successful after you launch it. Decide on what you want the blog to help you accomplish. Do you want to replace some of your existing customer service efforts with the blog? Are you launching a new product that needs some publicity? Whatever your direction, plan your purpose prior to launching the blog.

So many things could go into a blog, but you also have a business to run. Decide how much time is acceptable to devote to writing and maintaining your blog. Blogging is part of your business, but it can't take away from time you need to devote to other tasks.

Top five reasons why blogs work with business

Here are just a few reasons that blogs work so well as a business and marketing tool in today's Internet-enabled world:

✔ **Cost:** Lots of blogging software packages are open source and available at no cost, but even those with licensing fees are very reasonably priced. Hosted services can also provide you with an inexpensive platform to begin business blogging.

✔ **Communication:** A blog is an interactive way to communicate with potential and current clients in a direct and informal way. You can chat and communicate about your product or service without pressuring your client. It allows you to make sure your potential or existing clients are given the facts about your product without a heavy handed sales pitch.

✔ **Research:** Many companies are seeking ways to break into new markets and new demographics. Blogging is a method that allows for

collaborative discussion that can help you gather valuable information about how to position products and services.

✔ **Feedback:** Find out what you're doing right and wrong in your blog by just asking outright. Discover how to improve what you're currently doing or how you can deal with existing problems and get points for effort as you do.

✔ **Reputation:** Do away with that "corporate giant" personality most companies can't help but convey. Blogs can put a human, personal face on what has usually been a monolithic surface. If you let the public see how you respect and regard them, you reap the benefits of being honest and open. Smaller businesses and consultancies benefit from the publicity around their name and opinion.

You might choose to define success by

✔ Increasing traffic to your Web site

✔ Reaching a certain number of blog comments on a daily basis

✔ Seeing more conversation about your company/products/services in the media or on other blogs

✔ Earning money from product sales or blog advertising

You might want to define success for your blog in other ways, so don't think any of these are requirements. This is such a flexible medium that your blog might accomplish a goal I can't even imagine!

Choosing a blogger

Businesses have developed two approaches to company blogs: blogs written by one person and those written by multiple people from all over the organization. Either approach is valid as long as everyone posting to the blog has a clear idea of the goals, ideas, and style of the blog.

If you have a blog with multiple contributors, put a single individual in charge of content on a regular basis and encourage others from the organization to chime in when they have something to say. The responsibility for the blog is in one person's hands, but the door is open for wide participation.

Occasional writers are welcome, but don't suddenly give employees brand-new job duties that they can't meet. Having multiple voices in a blog can also help you to convey the culture of your company overall, giving readers a taste of what people at all levels of the organization think about and do.

If you spread the writing around, you might be able to create a blog with a huge amount of content that satisfies a very large readership. The multiple-voice perspective might also awaken ideas in the other writers and generate internal conversations.

Bryght (www.bryght.com) is a content and community management system that offers customers a custom installation of the open source Drupal system for managing Web sites. The staff of Bryght all contribute to a company blog (www.bryght.com/blog) to help keep its customers informed (see Figure 17-3).

No matter who blogs, you must decide internally whether their posts will be vetted before they're posted, and by whom. It's a good idea to have someone who isn't blogging keep an eye on things, just to get a second opinion sometimes.

When you are considering just who should blog on behalf of the company, give some thought to

- **Writing ability:** You need a blogger who is an effective writer, and who also *likes* to write.

- **Position within the company:** Who is the right person to reach out to the public? CEOs offer one perspective, and so do those on the factory floor. Try to match the goals and style of your blog with the right people within your company, and don't be afraid to give unexpected staffers a try. You might be surprised at how interesting readers find a behind-the-curtain approach.

- **Knowledge and expertise:** Be sure you choose a person who has sufficient knowledge and expertise to be interesting and engaging on the subjects being discussed. Preferably, you want people who really know what they're talking about and have information to share.

- **Time commitments:** Choose a blogger with the time to put into the site. Don't overload already busy staff with this new job requirement.

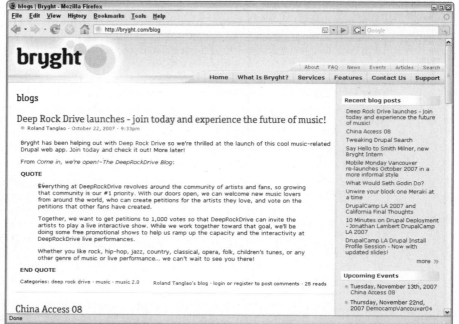

Figure 17-3:
Bryght
staffers put
their two
cents into
the
company
blog.

With a blogger chosen, you have a few more folks to identify. Don't forget to plan who will review comments, deal with spam, and fix technical issues.

Deciding what to write

As you think about topics for the blog, give some thought to how informal or personal your topics and style will be. Although the occasional personal post can help to humanize your blog, don't be tempted down the journaling path: This is a business blog, so look for creative ways of covering your industry.

The goal of many business blogs is to establish — or maybe reestablish — themselves as a leader in their industry. Think about how to demonstrate expertise while staying interesting and readable — you need to show that you know your stuff without becoming a stuffed shirt! Use the blog to persuade people that they should trust you without coming right out and telling people "I'm trustworthy!"

Whoever blogs for your business needs to have a keen understanding of the goals and culture of the company and know how much information can be put on the blog without going too far. Many companies find it helpful to set up some rules about topics that are appropriate for the blog, as well as defining what information should be kept confidential.

Here are some general guidelines to keep in mind for your blog content:

- **Keep it true.** Double-check blog posts for accuracy before making them live. Like a newspaper or any other publisher, you should have a process you follow to make sure you're publishing facts and not fiction. Opinions are okay as long as they're labeled as just that.

- **Keep it relevant and real.** Be as open and honest as you can in your blog. This approach to transparency can make some in your company nervous (hi, corporate lawyer!), but the more successful business blogs provide insight or communication from real people. Some even give the public access to the viewpoints and words of high-level staff the readers would normally never meet or talk to. Furthermore, whoever blogs should be sure to stay on topic and keep posts related to the subject of the blog, no matter how interesting that TV show was last night.

- **Keep it informative and educational.** One problem that many companies encounter when they start to blog is the fact that their blog is (ahem) boring. The information might be great, but if it isn't also interesting to read about, you won't get readers to stick around long. Try to write posts that educate with a light-hearted manner and that focus on information and news that will really be useful to those reading it.

- **Keep it positive.** Steer away from discussing your competition in your blog. If you can say something nice about another company, don't hesitate, but this probably isn't the place for pointing out just what other companies are doing wrong. That kind of approach can turn your blog into a giant argument, scaring off less opinionated customers who might otherwise be interested in your products and services.

- **Keep using keywords.** Part of the plan of a business related blog is to make sure the blog is useful to readers, but for that to work, you have to get readers from the search engine to your blog. Use your knowledge of your industry and topical news to find and use keywords that people are likely to use in search engines.

Pay special attention to the words you use in the titles of your blog posts: Search engines often weight these words most heavily, so it's important to hit the highpoints in your titles. Informative is better than cutesy!

✔ **Keep linking.** Business blogs should also link to related articles and Web sites. These resources can be on your own Web sites, but don't hesitate to point folks to good information that isn't on your Web site. If you're a source for information they need or can get them to the information they need effectively, you won't lose them for long.

Also, look for chances to link the blog to itself! Lots of bloggers are clever about linking to old posts on their own blogs so that new readers are pointed deep within the blog archives. This can increase traffic and also be a great service for your readers.

✔ **Keep posting.** Post on a regular basis and don't stop. There's no absolutely right number of posts per week, but most experts agree that two to three posts a week is enough to keep your blog active and useful without overwhelming your readers. Other bloggers post less frequently, and others post multiple times a day. Do what works for you and for your readers, but be consistent so that your readers know what to expect from you. Having long silences followed by short bursts of posting is a recipe for low readership numbers.

Generating sales or action

Asking potential customers to check out your services after having read something on your blog is always a good strategy. If you see a logical link to a product or service you offer, it only makes sense to let people know. But you need to do more than simply push sales. You tread a fine line between a blog that points out possible purchases along with providing content, and one that isn't anything more than a big ad.

Keep one idea in mind: meet the needs of your readers. If you can put yourself in the shoes of a blog visitor, you might be able to successfully discriminate between a reasonable link to a product sale and one that's too blatant.

Some blogs don't try hard to get people to pull out their wallets. Instead, the blog's purpose might be to gather feedback and get people to participate in an event or content. Again, try to be genuine and inviting, rather than pushy. Get readers involved and invested in your goal.

The Green View blog (www.greenviewblog.com) successfully negotiates between information and sales. This blog, shown in Figure 17-4, keeps readers up to date on news and information about lawn care, tracking the seasons, the environment, and other issues that impact lawns and gardens. When warranted, the blog links to some of the fertilizer products of Greenview Fertilizer, the Pennsylvania-based company that runs the blog.

A lawn care weblog covering everything that makes and keeps your yard beautiful.

the **Green** View

August 29, 2007

Zero Phosphate Fertilizers from Greenview

Do you want a healthy and beautiful green lawn this fall? With Greenview's Zero Phosphate Fall Fertilizer you will get the lawn you always wanted while being "Eco-Friendly" to the environment.

Phosphorous, which young grass needs for root development and seed production, is usually not needed by mature or well established lawns. Before choosing a fertilizer it is a good idea to perform a soil test to determine if your lawn needs additional phosphorous. A recent university study concluded that most home lawns have adequate amounts of phosphorous which is delivered naturally from the break down of leaves and plants.

So what are the benefits of using Greenview's Zero Phosphate Fertilizers with slow release nitrogen? Greenview fertilizers contain a patented slow release technology and are environmentally friendly because they release nutrients slowly over a period of weeks, allowing the grass plant to take up the nutrients. This means more food for the grass and no runoff into

About

The Green View provides news and information to help homeowners get and keep a great looking lawn.

This site is brought to you by Greenview Online.

Sign up for the Greenview Newsletter to receive lawn care tips and offers for your area.

Questions? Comments? Ideas? Email Us

Posts By Topic

Bird Corner

Disease/Insect Control

Equipment

Fertilizer

Gardening

Grass Seed

Greenview Diary

Hear From The Experts

Offers

Get the right fertilizer at the right time, delivered to your front door.

Build a plan and place your order Today! We'll ship when it's time to fertilize.

Spring Fertilizer

Fertilizer 26-4-12

Fertilizer with Crabgrass Preventer 26-4-12

Fertilizer Weed & Feed + Crabgrass Preventer 26-4-6

Weed & Feed w/Crabgrass Preventer 24-0-6

Zero Phosphate Fertilizer 27-0-12

Fall Fertilizer

Done

Figure 17-4:
Get lawn care advice and opportunities to buy fertilizer on the Green View blog.

Delivering with Technology

You might be thinking about how you, as a blogger, can make connections with potential customers using your blog. Words are a great start, but technology can also be your friend! Lots of the standard blog bells and whistles are designed to get people involved or to make it easy for them to consume your blog.

Use the tools in the following sections to get readers to come back to your blog again and again.

Enabling comments

Comments are a double-edged sword for companies who start blogs. On the one hand, they do a great job of starting conversation and interaction. On the other hand, they can be a source of lots of work to keep free of spam or inappropriate conversation. It's tempting for many businesses to start a blog and keep comments turned off, but that cuts out a huge part of the benefit of a blog: hearing from your readers and interacting directly with them.

My advice? Turn on the comments! But take precautions by setting up a good policy on what kinds of comments are deemed acceptable (see Chapter 3), and implement some of the very good spam-fighting tools discussed in Chapter 10.

Creating RSS/Web feeds

Before the advent of Web feeds, blog readers had to remember to visit to the blog periodically to see whether a new entry was posted. This was a dangerous method because it was easy for people to forget to visit. Web feeds, or RSS, give you a way to let people know quickly, easily, and automatically that you have new content available on your blog. Blog visitors simply subscribe to the feed by using a newsreader, which tracks the feed and updates it every time you update the blog, giving instant notification to the reader.

Web feeds, usually formatted as RSS (Really Simple Syndication), are quick and easy to set up. In fact, most blog software packages automatically include an RSS tool, so you can set it up once and never think about it again.

I talk more about Web feeds in Chapter 11, so be sure to read more about setting up these handy tools.

Tagging your posts

Tagging can also help business connections by organizing your blog posts into easy-to-find areas. Tag all posts related to each other by a central theme or topic with the same keyword, or *tag,* and readers can find all of them together easily. By adding tags, you streamline your blog and make it more efficient for readers.

Tags also help your blog become more noticeable in the blogosphere. Social networking sites thrive on the ability to sort content by using tags. FreshBooks, a Toronto-based online invoicing tool, uses tagging in its blog at www.freshbooks.com/blog. Figure 17-5 shows where the tags reside at the bottom of the post. Clicking a tag shows you all the posts on the blog tagged with the same keyword.

Many blogging tools come with tagging tools, but for more on this technology, jump to Chapter19.

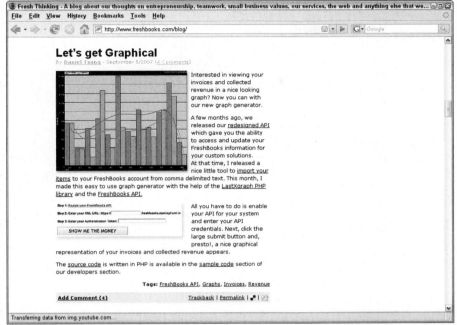

Figure 17-5:
The
FreshBooks
blog sorts
posts by
tagging, or
labeling
them, with
keywords.

Podcasting

Podcasting is a relative newcomer to the blogosphere but is proving to be a powerful blog ally. *Podcasting,* the recording and distribution of audio and video files to subscribers, has a tremendous potential to give your business blog a boost by providing multimedia presentations to your readers. You can add personality and a face to your blog. Posting interviews, discoveries, tutorials, and other adventures your company has had can boost your visibility higher than with only a text blog.

The tech television show The Lab with Leo Laporte (`www.labwithleo.com`) regularly produces a video podcast to solicit input and update viewers between shows. Staffers use the in-house studios to form short video segments, and broadcast them using the program's blog.

You can read more about creating a podcast in Chapter 14.

Starting a wiki

Wikis are collaboratively built Web sites, editable by any visitor. Businesses and organizations have found that the implementation of a wiki can complement blog sites nicely. Blogs allow for comments, but a wiki can provide a little more flexibility because visitors can both post pages and leave updates in a wiki, contributing to everything from documentation to news coverage.

Wikis are terrific collaborative tools, and if you've been trying to figure out a good way to share knowledge within an organization, this might be a great approach. Many companies have found them useful for group learning purposes, like building documentation or setting up procedural tasks. One of the most well-known examples of a successful wiki is Wikipedia (`www.wikipedia.org`), an online encyclopedia to which anyone can contribute content, or edit existing content. It is available in multiple languages.

The Northern Voice blogging conference (`www.northernvoice.ca`) used a wiki to allow attendees to a self-organized event called Moose Camp to create its own event schedule. Figure 17-6 shows the wiki.

Figure 17-6:
The attendees of the Northern Voice Moose Camp day organized sessions using a wiki.

Joining a social network

Adding your company to a variety of social networks can also help to boost your visibility in the blogosphere. Businesses tend to shy away from social networking as a valid form of online advertising, but using these mediums properly can add a viral component to your communication strategy. (*Viral marketing is advertising that consumers actually spread themselves. For example, when you forward a funny video created by a company, you've spread the "virus."*)

Lots of social networks exist, so be sure to choose those that are most pertinent for your industry and approach and not those frequented by 14-year-old girls (unless that suits your business!). LinkedIn (`www.linkedin.com`) and ryze (`www.ryze.com`) are good places to get started.

To get started with LinkedIn:

1. **Use your Web browser to go to `www.linkedin.com`.**

2. **Click the Join Now button.**

    LinkedIn loads the signup screen.

3. **Fill out the required fields, including your name, business information, and where you went to school.**

4. **Click Join LinkedIn.**

    LinkedIn creates an account for you.

    After you're a LinkedIn member, be sure to click the Expand Your Network button at the top right of any page in order to invite colleagues or see who in your address book already uses LinkedIn.

Social bookmarking

When you're blogging, you're likely to seek out reference material on the Web as source material for blog posts. What do you do with those references after you've checked them out and begun to share them?

Unless you choose to share those links in a blog post, it's likely that they live in your bookmark file and never see the light of day again. But that research is great informational material for your readers, who might be just as interested in Web resources for that information as you.

The solution is the use a social bookmarking tool like del.icio.us (`http://del.icio.us`) to share that research. You can post your link list on your blog. You can even ask your audience to review the links and provide you with feedback. del.icio.us helps you track your own favorite Web sites and links, and then to share those with others.

Because you're linking to these resources them from your business site, make sure any links you share are *work safe* — meaning safe to view at work.

Here's how it works:

1. **Sign up for a del.icio.us account at http://del.icio.us.**

2. **Click the Post link, and paste the URL (Web address) of a site you like or use frequently.**

del.icio.us also offers good tools you can install directly into your browser. Then, when you visit a site you like, simply clicking a button adds the site to your del.icio.us list. Visit the Help section and look for the tools area.

del.icio.us adds the link detail page.

3. **Fill out the description field, and tag your link (see Figure 17-7).**

Tagging a link means labeling it with descriptive keywords that might help you find the link later using a search box.

4. **Click Save.**

The link is added to your del.icio.us list.

Be sure to explore the Sharing section of the Help area to find out how to share the resources you gather on your blog or Web site.

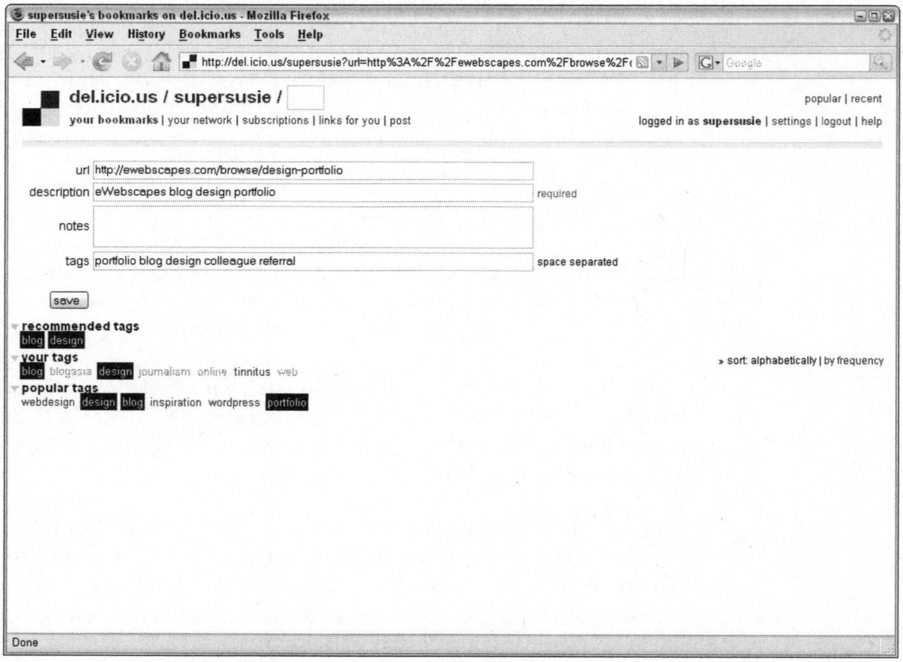

Figure 17-7:
Describe
and tag your
del.icio.us
links to
make them
easy to use.

Advertising on Blogs

Traditional marketing strategies include advertising, and blogs are no exception. But these aren't your father's ads: Blog advertising runs the gamut of everything from text links to full sponsorships.

In the past, taking out a typical advertisement meant that you would go the local newspaper, select an ad size, and choose a section you wanted your ad in. Maybe people saw the ad, maybe they didn't, but you got charged by how many newspapers got printed, not how many sales you made.

Online advertising offers the advertiser more accountability: Because of the way Web sites work, you can track how many times an ad is loaded, when it's clicked, and what the person does after he or she clicks the ad. The result has been a significant decline in the purchase of ad space in printed material, whereas online advertising has grown hugely. You can use several methods to get your name or even your blog URL seen on other Web sites and blogs.

Going contextual

Contextual advertising is the practice in which the advertisements are chosen based on the content being displayed. For example, a blog about candy would have ads for candy, and a blog about movies would show ads for upcoming films. The idea is that if the Web site visitors are interested in the content of the Web site, they're likely to be interested in goods and services related to the topic of the Web site as well, and thus they're more likely to click the ads.

The first major player in the contextual advertising game was Google AdSense. The program was popular from the start, and after a few rocky periods of users abusing the system, it has proven to be quite a money maker for successful bloggers. Many professional bloggers make their living almost entirely on the income received from Google AdSense revenue. Search engine marketer Alexandre Brabant uses Google AdSense on his company Web site, eMarketing 101 (www.emarketing101.net). The Google AdSense program ads appear below the navigation bar of his site, as shown in Figure 17-8.

Here are two ways you can get involved with Google's contextual advertising tools:

- ✔ **Sign up to put ads on your blog** or Web site using the Google AdSense program (www.google.com/adsense).
- ✔ **Submit your blog or Web site for display** in the ads displayed on other Web sites using the Google AdWords program (http://adwords.google.com).

Figure 17-8:
Put ads on
your site
quickly
using
Google
AdSense as
done on this
blog.

If you want to find out more about leveraging Google AdSense for your blog or business, check out *Building Your Business with Google For Dummies,* by Brad Hill; *Pay Per Click Search Engine Marketing For Dummies*, by Peter Kent; or *AdWords For Dummies*, by Howie Jacobson (all from Wiley Publishing).

Yahoo! and several other companies also have contextual advertising programs — do a Web search for *"contextual advertising programs"* to see what's on offer.

You can add contextual advertising to your Web (RSS) feed, or put yourself into other Web feeds, using the FeedBurner Ad Network (www.feedburner.com).

Using ad networks

A number of advertising middle men can help successful bloggers put ads on their blogs. In most cases, you can choose between text and graphic ads in a set of standard Web advertising sizes. You create the ad, the ad network serves it up, the blogger posts new content, and his or her visitors see your ad.

If you want to advertise on some of the most successful blogs around, check out one or more of these ad networks:

✔ **b5media:** (`www.b5media.com`) Offers ad placement on more than 290 blogs reaching more than 10 million readers; bloggers can sign up to be paid for blogging on the b5media blog network.

✔ **Blogads:** (`www.blogads.com`) Offers ad placement on 1500 blogs, and allows you to choose an audience to target (for example, parents or news junkies).

✔ **ClickZ:** (`www.clickz.com`) Offers ad placement on the ClickZ family of news, opinion, and entertainment sites.

✔ **Crisp Ads:** (`www.crispads.com`) Offers advertising across blog categories (such as autos and food) or on specific blogs. More than 3800 blogs enrolled.

✔ **FeedBurner:** (`www.feedburner.com`) Offers placement on blogs and in RSS feeds; choose from categories of blogs and/or target specific times of day or geographic regions.

Each of these services offers you an array of popular blogs and ad formats to choose from, organizes the deal, and handles the transaction. Rates are negotiated based on the level of advertising, the blogs you are placed on, and how many times your ads are viewed or clicked on.

Sponsoring a blog

For a splashy way to be seen on a blog or Web site, consider sponsoring the site. Sponsorships for popular blogs have gained a lot of notoriety in the blogosphere. Some bloggers call accepting sponsorships "selling out," but others regard it as a great way to get paid to do what they love. Sponsorships tend to get you coverage on other blogs, even if it's just speculation about the amount you paid to sponsor a blog, but as they say, "any publicity is good publicity."

Sponsorships usually entitle you to occupy any and perhaps all advertising slots on a blog, and they often earn you mentions in the text of the blog as well. Few blogs actually advertise that they accept sponsorships, but this is largely because they're still fairly rare. If you'd like to sponsor a blog, the best option is to contact the blogger directly with an inquiry. He or she will let you know whether the blog is open to a sponsorship, and you can go from there.

Sponsorships can be expensive to do. Be prepared to negotiate with the blogger about the length of your sponsorship and the amount of money you are willing to pay, but think bigger than you would for advertisement. In some cases, sponsors have been known to assume the operating costs of a blog in addition to paying the blogger for his or her time and audience exposure.

As a sponsor, you are entitled to more than just a prominent ad placement (though you should get that, too!). You can consider requesting exclusivity — that you are the only advertiser in your industry on the blog, the only sponsor, or the only advertiser. You can request mentions in the copy of the blog, or any other arrangement you think is good for both you and the blogger. For many sponsors, having a prominent logo placement and label at the top of every blog page, and no other advertising on the blog, fills the bill.

Here are some of the areas to discuss with any blogger you are considering sponsoring:

- ✓ **What topics will be covered:** Know what kinds of content are typical for the blog you are sponsoring, and what kind of language is used. Because your brand will be associated with the blog, you need to be comfortable with the way the blogger expresses him or her-self, and what subjects may be raised.

   You might also want to discuss how you will handle situations where the blogger has blogged about a topic with which you have a problem. Understand that the blogger is likely to resist giving you editorial control, and be clear about what, if any, say you want to have in the content of the site.

- ✓ **How you will be acknowledged:** Be sure to establish how your brand will be placed on the page, and when and where you will be mentioned and linked to.

- ✓ **How other ads or monetization will occur:** Talk with the blogger about other ways they earn revenue and decide what, if any, of those systems can remain in place during the term of your sponsorship. Be prepared to compensate the blogger for any revenue usually earned that won't be if you request them to remove it from the site. For example, if the blogger commonly uses Google AdSense advertising that you would prefer not be visible, ask for accounting statements showing the value of those ads to the blogger.

Bringing It All Together

Blogging for business reasons is a sensitive topic both in and out of the blogosphere. Old school bloggers don't like seeing blogging turned from a personal outlet into a professional one, and many businesses worry that the informality of a blog will look unprofessional. And that's not all — some businesses also have concerns about employees with personal blogs that might talk about their work or be perceived as representing the company.

As I mention at the beginning of the chapter, blogging isn't for every corporate culture. If your company has traditionally had an open hand with communication and outreach, blogging is going to be a great tool for you. But if your corporate culture is reserved, blogging might be too much of a stretch beyond "business as usual." Many companies who might not have been expected to use blogs for marketing or outreach have been happily surprised at the results they've obtained.

Businesses that need to keep information or trade practices confidential, or that stand to lose by having an open door policy, aren't good candidates for blogging. For instance, some government agencies and law firms are limited by their very nature in what they can communicate. You'll know best if your corporate culture or industry is one that won't benefit from the use of a blog.

At the very least, however, you should be tracking your company and what's said about it in the blogosphere. Just because you ignore blogs, that doesn't mean they'll ignore you! In Chapter 11, I talk about ways you can monitor the blogosphere for mentions of your company so that you can be on top of any praise or criticism that might surface. After all, this trend isn't going away, so you need to be knowledgeable even if you don't participate.

If you're still on the fence about starting a blog, try one with a set end point, for an event or a product launch. After the event occurs, you can end the blog's lifespan gracefully and have some real data to use in assessing whether blogging was a worthwhile endeavor for you. As well, take a look at your competitors — are any of them blogging? If so, does the blog appear to be reaching visitors effectively? Are readers leaving comments? Watch how these competitors are making use of a blog and give some thought to whether you might be able to do something similar (but better).

Part VI
The Part of Tens

The 5th Wave   By Rich Tennant

"Hi all. Turns out that the rash I posted about last night is contagious..."

In this part . . .

Bring it all together in The Part of Tens by touring some top blogs and blog technologies. Chapter 18 covers some excellent ways to grow your audience into a true community, encouraging feedback and discussion and handling dissension in the ranks. In Chapter 19, get a cool list of technologies that you shouldn't miss. This isn't the cutting edge; it's the bleeding edge! For good measure, I leave you with ten outstanding and successful blogs you must check out in Chapter 20. And, finally, don't miss the glossary, where all the technical mumbo-jumbo gets defined clearly

Chapter 18

Ten Ways of Growing Community

In This Chapter

▶ Putting in the time to keep your community active

▶ Encouraging conversation and ideas

▶ Asking for help diagnosing problems or building interaction

*E*very online community needs leaders or facilitators to keep the topics lively, upbeat, and on topic. Playing "mom" can be the hardest job in any community, and sometimes, the rewards come slowly. Don't let this discourage you, though. Encouraging growth in any community requires a certain level of patience, persistence, and attention — but when it works, it really works.

This chapter offers a few simple tricks for developing your blog from your soapbox into a real community, with true interaction between you and your readers, and among the readers themselves.

If you're lucky, in the process of getting people to read and comment on your posts and on each other's comments, you'll even discover how to convert readers into community evangelists who will take the community even further.

Write

Get writing (or podcasting, or posting photos, or whatever it is you're doing on your blog)! If you're writing actively in your blog, do the same thing in the comments you get on your posts by joining the conversations that start within the comments.

Establish a regular schedule for maintaining your blog; this really helps readers to know what to expect and when. A regular schedule can even build some anticipation and excitement. Be open to ideas, provide a welcoming environment, and keep yourself on topic so that interested, engaged readers get what they're looking for when they visit.

Write on other Web sites as well. See whether other blogs might need a little help with a few additional posts. Also, help keep the conversations going on other blogs you enjoy. Each time you comment on another blog, you get exposure to a few more potential readers for your own blog, and you build links back to your blog (which can help boost your search engine rankings).

Reply

If someone asks you a question, either in the comments or through e-mail, make sure to reply. Acknowledge what the person says in your reply and take the time to answer properly, even if only to thank him or her for the comment. Thoughtful responses to these kinds of questions and comments can do as much to build your community as original blog posts.

Some bloggers take the attitude that reader comments aren't important or don't count as much as the blog posts. If you actually want to build a readership that interacts with you, this is dead wrong. These folks want your attention and encouragement.

Keep on top of what people are saying within your blog domain, and don't be a stranger to those who like what you do. Embrace their enthusiasm for your blog. Give them a reason to keep coming back. Interaction will keep those who might shy away feeling that they're really part of the community you're developing.

If you reply to comments and criticism on both your blog and in other online communities, you'll go far with attracting others to your own site. Get involved as much as you would in any offline community group.

Visit and Participate

Join other communities. It's that simple. If you want to build a community around your blog, you need to participate in others. Find blogs that are related to the topic areas of your blog. Jump into the conversation by offering a different perspective or some feedback to the blogger or to the folks who leave comments. Mentioning your site on other blogs is fine, as long as you make sure that your comments relate to the subject at hand and add to the conversation.

Also, don't just write and leave. Keep active in the communities in which you are a member and use that time to connect with others. Take what you can from the community, but also give back what you think will benefit everyone as a whole. Remember that participating in these communities might even give you ideas for your own blog, so you're likely to benefit in several ways from the time you spend on these blogs.

You can also share links between your blog community and related blogs that you want to support. Offer to set up a type of network where you can share content between sites. Anything is possible; all you need to do is ask.

Add Guest Bloggers

If your blog readership is up and running and you're attracting a significant number of daily readers, you can request members of your community to help you out by guest-blogging on your site. Depending on the software you're using, you can either set up private subblogs or allow them to post to the main page of your site. Being able to get other perspectives and comments from your community "experts" is incredibly cool, and you might be able to build a series of posts from other bloggers into your site.

This kind of blogging trade off is a great way to have multiple voices filling out the content on your site and providing a richer experience for your readers.

These relationships are great to have when you get sick or want to take a vacation — tap your guest-blogging community for help covering your blog while you aren't around to do it.

Try E-Mail and Newsletters

As spam-ridden as electronic mail can be, it's still a useful tool that you can use to stay in contact with your community. Offering e-mail delivery of some or all of your blog content to your readership is something that can attract users who aren't comfortable with some of the fancier technologies such as RSS. Try these three tactics in this arena:

- ✔ Let your readers send a blog post to a friend that might also be interested.

- ✔ Let your users sign up for e-mail notifications when you post something new to your blog.

- ✔ Let your readers sign up for an e-mail newsletter that supplements your blog or recaps recent blog posts of interest.

Many blog software programs have a built in "Tell a Friend" or "Email a Friend" functionality. If you turn this on, every blog post is accompanied by a small icon or link that, when clicked, lets your reader fill out the name and e-mail address of a friend and send an e-mail notification about your blog post to them. It's like free marketing. Figure 18-1 shows an E-mail This Item form on the Vacant Ready blog (www.vacantready.com).

Figure 18-1:
The Vacant Ready blog offers an "Email This Item" feature to let you clue in friends about a great blog post.

Setting up your blog to allow users to sign up for e-mail notifications when a new blog entry is posted is an easy way to reach users who have mastered e-mail but aren't up on newsreaders and RSS. Allowing them to sign up and also to remove themselves from your e-mail system puts them in control of the situation, too, which means you won't be contributing to the spam problem. The FeedBurner site (www.feedburner.com) lets you set up an e-mail notification/subscription tool.

Taking the time to create some kind of additional e-mail newsletter is another way of getting people interested in your Web site. One approach is to take a little time at the end of each calendar month and pick out your best or most popular blog posts. You can forward the links to your blog posting, or you can copy and paste the text into an e-mail and send it off.

You can create this kind of newsletter in several ways, but it's most effective for you to sign up for an e-mail service provider like Constant Contact (www.constantcontact.com), Topica (www.topica.com), or Email Labs (www.emaillabs.com). These services can handle subscription requests, unsubscribe requests, and change of e-mail addresses, all without your needing to do anything. In addition, most of them offer you the ability to track click-throughs on links in your newsletters and track who you e-mail and when.

There are a few free mailing list options out there, but most of them involve a monthly fee. Shop around to find one that fits your price range.

Track and Customize

What does your community like to read? Do the members like your posts about your personal life, or are they more interested in what you're doing in your daily job? Or is it your opinion about some other topic you've discussed?

Watch to see what element of your content is most popular and what gets the most comments and responses. Don't confuse this with what people like — you want to know what people are interested in and willing to comment on, not what they like. Controversial blog posts are most likely to generate conversation and feedback.

Knowing what's popular can help you with writing later on because you can draw on this knowledge to create more posts that get responses.

Also pay attention to what posts are unpopular and try and refrain from covering that content again.

You can also turn this information into additional resources for your readers. Engadget (www.engadget.com), for instance, tracks the posts that get the most comments and displays them in a Most Commented On box, which is shown in Figure 18-2. If you assume that the blog posts with the most comments are the most interesting, this is a shortcut for readers to find the best content on the blog.

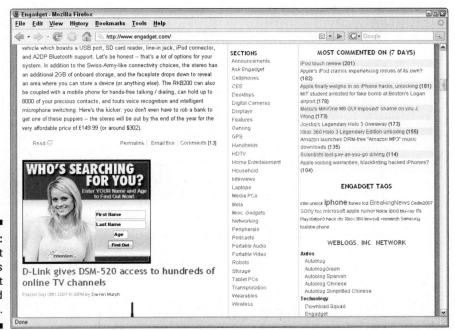

Figure 18-2: Engadget highlights the Most Commented On posts.

Develop Solutions

Pay attention to what's going on in your community so that you can find solutions to problems as they arise. Communities grow and change, but they won't thrive unless you resolve issues like spam or technical problems.

This is a tough one to describe because each community's problems will be unique. Just know that you need to keep on top of any problems that do come up.

For instance, if your blog readers start complaining about seeing too many spam comments on your blog, it's your responsibility to find and implement some of the spam prevention tools and techniques that are available. If you fail to do so, you risk losing your readers who get frustrated with skipping every other comment on your blog.

Other possible problem areas might include flame wars between overheated readers, slow Web servers, or too long a turnaround between when a comment is submitted and when it's moderated. (For the full scoop on comments and moderation, see Chapter 10.)

Check Your Code and Software

Your blog should be accessible to all Web users. This means that your HTML code needs to be flexible enough to display in the many Web browsers, and it must be written to accommodate browsers used by the blind. From keeping the Web site design code clean and offering RSS feeds, you're ultimately responsible in making your site work for your readers.

It's a hard thing, but true: Your blog won't look the same on your monitor and in your browser as it does on other computers and in other browsers.

Test your designs and test your RSS feeds in as many places as possible. Keep checking back and see whether anything changes over time. For instance, when Microsoft upgraded the Internet Explorer from version 6 to 7, many Web sites experienced display problems that had to be resolved. And of course a blog grows, which means that the load your site puts on your Web server changes over time.

Here are some important questions to ask yourself:

- How does your site behave with 500 blog posts and not the 10 or 20 you started with?

- Can your RSS feed be displayed in Google's newsreader? What about Bloglines? How about . . . you get the picture.

✏ Is the podcast you listed with iTunes still displaying? Can it be subscribed to? Is it being delivered?

✏ Are the images in older blog posts still available and viewable on the site?

✏ Are you regularly exceeding your bandwidth allowances provided by your Web host? Does your site run slowly at certain times of the day?

Changes, no matter how small, in design code or blog software programming can have unintended results. Be sure to look at your own blog on several computers every few weeks. Try leaving comments, using the search feature, clicking links, and generally kicking the tires on a regular basis.

Have Contests

Everyone loves to get free stuff! If traffic is lagging and needs a boost, try holding a giveaway or contest to spur more interaction. You could have a candy give-away or, give away that rusting Chevy in your backyard. The thing is you need to make your community members do something in order to get this free stuff you see fit to give away.

The Writing Publishing Program of Simon Fraser University posted a last-minute contest in October 2007, only days after launching its blog (`http://sfuwpp.wordpress.com`). The contest was for tickets to a local literary event (shown in Figure 18-3). Within two days, the program received 75 entries.

Having contests on your blog is one way that you can build your site traffic. The contests can be almost anything: writing contests, reward points for different levels of activity, writing and submitting blog posts, and so on. Hold a seasonal contest like best costume during Halloween or most romantic date idea on Valentine's Day.

The possibilities are practically endless. Get hokey and create memorable contests. Sometimes the sillier you get, the better response from your readers.

If you're running a business blog, be sure you understand the legal issues surrounding contests; rules can vary state by state, and there might be national issues as well.

Figure 18-3:
Bring
people to
your blog
fast with a
giveaway.

Ask Your Readers

One of the best things that you can do for the community is to make sure that everyone is having the best time that they can. How do you know this is happening? Why not just ask?

Giving people a way to let you know whether the community aspects of your site work for them is important, so a Contact Me page is a great idea. But if you really want to hear about how things are going, try just posting a blog entry asking people for their thoughts and criticism about what you're doing.

You're likely to get some great new ideas as well as some help identifying real problems, and best of all, it'll be free. In fact, you'll get bonus points for asking for this kind of input.

Chapter 19

Ten Cool Tricks for Making Your Blog Shine

*W*hen you're committed to the blogging lifestyle, the daily grind might feel overwhelming at times — writing, tinkering with blog software, preparing images, and repeating the process over and over. What a grind! Luckily for you, a series of Web sites and software can spice things up and banish any boredom you're experiencing, all while attracting new readers to your blog.

These tools are fun to play with. Some help create more links, keep people up to date, or just add a little silliness. Others are truly useful services to add to your blog. Adding *tag clouds* (a visual representation of the keywords used to describe your blog posts), throwing in some social bookmarking tools, adding a notification service, and sharing your musical tastes are but a few of these new aspects of the blogosphere.

This chapter highlights a few of these interesting methods of attracting like-minded individuals to your blog and how users can benefit from using these services.

Twittering Your News

Twitter, shown in Figure 19-1, is a social networking tool that allows individuals (be they bloggers or not) to broadcast short messages to fellow Twitterers or to the general public. Twitter is all about keeping people updated. The updates are tracked and can be subscribed to through the Twitter Web site (`www.twitter.com`) or followed using RSS and your newsreader. Messages can be informative, entertaining, Web links, dates, times, suggestions — just about anything if it will fit into 140 characters of text. When I looked at Twitter's home page while writing this, I found twitters about one user's plan for dinner and a link to a Web site about a missing child.

Each time you post a message on the Twitter Web site, several things happen:

- ✔ It's displayed on the Twitter Web site at `www.twitter.com`.
- ✔ It's delivered to anyone following your Twitters via SMS messages to a mobile phone or to an e-mail address.
- ✔ It's displayed in any Twitter "badge" that you've created and placed on your blog.

You can update your messages using e-mail, many instant messenger programs, or your phone. When you put the Twitter badge on your blog, you can create very quick updates for your readers, even when you can't take the time for a full blog post.

Figure 19-1:
When you visit the Twitter Web site, you can see recent updates from Twitterers all over the world.

Blogmapping

Blogmapping (or feed mapping) is a service that displays the geographic locations of bloggers on a mapping system like Microsoft Live Map or Google Maps. You can map your location based on your ZIP or postal code and, depending on the implementation, add your Web site address and RSS feed so potential readers can easily reach you.

One of the great things about this kind of service is finding bloggers in your own neighborhood, so you can turn your online relationships into offline friendships.

Some blogmapping services also allow you to create *tag clouds* (a visual representation of the keywords used to describe your blog posts) and keywords, so you can easily view the subject of the blogs on your map.

Just think of all the great blog posts you can write about meeting and getting to know other bloggers in your neighborhood, thanks to your blogmap! Figure 19-2 shows a blogmap implementation on a knitting club blog.

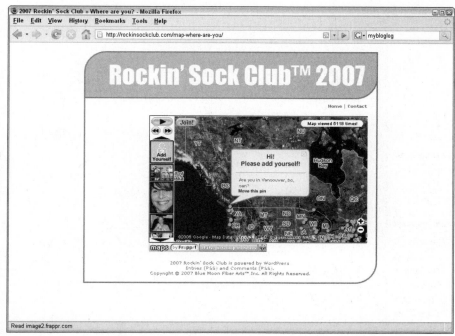

Figure 19-2:
This blogmap is on the members-only Rockin' Sock Club 2007 blog run by Blue Moon Fiber Arts.

Put a blogmap on your blog using one of these blogmapping tools:

- FeedMap, `www.feedmap.net`
- Frappr, `www.frappr.com`

Sharing the Weather

Let your readers know just what kind of weather you're experiencing today with iBegin Weather (`http://ibegin.com/weather`). This little widget lets you choose a Canadian or U.S. city with a simple browsing interface, and then displays today's temperature and cloud conditions, along with forecasts for the next few days.

You can customize iBegin Weather (see Figure 19-3) and choose what size icons to use, and whether you want to show today's weather, a forecast, or even a search box your readers can use to get a weather report themselves. You can also customize the text, link and background colors, as well as the fonts used in the box to match your blog.

Figure 19-3: Give your readers a weather forecast with iBegin Weather.

After you customize your weather box, simply copy the code iBegin Weather provides into your blog post or templates. Once set up, the widget stays current on its own, so you always have the current conditions and forecast.

If you have a weather-related blog, this is the perfect sidebar addition for you! Bloggers who aren't weather-focused might also enjoy letting others know when an umbrella is needed, especially those who write about the area they live in.

Polling the Masses

Polls aren't new to the Web — some of the most popular sites have attracted visitors with fun polls that promise to tell you what color you are, what superhero you are, or what your personal song is. Bloggers have used polls, too, getting readers to provide useful feedback and making them happy about doing it.

In fact, polls have proven to be a great way of increasing your blog traffic; no one can resist talking about themselves, especially if there's a button to push along the way!

You can use polls on your blog in a couple of ways:

- ✔ **Create a poll for your blog.** PollDaddy (www.polldaddy.com) offers a free poll service that you can use to create a poll and then display the results. You can even customize the poll so that it matches the rest of your Web site design. Some blog software actually has poll functionality built right in.

  Figure 19-4 shows how blogger Cybele May uses polls to find out what her readers want to know about on Candy Blog (www.candyblog.net).

- ✔ **Take a poll, test, or survey, and embed the results in a blog post.** This doesn't sound super fun, but it actually is! Many of these polls are light-hearted, so they're fun content for lazy Fridays. Best of all, when you create the blog post, you create a link back to the poll, so your visitors can find out what pie flavor they are, too.

Quiz Meme (www.quizmeme.com) is a great source for some of these quick, fun polls.

Figure 19-4:
Let your readers tell you about themselves with polls, as with this sidebar poll on Candy Blog.

Tying in Social Bookmarking

Social bookmarking systems like del.icio.us (`http://del.icio.us`) and Ma.gnolia.com (`http://ma.gnolia.com`) are great ways of collecting, saving, and sharing your bookmarks. You have access to all of your Web site bookmarks from any computer from anywhere, and those bookmarks are organized and labeled in ways that make sense to you so they're easy to find again (and not how a search engine thinks they ought to be labeled). Conveniently, your bookmarks are saved on the Web, so you always have access to them, no matter what computer or browser you're using.

So, what else can you do with those bookmarks? The answer to that question lies in the word *social* that's used to describe these services: When you create a catalog of links you want to bookmark on a social bookmarking site, you can share that list with others.

Social bookmarking is especially cool for groups who are researching the same topic — imagine working on an academic project with a group where you all pool your Web research, or planning a family vacation.

Because bloggers have long shared lists of links with each other (usually in the form of blogrolls), this a great service to use for your audience. For some link bloggers (link bloggers blog mainly about cool or interesting Web sites they find), social bookmarking has come close to replacing the need for a blog. Social bookmarking can even be used to generate your blogroll.

Both Ma.gnolia and del.icio.us (see Figure 19-5) turn your bookmarks into an RSS feed that can be followed using a newsreader or any software that understands RSS. Ma.gnolia even publishes a feed that can be understood by phones!

Some blog software can aggregate content using RSS and display it on your blog; you can use that functionality to display your Ma.gnolia or del.icio.us feed.

Flying High with Tag Clouds

Tagging has been all the rage over the last couple of years. Bloggers use tags to label and sort blog posts, images, or podcasts with contextual keywords, in the process creating a kind of personal dictionary to the topics on the blog. These keywords allow users to sort and organize content in different configurations — tag clouds are one way to view this kind of organization.

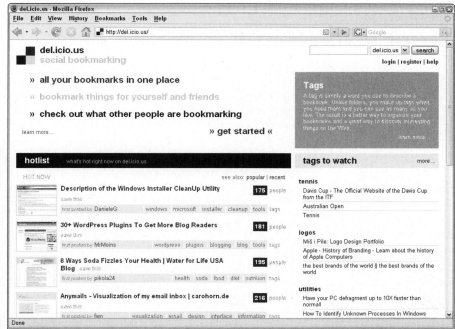

Figure 19-5: With social book-marking, you can share all the strange and curious Web sites you stumble upon.

Essentially, a *tag cloud* is a collection of keywords that grow or shrink in size, depending on the number of posts tagged with the individual keyword. If you have ten blog posts with the keyword *bunny* and five blog posts with the keyword *music,* the *bunny* tag appears larger in size than the *music* tag in the cloud. This makes the cloud a visual representation of how often the *bunny* tag is used. A tag cloud generated by the photo tags of the Flickr community is shown in Figure 19-6. Flickr was actually the first site to use a tag cloud to represent content.

Any kind of content can be tagged — images, blog posts, audio, or any other kind of content that is available on a Web site.

You can read more about tag clouds at `http://en.wikipedia.org/wiki/Tag_cloud`. If you want to install a tag cloud on your blog, check to see whether your blogging software has such a feature. If it doesn't, check out Make Cloud (`www.makecloud.com`), which permits you to build a tag cloud from your RSS feed that can be displayed on your blog.

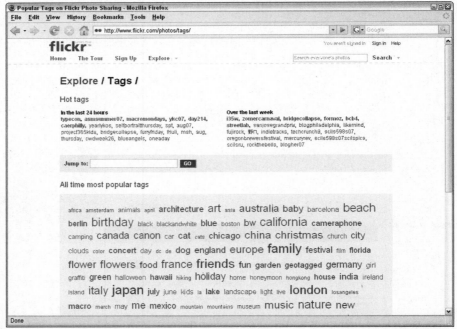

Figure 19-6:
Flickr pioneered the use of tag clouds to represent content on its Web site.

Reproduced with permission of Yahoo! Inc. ® 2007 by Yahoo! Inc. YAHOO! and the YAHOO! logo are trademarks of Yahoo! Inc.

Going Web 2.0 with Big Footers

If you're even remotely interested in how your blog looks, a great place to get ideas is from other blogs! I check out other blogs all the time for design ideas, cool new functionality, and also great content. One of the latest Web 2.0 trends is the creation of large footers at the bottom of blog sites.

Web 2.0 is a generation of Web sites, especially blogs, that featured interactive functionality and community content. Newspapers that solicit news stories from readers, blogs with comments, wikis, and other kinds of social interactivity all qualify a Web site to have the descriptor "Web 2.0." The phrase has been around since 2004, long enough for some Web developers to get a little jaded by it, so it is sometimes used facetiously today.

Most Web sites have a *footer,* an area at the bottom of each page that contains things like copyright notices, navigation, and other information that needs to be consistently displayed across an entire Web site. The big footer is just that — a footer, but bigger.

These large footers contain information such as the latest comments, the most read posts, pictures from photo galleries, and author information. One of the reasons for the big footer is that it provides visitors a "one-stop shop" section of the page when they read all the way to the bottom. It also means that these elements don't have to be displayed in the sidebar of the blog, reducing clutter. The biggest benefit of a big footer, though, is that it puts fresh content links on every page of the site, so no matter what page your visitors pulls up in a search engine, they can quickly access the latest and greatest.

On Chris Clarke's Vacant Ready Web site, shown in Figure 19-7, the big footer area is used to promote fresh content from three different blogs, along with some site navigation.

Footers don't require any special functionality or software; you just need to set up your blog template, which might mean getting a little crazy with HTML.

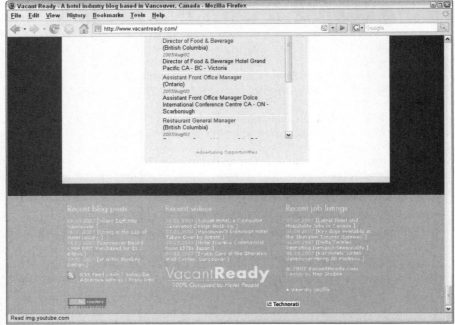

Figure 19-7:
Vacant
Ready, a
blog for
hotel
industry
professionals,
uses the big
footer to link
to fresh
content.

Digging It

Digg (`www.digg.com`) is a Web service dedicated to "user powered content." Digg specializes in user community rating and voting, which allow users to submit and vote on what content, comments, videos, or images are important and what are not.

Think of a newspaper that's created by what you and your friends think is interesting and important. In theory, Digg users select the most interesting content found on the Internet — hopefully, content that's worth paying attention to.

Digg is a great tool for keeping tabs on what is popular and interesting online, especially in blogs, but the ultimate goal is to have your own posting featured on the front page, and benefiting from the flood of traffic and visitors that then comes your way. This is called being *dugg*.

Getting dugg is a blogger's dream come true and worst nightmare rolled into a single moment. Getting a blog post dugg on the Web attracts attention and traffic, and your blog gets lots of visits from people who might never have come to your blog otherwise. But nothing is ever free: All that extra traffic can put a real load on your Web server. Web sites have been known to crash, taking the site offline. Even if that doesn't happen, your Web host might have to charge you extra bandwidth costs for the additional pages of your blog that get served.

To encourage people to Digg your site, customize your blog software to include a Digg This icon next to your blog posts, as the Truthdig online magazine (www.truthdig.com) does, as shown in Figure 19-8. Blog visitors can simply click the Digg icon (found on the Share drop-down menu on Truthdig) and blast your blog to the front page of Digg.com!

Dressing Up with Avatars

Many blogs encourage visitors and content creators to set up a profile with some basic biographical information and a photo. For some Web users, this is a chance to have some fun. Instead of a photo, you can use an avatar! An *avatar* is a visual representation of yourself, often a comic or cartoon.

Figure 19-8:
Truthdig, an online magazine that uses many blogging features, encourages visitors to digg their posts.

You can use your avatar on any Web site that lets you set an avatar or photo for use with a profile, like Facebook, Digg, Flickr, and so on. And of course you can use your avatar on your own blog.

Here are a couple of places you can use to create an avatar:

✔ Zwinky (www.zwinky.com) is a fun Web site that lets you a build cartoon version of yourself, customizing everything from skin tone to hairstyle to clothing accessories.

✔ Meez (www.meez.com) offers a fun interface with lots of customization to help you build a virtual you. Use the Meezmaker to pick skin color, hair color, clothes, jewelry, even the right environment.

✔ Another site you can check out is associated with the release of *The Simpsons Movie*. At www.simpsonizeme.com, you can replicate yourself as a Simpsons character, right down to Moe's hair and Homer's nose.

If those sites aren't what you're looking for, try searching for *"free avatar"* using your favorite search engine.

Connecting with MyBlogLog

MyBlogLog (www.mybloglog.com) is a tracking and community tool that allows bloggers to bookmark and share favorite blogs, display cool widgets, and keep track of what blog visitors find interesting. MyBlogLog says it's in the business of helping you identify what your readers like about your content, but the side result has been to create a community-building service, which the folks at MyBlogLog are pretty happy about, too!

Using a combination of RSS, tagging, and other tools, MyBlogLog tracks what links your visitors click when they visit your blog (and not the ones to your own site), letting you know where you're sending people. If you keep a blog where you refer folks to other Web sites, MyBlogLog can help you know whether you're doing a good job of choosing resources to share.

The key feature of this service is the MyBlogLog community badge that can be displayed on your blog. As a MyBlogLog member, when you visit a site with this badge, you're added to a badge displaying your profile information. It's an instant community!

MyBlogLog, shown in Figure 19-9, is still fairly new at the time of writing this book, so I expect to see a lot of change in how people are using it; it should be an exciting service to watch. Yahoo! recently purchased MyBlogLog to add to their Yahoo! services. It can only get better!

Figure 19-9:
Use
MyBlogLog
to track
visitors to
your blog
and find out
what they're
interested
in.

Reproduced with permission of Yahoo! Inc. ® 2007 by Yahoo! Inc. YAHOO! and the YAHOO! logo are trademarks of Yahoo! Inc.

Chapter 20

Ten Blogs You Should Know

In This Chapter

▶ Blogs that talk about technical stuff and gadgets

▶ Blogs that discuss politics

▶ Blogs that help you with your blog

*B*ecause so many blogs are floating about in the blogosphere, you can't possibly read them all. In the beginning, only a handful of blogs were known well enough to attract solid audiences. Only a few short years later, well over 100 million different blogs exist, and each one attracts its own audience. This book has made reference to a number of blogs, but there's always room for more. This chapter includes a short list of some of the blogs I find most interesting and useful.

Take some time and visit each of these blogs. Not only do they feature some great content, but you also can discover more about what types of things these bloggers do to achieve blogging success.

Engadget

www.engadget.com

In March of 2004, Peter Rojas, cofounder of the blog Gizmodo, launched Engadget. Engadget is a contributor-supported blog with posts written by several writers; it features articles about consumer technology and boasts lively discussions in the comments section.

Engadget, shown in Figure 20-1, is one of those blogs you can't live without. It has won a number of awards and has been translated into several different languages. If you have any interest in gadgets (I know you do!) and you want to find out more about them, you can't go wrong in subscribing to Engadget.

Figure 20-1:
Engadget
talks
gadgets,
consumer
products,
and other
technology.

And should you be interested in exploring the podcast milieu, Engadget also hosted a podcast that ran from 2004 until 2006, which you can find by searching the site.

defective yeti

www.defectiveyeti.com

If you like reading funny blogs, you'll love defective yeti, written by Matthew Baldwin and "Haphazardly Spellchecked Since 2002." defective yeti, shown in Figure 20-2, is a classic personal blog — the personal diary of an amusing writer who blogs when he feels like it, about whatever he wants to. Baldwin is a programmer, but he blogs frequently about his family life, games, fiction, and entertaining news stories.

Figure 20-2:
defective
yeti is sure
to entertain.

Daily Kos

www.dailykos.com

Daily Kos, shown in Figure 20-3, is possibly the most popular political blog in the blogosphere. It discusses American politics and news, and it produces opinion pieces about the state of the United States from a liberal perspective.

Founded by Markos Moulitsas Zuniga in 2002, Daily Kos has helped small groups of like-minded individuals to use discussion forums and blogs to create momentum around different causes. If you want to be a part of Daily Kos, you can create an account that allows you to post comments and also to post diaries that become part of the online community (though not usually on the front page). The main front page blog is the work of several contributors from Daily Kos; if a post from your diary is highly recommended by other readers in the community, it might be promoted to the front page.

According to the Web site, Daily Kos has about 600,000 unique visits every day, averaging 14 to 25 million visits per month. And it offers a special subscription to anyone interested — you can become a paying subscriber to help support the community and get the benefit of having the ability to turn off the advertising!

Figure 20-3:
Daily Kos supports grassroots organizations and discusses politics.

Pug-A-Day

www.pugaday.com

Pug-A-Day is a brand-new blog (at least at the time when I was writing this book). It was started in April 2007 by a Web developer who owns two pugs, Roy and Gwen (who have their own dedicated blog site at www.royandgwen.com). The Pug-A-Day photo blog is intended to bring a smile to your face with a new cute pug for each and every day.

Pug-A-Day readers provide the majority of the content by submitting pictures of their puppies. The blogger requests that readers send in photos of their own pugs that are eventually posted as the pug of the day. Figure 20-4 shows a sweet pug living in the lap of luxury. And might I suggest that you check out my dog Serendipity on May 4, 2007 . . . she's extra cute!

This daily blog is increasing in popularity so much so that it could take up to a month for your pug photo to appear. It's an excellent example of a simple blog site that offers a wonderful return for the community who visit and share in the love of pugs.

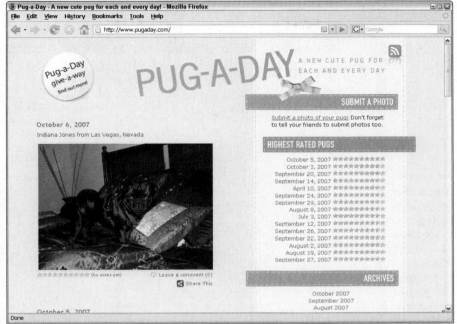

Figure 20-4:
Pug-A-Day
brings a
smile to
your face
with a new
cute pug
every day!

Problogger

www.problogger.net

ProBlogger was founded by Darren Rowse in 2004 and is one of the main landing spots for bloggers who want to know how to improve their blogs with tips on making money, writing solid content, and other simple tricks of the trade.

Since 2003, Darren has started many different blogs and more recently has cofounded the blog network b5media. He's the manager of many other blogs and writes daily on his Problogger Web site, helping new bloggers find new ways of monetizing their blogs.

If you want to find out more about blog design, blogging tools and services, social media, blogging for dollars, podcasting, RSS, writing content, business blogging, advertising, blog promotion, video posts, affiliate programs, and other miscellaneous blog tips, this site is for you.

Problogger, shown in Figure 20-5, is a great resource and should not be missed!

Figure 20-5:
Problogger
helps you to
become a
better
blogger and
make
money
doing it.

TreeHugger

www.treehugger.com

TreeHugger is a blog about how you can make the world a better place (see Figure 20-6). This blog is written by many different writers, all with the simple goal of helping readers find ways to establish a more sustainable world. It has a great collection of "green guides" that cover topics like greening your summer and how you can green your wedding.

You can submit your own tips on green living to TreeHugger. Check out its blogroll first if you need some inspiration!

This comprehensive lifestyle blog feature a main blog, a user-generated blog, videos, and a weekly podcast. And if you're not quite into RSS feeds yet, you can even sign up for a weekly or daily e-mail newsletter.

Figure 20-6:
TreeHugger
shares how
you and
others can
make the
world
sustainable.

TMZ

www.tmz.com

TMZ is an entertainment blog that takes its name from "thirty mile zone," a Hollywood term from the 1960s. The Web site is a juicy place to go for those who want the most up-to-date information about what is going on in Hollywood.

This blog, shown in Figure 20-7, is very much a guilty pleasure because it fulfills the celebrity addiction that a lot of people have. The blog is deep in the trenches and is always producing good content for people who like to keep on top of what celebrities are doing, what gossip is floating around, and how many times so-and-so goes to your local coffee shop.

I mean, who can resist a blog that has categories for Fashion Police, Celebrity Justice, Wacky and Weird, Train Wrecks, Paparazzi Video, Baby Watch, Full Throttle Fashion, Star Catcher, and Let's Get This Party Started? Not to mention the fabulous photos of your favorite stars at their *worst*.

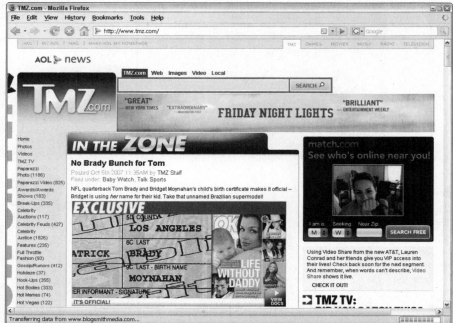

A List Apart

www.alistapart.com

A List Apart is a blog and Web site that talks about nothing but how to make Web sites. This blog features articles, tutorials, and community conversation about how Web sites are made, how they should be created, and how you can use new tricks to improve your Web development skills.

This blog is important to bloggers who like to get into the muck of their blog software because it provides many techniques for making your blog accessible and friendly to both computers and human beings.

A List Apart, shown in Figure 20-8, started as a simple mailing list in 1997 and has grown to a hugely popular Web site and has spawned a conference called An Event Apart. The main topics that are covered in this blog include code, content, culture, design, process, and user science. And when you become a blogging expert and you want to contribute, you can even submit your own articles for publication on this popular blog.

Figure 20-8:
A List Apart
is a blog for
people who
make Web
sites.

Copy Blogger

www.copyblogger.com

Copyblogger is the brain-child of Brian Clark, an Internet marketing specialist who develops content, helps people to write better, designs online communication strategies, and is a "recovering attorney."

Brian founded Copyblogger in January of 2006 and has written hundreds of blog posts that are concise coverage of topics ranging from copyright discussions to how you can "pimp" your blog. He blogs in a no-nonsense style and isn't afraid to tell people about the real state of writing on the Web.

This personal blog shows one person's thoughts and creativity. Brian stands out and gets noticed in the blogosphere for his forthright opinions. Read his blog to find out more about how to make yours great. Figure 20-9 shows the Copyblogger home page.

Figure 20-9:
Copy
Blogger
helps you
write better
copy.

Improv Everywhere

www.improveverywhere.com

Improv Everywhere is a blog (see Figure 20-10) that documents "scenes of chaos and joy" organized in New York City public spaces by Charlie Todd. Todd brings together volunteers for lighthearted "missions" that take them into public spaces to do unexpected activities.

In October 2007, Todd led a group of 111 men into the 5th Avenue Abercrombie and Fitch store. After a few minutes of shopping, all the men removed their shirts and then continued to shop. Todd and his crew documented the ensuing hilarity as actual shoppers and store personnel reacted to this gentle satire of the company's marketing imagery.

Todd organizes these events irregularly, but they all make great, entertaining reading.

Figure 20-10:
Poke a little fun at society with Improv Everywhere's antics.

Courtesy Improv Everywhere

Glossary

aggregator: A collector of information about a topic or idea. An aggregator can be a person, blog, or Web site. Technologically speaking, RSS is an aggregation format for individual blogs. Google News is an example of a Web site that aggregates news for many sources.

audio blog: A blog consisting of audio files, or the practice of placing an audio file in a blog post.

blog: A chronological log of information kept by an individual, a group, or a business. The term *blog* is a merging of the words *Web log*. On a typical blog, the most recent post appears at the top of the page, usually time-stamped. Scrolling down the page takes the reader to older posts. Each post usually offers an opportunity for readers to interact by adding their comments and might also display Trackback information about other blogs that have linked to this post. Blog content is determined entirely by the author(s) of the blog, so many are personal journals, but others are focused aggregations of news or commentary.

blogger: The author of a blog.

blogging: Producing blog posts. A blogger blogs on his or her blog.

blogosphere: The community of blogs and bloggers around the world.

blogroll: A collection of links used or recommended by an individual blogger. A blogroll is usually shown in a column on a blog.

buzz marketing: A no-cost or low-cost method of marketing associated with people telling other people about a company's products or services. Buzz marketing is based on peoples' direct experiences with specific products or on the experiences others have related to them.

comment: A piece of feedback left by a reader on a blog post.

CSS: This acronym stands for Cascading Style Sheets, an advanced HTML technique that permits fine control and layout of a Web site and quick changes in formats across the site.

entry: See *post*.

feed: See *RSS*.

feedreader: See *newsreader*.

FTP: File Transfer Protocol is the mechanism that allows transfer of files and data from one computer to another.

hit: A request to a Web server for a file. When the Web page (which often consists of multiple files) is downloaded from a server, the number of hits is equal to the number of files requested. Thus, one page view can often equal more than one hit, which means that counting the hits is typically an inaccurate measure of Web traffic.

HTML: Hypertext Markup Language is the computer coding used by Web designers to create Web pages.

keyword: The content and/or type of meta tag included in a Web page's HTML code to help index the page. The term *keyword* also refers to terms or phrases that a user submits to a search engine when looking for content on the Internet.

links: A link, or hyperlink, is a navigation tool that allows a user to go from one Web location to another by clicking. They typically are underlined.

meme: Memes are ideas that evolve virally. As bloggers post, comment on other blogs, post about posts on other blogs, and add their own thoughts, a meme spreads across the Internet, changing as it goes. Some groups spread memes consciously by participating in answering a set of questions or posting on a topic, but most memes are a natural byproduct of interesting topics.

meta tag: HTML tags used in a Web page to describe the document to search engines. Common tags are title, keyword, and description. Title and description are frequently displayed in search results; keywords are used to determine when a site should be returned as a search result.

moderation: The regulation of an online community, specifically the contributions made by users to discussion forums or blog comment threads. Moderation might include removal of content if deemed inappropriate.

moderator: A person granted special privileges to enforce the rules of an online community by removing or changing content from individual posts.

newsreader: Software used to subscribe to and then read blog and Web site RSS feeds.

page view: A request to load a single page of a Web site. Counting page views can help determine whether any change made to the page results in more or less visits.

permalink: Short for permanent link. This is a page of a blog that contains a single blog post and usually any comments on that post. Permalinks allow users to link directly to a single post for more accurate reference.

photoblog: A blog composed entirely of images, sometimes with caption information.

ping: A ping occurs when one computer asks another whether it's there; the second computer confirms its presence. In the blogosphere, many bloggers alert blog aggregation Web sites when posting a new entry.

podcast: A digital media file that is distributed over the Internet using feeds and is intended for download and playback on portable media players and personal computers.

post: A publication to a blog, possible containing text, images, and other media. A post can also be called an *entry*.

RSS: RSS stands for Really Simple Syndication, an XML-based feed of a blog's postings that's picked up by blog aggregation sites or software.

sidebar: A column to the right or left of the main content of your blog. Usually blog software comes with some content already in the sidebar, such as links to your categories, archives, and RSS feed. Sidebars can be customized with additional common and uncommon elements.

spam: Unsolicited electronic messages sent in bulk that may be commercial, nonsensical or malicious. In addition to e-mail spam, blog comments and blog forums can be targeted by spammers.

syndication: See *RSS*.

tag: A relevant keyword that is associated or assigned to a piece of information such as an image, a blog entry, or a video clip. Tags are usually chosen informally by the content creator or by the online community; they help give to context to nontext media and organize information for ease of searching.

tagging: The act of adding tags to a photo, video, audio file, or blog post.

Trackback: A mechanism that tracks references to a blog posting that occurs on other blogs. Trackbacks are designed to help readers find other blogs discussing the same topic. They also let bloggers know that another blogger has blogged about and linked to a post.

troll: A blog reader that posts offensive, personal attacks that interfere with the conversation between blogger and readers.

unique visits: A statistic used to count the visitors to a Web site, counting each visitor only once in the time frame of the report. The number of unique visits are a measure of a Web site's true audience size.

video blog: A blog consisting of video files, or the practice of placing a video file in a blog post.

video podcast: A digital video clip shared on the Internet that can be downloaded and viewed on a mobile device or personal computer.

Web content: Anything that can be read, seen or heard as part of the user experience on web sites. It can include text, images, sounds, videos and animations.

Web log: See *blog.*

WYSIWYG: An acronym for What You See Is What You Get, this term refers to a system in which the content during editing appears very similar to the end result.

XML: XML stands for eXtensible Markup Language, and it allows publishers to build their own structures into markup languages. XML can be used for any kind of structured information and is intended to allow information to be passed to any computer system, regardless of the platform that the computer uses.

Index

• C •